Avoiding the Enemies to HAPPINESS

This isn't a book that will tell you everything there is to know about happiness. This is a guide book of specific techniques and practical strategies that you can apply immediately to avoid the enemies to human happiness and create more meaning and success in life. It's easy to learn. It's easy to use. It works.

Avoiding the Enemies to Happiness combines the latest research from the new fields of *m*BIT (multiple Brain Integration Techniques) and Positive Psychology, along with deep insights from behavioral technologies such as Accelerated Learning and Neuro Linguistic Programming (NLP), and blends these with time-honored practical wisdom.

This book is powerful. And has been designed to guide and teach you how to gain more satisfaction, meaning and happiness in your life. If that interests you, then let's get started now.

Avoiding the Enemies to HAPPINESS

Grant Soosalu

www.avoidingtheenemies.com

Copyright © 2014 Generative Designs Pty Ltd

ISBN 978-1500251703

All rights reserved. No part of this publication may be reproduced, stored in a retrieval system, or transmitted in any form or by any means, electronic, mechanical, recording or otherwise, without the prior written permission of the author and/or copyright holder.

The materials and information in this publication are provided as is, without representation, endorsement or warranty (express or implied) of any kind. This publication is designed to provide accurate and authoritative information about the subject matter covered, and best attempts have been made to provide the most accurate and valid information, but the publisher and author do not warrant that the information is complete or free from inaccuracies. The publication is sold with the understanding that the publisher and author are not engaged in rendering medical, psychological, financial, legal, or other professional services. If expert assistance or counseling is needed, the services of a competent professional should always be sought. For further legal information please refer to the Legal section at the back of this publication.

Warning: If you suffer from serious medical or psychological conditions, please consult your doctor or health-care professional before utilizing any of the patterns or information contained in this publication to ensure it is appropriate to do so.

Trademarks: All brand names and product names used in this book are trade names, service marks, trademarks, or registered trademarks of their respective owners. Neither the publisher nor the author are associated with any product or vendor mentioned in this book. For permissions and specific trademark acknowledgements please refer to the Acknowledgements section at the back of this publication.

First Published 2014
TimeBinding Publications

Contents

    Intro — Read me PLEASE! 7
0.   What's it all ABOUT? 9
1.   It's YOUR world 57
2.   I don't BELIEVE it 93
3.   Ignorance is NOT bliss 151
4.   Warning: Slow Suicide will kill YOU 187
5.   It's all THEIR Fault 233
6.   Too much, too SOON! 277
7.   Piss me off, pay the PRICE 317
8.   HALF way there… 357
9.   More GREED is better? 391
10. Life is FANTASTIC! 427
11. HAPPINESS is a verb 391

Acknowledgements and thanks 515
Legal stuff 518
About the author 519
References and resources 521

Avoiding the Enemies to HAPPINESS

Intro

Read Me... PLEASE!

Have you ever looked on the back of your birth certificate???

Well, I have, and there's nothing there. Nothing! No instructions at all on how to run your body, your brain and mind, or your life. You pop into this world, and the most important information and skills — how to get happiness and how to stay away from the enemies to happiness — are never explicitly taught to you. There's no Happiness 101 at school. Nothing!

Me, I'm passionate about life and learning. And I'm passionate about sharing knowledge and learning with other people. I'm also concerned about making this world a better place.

So I wrote this book to share with you the skills of happiness-ing. It's not a popularist personal development story-book filled with lots of tales and anecdotes about happiness. If you like those sorts of books, then put this down and go grab one off another shelf. I personally can't stand books where you have to wade through chapters and chapters of stories about this person and that person, before you finally get any practical info. I don't want to be tricked into learning.

Instead, this is a practical field guide for your own personal war on the enemies to human happiness. It's a reference book that shows you how to hunt down, remove and replace those enemies with explicit strategies for happiness success. It teaches you the pragmatic concepts and explicit techniques you'll need to run your brain, body and life. It's a little bit like an owner's manual for happiness; it's based on the latest science and behavioral technologies, but written in easy to understand language, with a light-hearted and conversational approach.

This book is simple, practical and well-structured. It's designed to allow you to either dip and skim, reading those areas that are of immediate concern and interest, or you can read it from cover-to-cover. It's structured in chunk-sized sections that are simple to read and learn. And the information is specific and explicit so you can learn, remember and use it easily.

So it's your choice. Decide if this is a book you can use to make a difference to your life or the life of someone you love, and if so, grab and read it. Share it. Apply it. It's a guide book to happiness! I'm passionate about learning and creating more happiness in life. Are you?

Wishing you all the best,
Grant Soosalu

June 2014

Avoiding the Enemies to HAPPINESS

Chapter 0

What's it all ABOUT?

You will learn about

- ✓ The new fields of Positive Psychology and *m*BIT — multiple Brain Integration Techniques
- ✓ Practical tools and insights from Cognitive Behavioral Therapy
- ✓ The behavioral technology of NLP — Neuro Linguistic Programming
- ✓ Your unconscious mind and the processes of learning and change
- ✓ The structure of this book and how to use it to avoid and overcome the Enemies to Happiness in your life

About the Enemies to Happiness

Did you know there are enemies to your happiness, enemies waiting to trip you up and destroy your joy and meaning in life? Some of them are obvious, but many are elusive and insidious.

By learning about these enemies, their signs and symptoms, you can defeat and destroy them before they impact your day-to-day and long-term happiness. What's more, by learning how to build strengths and supportive patterns and habits in your life, you can transcend these enemies and create a life filled with deep joy, purpose and meaning. A life of happiness and the skills to enjoy and share it.

You know, for most people the cause of unhappiness in their life is *not* due to them *not* doing things that make them happy. That's quite a mouthful of a sentence, isn't it? Let's unpack it. Most people have a general idea of what makes them happy and they put in place things and processes in their life to increase their levels of happiness. For example, most people get enjoyment and happiness out of holidays, hobbies and leisure activities. So they save for and build these into their lives.

What most people don't realize is there are behaviors, thoughts and feelings that are enemies to happiness; that destroy peace of mind and long-term enjoyment of life. Not realizing and being aware of these enemies, people typically do the things they believe will make them happy, but at the same time, don't remove and destroy the enemies to this very happiness. They literally shoot themselves in the foot and hobble their chances of lasting and ongoing happiness.

It's like wanting to be an Olympic long-distance runner. If you did all the positive things to support running success, like training, and eating correctly and exercising and studying running strategies, you'd likely become a victorious runner. However, if while doing these you allowed a huge weight to be chained to one leg, this would be an enemy to running success. No matter how much training you did, you'd end up damaging your leg muscles and draining your strength. You would never win a race with that enemy chained to your body.

Achieving happiness in life is similar. You need to do the positive supportive actions of success whilst at the same time ensuring you stay away from the enemies to that. And that's why this book will teach you about the Enemies to Happiness and how to avoid them, it will also provide you with positive strategies and skills to generate more focus, meaning and joy in life. That way you have all bases covered and are maximizing your chances for true happiness success.

Sound good? Ok, let's get started by learning about the technologies and concepts this book is based on. Remember, knowledge is power and the greater your understanding of how your mind works, the greater your choice and chances of success.

Now just before you begin… a couple of suggestions to help as you work through this chapter. If the fields of *m*BIT, Positive Psychology and NLP are new to you, then it's important that you read this chapter carefully as it introduces you to an overview of these fields and teaches you very important models that will be referred to throughout the book. While I've done my best to make this an easy read, nevertheless, this is reference material and you'll just have to roll up your sleeves and get into it. The more you understand the concepts and principles of the technologies we are using, the better equipped you'll be to begin to generate amazing levels of happiness in your life.

On the other hand, if you are already cognizant and skilled in *m*BIT, Positive Psychology and NLP then you can probably skip straight ahead to Chapter 1. However in my experience, reviewing the following material can help refresh your memory and provide additional distinctions. At the very least it will get you on the same page with respect to how I am using these powerful models and techniques. The choice is yours.

> According to the Dalai Lama, the process for achieving true and lasting happiness is: *"one begins by identifying those factors which lead to happiness and those factors which lead to suffering. Having done this, one then sets about gradually eliminating those factors which lead to suffering and cultivating those which lead to happiness. That is the way."*
>
> Dalai Lama and H. Cutler
The Art of Happiness

Pos ψ   Positive Psychology

In recent years, Prof. Martin E. P. Seligman along with a group of his professional colleagues commenced what has now become a revolutionary new direction in Psychology. Known as Positive Psychology it focuses on strengths rather than weaknesses, and claims that happiness can be measurably increased through the cultivation of appropriate strengths and various exercises and practices.

Prof. Seligman is a famous researcher in the field of traditional Psychology and has written many books on the subjects of Learned

Helplessness and Learned Optimism. He recently headed up the American Psychological Association and along with a growing team of researchers across the world, continues to develop groundbreaking insights into the structure of happiness and how purpose, meaning, flow and pleasure can be utilized for greater happiness.

As Prof. Seligman describes it, the field of Psychology has traditionally maintained a narrow-minded focus on pathology, victimology and mental illness. Positive Psychology instead focuses on positive emotions, virtues and strengths. It's based on the concept of providing and supporting mental health and increased happiness for normal people.

Evidence Based, Scientifically Validated Techniques

Positive Psychology is fundamentally a scientific endeavor. It seeks to examine and determine the causes and behaviors that generate and support happiness. Researchers in the field have examined hundreds of personal development techniques and exercises looking for scientific evidence that these produce objective changes in measurable levels of happiness. The techniques that have been shown to work have been validated using placebo based, blind controlled studies. This means that you can have a solid level of confidence that they work.

Authentic Happiness

Research in Positive Psychology has also shown there are three major components to Happiness: Pleasure, Engagement and Meaning.

The Pleasurable Life

The more you increase and experience pleasure in your life, the more happiness you'll feel during and immediately after these experiences. However, these positive feelings are short-lived. Think about relaxing in a warm bath, or enjoying a massage; in the middle of the experience, you are filled with relaxation and positive feelings. A couple of days, a week, or a month later, the experience is merely a dim memory and doesn't contribute to lasting feelings of happiness.

The Engaged Life

Engagement is about flow, absorption and gratification. Whenever you engage fully in an experience, with total involvement and concentration, you'll usually find you are left feeling strong, alert, refreshed and invigorated. Indeed, the research in Positive Psychology has shown that engagement and flow measurably increase levels of happiness and life satisfaction. The positive effects of engagement are not short-lived either. Flow builds psychological and emotional capital. It can bring exhilarating feelings of transcendence, and help dissolve emotional problems and challenges.

The Meaningful Life

Of all the components to happiness, meaning provides the longest lasting, strongest and most durable effect. By having a purpose that is bigger than yourself, by living a life of meaning and significance, you can measurably increase your levels of happiness and life satisfaction.

The Components of Happiness

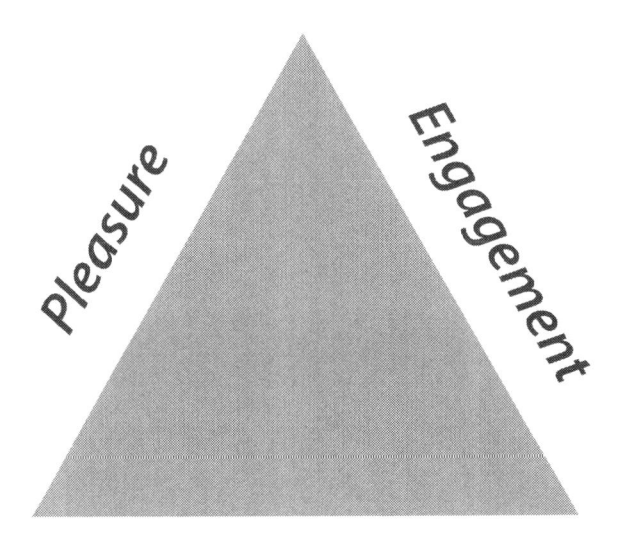

Pleasure

Engagement

Meaning

As you can see from the diagram above, to create a life of happiness and satisfaction, you need to focus on all three components of happiness. You need to put in place activities and processes that increase the amount of pleasure and engagement you experience. Most importantly though, these need to be underpinned with a foundation of meaning and purpose. This book will help you understand what this means and guide you in achieving this. In addition, you will learn about the enemies to these three components of happiness and how to avoid them.

Values In Action (VIA) Strengths and Virtues

One of the key insights of Positive Psychology is that happiness and satisfaction are markedly increased through the exercise of virtues and strengths.

Positive Psychology has identified six core virtues:

1. Wisdom and knowledge
2. Courage
3. Love and humanity
4. Justice
5. Temperance
6. Spirituality and transcendence

These core virtues in turn are comprised of 24 strengths or values in action. The research has shown that each of us has relatively enduring preferences and propensities for certain of these strengths and that satisfaction and happiness are increased whenever we utilize these strengths and values in our daily lives.

Prof. Seligman and his colleagues have developed a test to measure your key or signature VIA (Values In Action) strengths. You can access it from the following web page:

http://www.authentichappiness.sas.upenn.edu/testcenter

Once you have registered, select '*VIA Survey of Character Strengths Questionnaire*'.

Take a moment to complete the test and determine your top 5 or so strengths. Alternately, look through the following list of strengths and pick out 5 or so that really speak to you; that you consider to be the most important and valued for you.

VIA Strengths

Creativity	Curiosity	Open-mindedness
Love of Learning	Perspective	Bravery
Persistence	Integrity	Vitality
Love	Kindness	Social Intelligence
Citizenship	Fairness	Leadership
Forgiveness & Mercy	Humility & Modesty	Prudence
Self-Regulation	Appreciation of Beauty	Gratitude
Hope	Humor	Spirituality

Later in this book you will use these strengths to combat the enemies to your happiness. By focusing on these and other strengths and virtues in your life you will build emotional resources and resilience. Using these will strengthen your ability to create and enjoy happiness, both in your own life and the lives of others. Strengths based living is definitely a crucial step to avoiding the enemies to happiness.

Positive Emotions and Time

The temporal or time components of happiness have also been studied. Not surprisingly, the process of happiness has been found to be different for the aspects of past, present and future.

Positive emotion about the past for example has been found to include contentment, satisfaction, fulfillment, pride and serenity and can be increased by gratitude, forgiveness and freeing yourself from irrational dogmatic beliefs.

Positive emotion about the present includes joy, ecstasy, calmness, zest, pleasure and flow and can be increased by savoring, mindfulness and overcoming habituation.

Finally, positive emotion about the future has been found to be made up of optimism, hope, faith and trust and can be increased through learning to dispute pessimistic and negative thoughts.

Broaden and Build Hypothesis

Research by Dr. Barbara Fredrickson and others has lead to the development of the *'Broaden and Build'* theory of positive emotion. According to this theory, positive emotions broaden the scope of attention and cognition, and initiate upward spirals of increasing emotional well-being.

The findings suggest that positive emotional experiences lead to the building of enduring personal resources and psychological resilience and that positive emotions, through their effects on broadening thinking and creativity, lead to future increases in positive emotions. People who achieve such upward spirals build coping mechanisms for better handling future adversity. So by focusing on and creating positive experiences in your life, you'll do much more than simply make yourself feel good in the present. You'll be building lasting resources. Indeed, the research also shows that positive emotions promote greater health and longevity. So by focusing on positive emotions, strengths and virtues, you'll be helping yourself to create both a happier and longer life.

Cognitive Behavioral Therapy

The field of Cognitive Behavioral Therapy (CBT) and its allied field of Rational Emotive Behavioral Therapy (REBT) have for many years provided rich and powerful models for behavioral change. There is much research and evidence to support the ideas from CBT and REBT that our thoughts and feelings are linked, and that through changing our habitual thought and belief patterns we can make lasting changes in our emotional and behavioral responses that are instigated by them.

The key notion from these fields is encapsulated by the ABC Model, first developed by Dr. Albert Ellis. In this model the A stands for **A**ctivating Event, B stands for an Irrational **B**elief and C is the Emotional **C**onsequences.

Activating Event ⇨ **B**elief ⇨ Emotional **C**onsequences

According to this model, most people erroneously believe that A causes C, that negative events cause negative emotions. They miss the intervening, and often unconscious beliefs that actually cause the emotional response. It is negative, irrational and un-useful beliefs that mediate your negative response to any event. These irrational beliefs are beliefs that are illogical, unrealistic, and which hinder you from achieving your goals.

The key insight is that beliefs and attitudes cause and amplify feelings. By surfacing and actively questioning these irrational ideas and beliefs you can change your emotional responses and gain more choice over how you experience your world.

According to Dr. Ellis, there are three main underlying irrational beliefs that people in western cultures are indoctrinated into accepting. These are:

1. I MUST ALWAYS do well, and be liked or else I am a totally rotten, no good person

2. Others MUST ALWAYS treat me how I want to be treated, or else they are no good rotten people, who deserve to suffer

3. The world MUST ALWAYS treat me well — I MUST have everything I want quickly and easily, and nothing I do not

want, or else EVERYTHING is awful and terrible

Obviously, none of these 'MUSTS' are true or scientifically valid, nor are the conclusions that are drawn from them either true or useful.

Through the conscious and unconscious use and acceptance of such beliefs, people tend to upset themselves and thereby create anxiety, self-deprecation, the damning of others and intolerance of life conditions. Such thoughts and beliefs are self-defeating and lead to negative emotions and actions, creating a negative spiral of failure, pain and unhappiness.

Negative Belief Patterns

Some of the other important negative belief patterns that Cognitive Behavioral Therapy has uncovered are:

- **Over-Generalization** — taking a single negative event as a never ending pattern of defeat

- **Absolute *'All or Nothing'* Thinking** — seeing things in black and white, as totally true or totally false, when most of life is far more complex and varied than this

- **Perfectionist Thinking** — expecting and requiring things and people to be perfect; and when they aren't, seeing yourself or others as totally worthless, hopeless or useless

- **Magnification and *'Awfulizing'*** — making things worse or more horrible than they really are

- **Should and Must Statements** — creating rules and directives that eventually lead to guilt, anger and frustration

- **Negative Interpretation** — using pessimistic and negative thinking to always find the worst in any situation or person

By becoming aware of these patterns in yourself and others and by actively working to refute and interrupt these patterns in your own thinking and life, you can begin to think and live more positively and more rationally. This can and will lead to more balance and happiness in your life and the life of those you interact with.

A Guide to Happiness Using CBT

According to Dr. Albert Ellis, founder of REBT, the following provides a concise guide to achieving personal happiness.

Throughout this book we will be using these insights and a number of techniques from the fields of CBT and REBT to help you overcome Enemies to happiness.

1. Strive primarily for your own happiness
2. Put other people's happiness as a close second to your own
3. Decide you largely control your own emotional destiny
4. Look for any self-defeating or disturbance-creating Beliefs
5. Actively dispute and surrender any self-sabotaging 'Musts'
6. Create a set of rational Beliefs that will help you to live happily
7. Use cognitive methods (problem solving, researching, cognitive restructuring, imaging, humor) to surrender any irrational Beliefs
8. Work on your emotions to change them from inappropriate to appropriate feelings

9. Forcefully act against irrational Beliefs
10. Make the change and acknowledge that change isn't always easy, and keep working to ensure change.

mBIT — multiple Brain Integration Techniques

*m*BIT is an exciting new coaching, leadership and personal evolution field, based on startling new insights into human intelligence and wisdom. Over the last decade or so, research in the field of Neuroscience has uncovered that we have complex, adaptive and functional neural networks, or *'brains'*, in our heart and gut regions. Called the cardiac and enteric brains respectively, these neural networks exhibit memory, intelligence and adaptive processing — they learn, change and adapt. For example, with around 500 million neurons in the gut, (about the size of a cat's brain), the enteric brain is able to perform a number of vital functions and competencies that go way beyond mere digestion. And not surprisingly this explains why we intuitively know that we have a *'gut wisdom'* that we ignore often at our peril.

The Developing Brains

It's interesting to note that the heart and gut brains are primal in both an evolutionary sense and a developmental sense. The gut brain for example evolved long before the head brain, and can be found in organisms such as sea slugs, sea cucumbers and spineless helminthes (a type of parasitic worm).

Fascinatingly, the development of our brains during gestation mirrors evolutionary sequencing. As the fetus begins to grow, cells form that will eventually become the various brains. A neural plate first forms and then rolls into a neural tube. This tube eventually becomes the spinal column and goes on to generate the cephalic head brain. However, at the point where the edges of that neural plate meet an out-poaching called the neural crest forms and this develops and begins the process of generating the gut brain as the crest derived cells colonize the developing gut. So before the neural tube has elongated and rolled up to form the encephalon and ultimately the complete head brain, the gut brain has already begun forming and populating the visceral region. Along the way, as the neural tube develops there is another out-poaching of what ultimately becomes the vagus nerve system and this forms the cardiac plexus and the innervation of the heart.

Dr. Michael Gershon is one of the leaders in the newly emerging field of neurogastroenterology, and has published a groundbreaking book entitled, *'The Second Brain: Your Gut Has a Mind of Its Own'*. Dr. Gershon's book is being hailed as *"a quantum leap in medical knowledge"* and that it provides *"radical new understandings about a wide range of gastro-intestinal problems."* Gershon and his colleagues have shown that the enteric brain sends and receives nerve signals throughout the chest and torso and that it innervates organs as diverse as the pancreas, lungs, diaphragm and liver. The gut brain is also a vast chemical and neuro-hormonal warehouse and utilizes every class of neurotransmitter found in the head brain. According to Dr. Gershon over 80 percent of the serotonin used throughout the body and brain is made in the gut. Diseases of the head brain also affect the neurons in the gut and heart brains. Patients with Alzheimer's and Parkinson's diseases often suffer from constipation due to the same damage to their gut brains as is occurring in their cranial brains.

Neuroscience meets Ancient Wisdom

Yes, the heart and gut have their own deep intuitive intelligence and what's amazing is that we've known about this for thousands of years. Now finally science is catching up and validating what wisdom traditions have been saying for millennia. Indeed, in a review of the last 100 years of ethnographic data on spiritual traditions, researchers Frecska, Moro and Wesselman found that a tripartite concept of soul was the rule rather than the exception in aboriginal spiritual traditions, with the three *'souls'*, or intelligences, typically imbued in the head, heart and gut.

So yes, we have three brains, and each of them brings to life its own form of intelligence and its own set of prime functions and core competencies. Your multiple brains also communicate with one another, and can be aligned or not-aligned. Using methodologies from NLP (Neuro Linguistic Programming), Cognitive Linguistics and Behavioral Modeling, (more on this coming up) and informed by the latest Neuroscientific discoveries, the field of *m*BIT has codified a powerful system for communicating with and integrating the wisdom and intelligence of your multiple brains. I've written about this in detail in my book *'mBraining — Using your multiple brains to do cool stuff'*, and you can find out more details at my website www.mbraining.com.

As one of the original co-developers of this exciting new field of *m*BIT, I am well placed to share the insights it brings to human happiness. We all know what it's like to have our head saying one thing, our heart another and our gut screaming out, *"Warning, warning, warning!"* In the work on *m*BIT, we found that wisdom requires alignment of the three brains and that the neural networks need to be operating in what is known as an *'Autonomically Balanced Mode'* (we'll get into this in more detail shortly). When these conditions aren't met, and our brains are in conflict, we end up sabotaging our own success and happiness. We make un-wise decisions, we aren't able to motivate ourselves, and we make mistakes that we end up regretting. All enemies to happiness.

On the other hand, when all our brains are aligned and working together, when we are operating from a balanced and calm mode, our life runs smoothly, we bring innate and intuitive wisdom to our decisions, and our human spirit comes alive. This is the power of *m*BIT and *mBraining*.

*m*BIT Prime Functions

What *m*BIT uncovered is that each brain has a fundamentally different form of intelligence; they utilize different languages, have different goals and operate under different criteria. In other words, your head, heart and gut have different ways of processing the world, communicating, operating and addressing their own concerns and domains of expertise.

Our findings indicate that there are three core Prime Functions for each of the three brains:

HEART BRAIN PRIME FUNCTIONS

- **EMOTING** — emotional processing (e.g. anger, grief, hatred, joy, happiness etc.)
- **VALUES** — processing what's important to you and your priorities (and their relationship to the emotional strength of your aspirations, dreams, desires, etc.)
- **RELATIONAL AFFECT** — your felt connection with others (e.g. feelings of love/hate/indifference, compassion/uncaring, like/dislike, etc.)

GUT BRAIN PRIME FUNCTIONS

- **CORE IDENTITY** — a deep and visceral/bodily sense of core self, and determining at the deepest levels what is 'self' versus 'not-self'
- **SELF-PRESERVATION** — protection of self, safety, boundaries, hungers and aversions
- **MOBILIZATION** — motility, impulse for action, gutsy courage and the will to act

HEAD BRAIN PRIME FUNCTIONS

- **COGNITIVE PERCEPTION** — cognition, perception, pattern recognition, etc.
- **THINKING** — reasoning, abstraction, analysis, synthesis, meta-cognition etc.
- **MAKING MEANING** — semantic processing, languaging, narrative, metaphor, etc.

The importance of this to the realm of happiness is two-fold. First, it's crucial when making decisions and taking action in life that all three intelligences are accessed and incorporated into the process. Without the head intelligence, things will not have been properly thought through and analyzed. Without the heart intelligence, there won't be sufficient values-driven emotional energy to care enough and prioritize the decision against competing pressures, or to take into account the impact on others. Without the gut intelligence there will not be adequate attention to managing risks nor enough willpower to mobilize and execute the decision once challenges arise.

The second implication for happiness is that you need to ensure that you are not using one brain to do the function of another. Each brain has its own domain of competence and therefore is not the most competent in the other prime functions. This mistake can be typically seen in people's lives where they use their head brain to logic their way into a relationship decision that their heart brains don't really care about, or the head brain is used to design goals and action plans that the gut brain just doesn't fully engage with.

Understanding the ANS

As hinted at above, the Autonomic Nervous System (ANS) is an important component in how your brains work together. The ANS innervates and connects with each of your brains and influences their overall mode of processing. So it's imperative to understand something about the ANS and how it works.

Your overall nervous system has two major divisions, the Voluntary and the Autonomic. The Voluntary System is mainly concerned with movement and sensation. The Autonomic Nervous System on the other hand is responsible for control of involuntary and visceral bodily functions. The functions it controls include:

- Cardiovascular
- Respiratory
- Digestive
- Urinary
- Reproductive functions
- The body's response to stress

It's called '*autonomic*' because it is operates largely automatically and outside of conscious control. It's divided into two separate branches — the Sympathetic and Parasympathetic. These two branches work in a delicately tuned, reciprocal and (usually) opposing fashion. Simplistically, the Sympathetic system can be considered to be the *'fight or flight'* system. It allows the body to function under stress and danger.

The Parasympathetic system is the *'feeding and fornicating'* and *'rest and repose'* arm. It controls the vegetative functions of feeding, breeding, rest, recuperation and repose. The Parasympathetic system also typically provides ongoing opposition to the Sympathetic system to bring your total system into balance or homeostasis. Where the Sympathetic system is like the accelerator of a car, the Parasympathetic is akin to the brake.

In times of danger or stress, the Sympathetic system, which has a very fast onset and response, kicks in and gets you moving to handle or resolve the situation. The typically slower acting Parasympathetic system begins to operate after the danger has passed, and brings you back to normalcy. Without the opposing function of the Parasympathetic system your body would stay amped up, burning energy and fuel and eventually exhaust itself.

The ANS and Your Multiple Brains

As highlighted above, it's crucial to know about the Sympathetic and Parasympathetic systems because they innervate and deeply influence the operating mode of the heart, gut and head brains. There are major connections between the head brain hemispheres, the heart brain, the gut brain and these Sympathetic and Parasympathetic arms of the ANS, and since the two ANS components work in opposing ways, the dominance of one or the other leads to very different modes of processing throughout our multiple brains.

For instance, Parasympathetic activity generally slows the heart, whereas Sympathetic activity accelerates it. In the gut,

Parasympathetic activity enhances intestinal peristaltic movement promoting healthy digestion and elimination whereas Sympathetic activity inhibits such activity during times when physical exertion requires catabolic (energy) mobilization. The following are some of the main influences of the two systems:

Sympathetic Activation

Activation of the Sympathetic nervous system has the following effects:

- Dilates the pupils and opens the eyelids
- Stimulates the sweat glands
- Dilates the blood vessels in the large skeletal muscles
- Constricts the blood vessels in the rest of the body
- Increases heart rate
- Relaxes and opens up the bronchial tubes of the lungs
- Contracts the sphincter of the bladder and the bladder wall relaxes
- Shuts down and inhibits the secretions in the digestive system
- Can lead to involuntary defecation
- Is associated with Right Hemisphere activation and dominance in the head brain (and therefore concurrent style of cognitive and emotional processing)

Parasympathetic Activation

Activation of the Parasympathetic Nervous System has the following effects:

- Constricts the pupils
- Activates and increases the secretion of the salivary glands

- Decreases heart rate
- Stimulates the secretions of the stomach
- Constricts the bronchial tubes and stimulates secretions in the lungs
- Stimulates the activity of the gastro-intestinal tract
- Is involved in sexual arousal
- Is associated with Left Hemisphere activation and dominance in the head brain (and therefore concurrent style of cognitive and emotional processing)

You'll notice here that a powerful functional principle is in play. That is, two modes of *opponent processing* are operating for autonomic control across your total system. Consequently, your multiple brains can function in ways that are Sympathetic dominant, Parasympathetic dominant, or some combination of the two (and for more details on how these two systems can combine, see my book *'mBraining'*). The end result is that your Sympathetic and Parasympathetic systems dramatically affect how each of the Prime Functions of your multiple brains express themselves to create your subjective world, and in particular what happens when the two systems are operating in what is known as a coherent or balanced mode.

The Consciousness of Highest Expression

One of the many powerful models emerging from *m*BIT action research is that each of our brains has what is known as a *'Highest Expression'*. This is an emergent competency that represents the highest, most optimized and adaptive class of intelligence or competency of each brain. The Highest Expressions of each brain are:

- Head brain — **Creativity**
- Heart brain — **Compassion**
- Enteric brain — **Courage**

What's crucially important is that these Highest Expressions are only accessed and activated when a person is in an optimal state of neurological balance, or what is defined as *'autonomic coherence'*. This is when the person is neither too stressed nor too relaxed, but is in a flow state. And it makes sense doesn't it, that unless someone is in a neurological flow state with all going well, their perceptions of any particular issue or situation along and their subsequent decision-making will likely be impaired.

For example, if your ANS is functioning in an overly Sympathetic (e.g. stressed) state, your perceptions and decision-making will typically default to reactive conditioning. Conversely, if your ANS is functioning in an overly Parasympathetic (e.g. apathetic, depressed or *'freeze response'*) state, you'll exhibit an inability or lack of desire to act, or at best make timid decisions. Whereas in an optimum state of autonomic balance you are able to bring a higher order of consciousness to your decision-making and consequent actions. The insights of *m*BIT are that the wisest forms of Highest Expression only occur when your ANS is in a balanced coherent mode.

The Highest Expressions are also naturally integrative. Each relies upon the others in order to express itself fully and wisely. In actual practice, these *'virtues'* are neurologically integrative by their very nature and when expressed together enable the emergence of a higher order level of consciousness and wiser way of being.

For example, courage without compassion can quickly turn to cruelty, belligerence or domination. Compassion on the other hand, without generative creativity is what the Buddhists call *'dumb compassion'*; it can quickly lead to *'shared misery'* and do more harm than good. Creativity that is not connected to courageous action is mere mental masturbation; it generates great ideas but changes nothing in the world due to inaction or ineffective action. Alternately, courage without creativity can become bull-headedness and inflexibility, leading to courageous stupidity. Finally, compassion not channeled through a gutsy will-to-action helps nobody in any tangible way. So each Highest Expression of the three brains only fully express wisely into the world when all three brains are aligned and working together.

Controlling your Autonomic Mode — Balancing the ANS

When a nurse or medical practitioner measures your heart rate, they typically count the number of pulses over a period of 15 seconds and then multiply by 4 to get the average number of beats per minute. They might then write on your chart that your heart is beating at say 76 beats per minute (bpm). But in reality it's almost never exactly at that average rate. Your heart is constantly speeding its rate up and slowing its rate down.

This is because, when your Autonomic system has Sympathetic dominance, your heart rate speeds up, and then as your Parasympathetic kicks in to bring the ANS back to homeostasis, your hear rate slows back down.

Heart Rate Variability (HRV) is the measure of the beat-to-beat changes that occur in your heart rate. Because of the links to the ANS and the effects that thoughts, feelings and impacts from the environment have on your multiple brains (head, heart and gut), your pulse rate and HRV are affected by all of these. Researchers

What's it all ABOUT?

have found that HRV is a very useful measure of how you and your heart are coping with stress and what sort of state your ANS and brains are in. The graph below shows the heart rate of a person who is under stress.

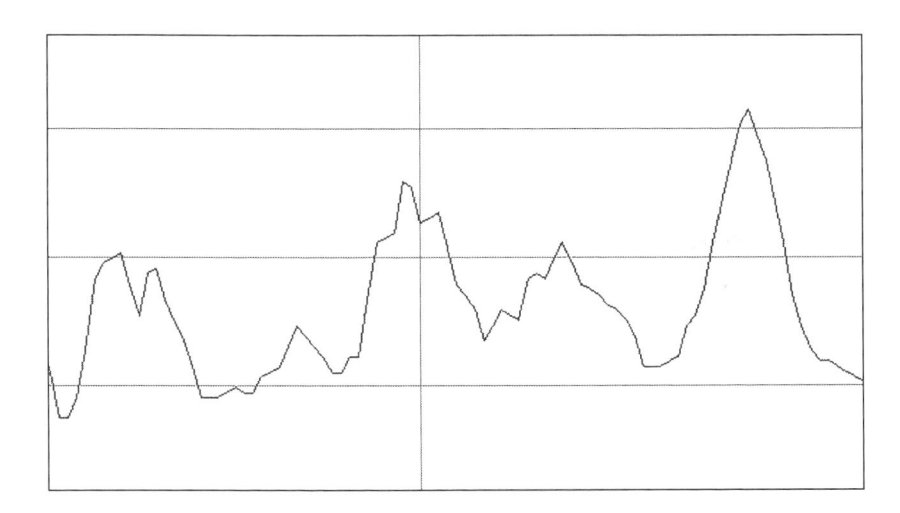

Contrast this with the one below from someone who is meditating and in a calm state, where they are focusing on feelings and thoughts of compassion and loving-kindness. Notice how smooth and even the changes in the heart rate are for the calm state. The graph almost looks like a sine wave. This sine shaped graph is one that has *'high coherence'*. Coherence is a mathematical measure that describes how evenly repeatable from moment to moment a wave-form is. A chaotic, sharply changing wave has low coherence, it is not evenly repeatable. In high coherence however, the Sympathetic and Parasympathetic systems are working nicely together, in balance, gently keeping your mind and body in an optimal state, and this shows in the smoothly changing wave.

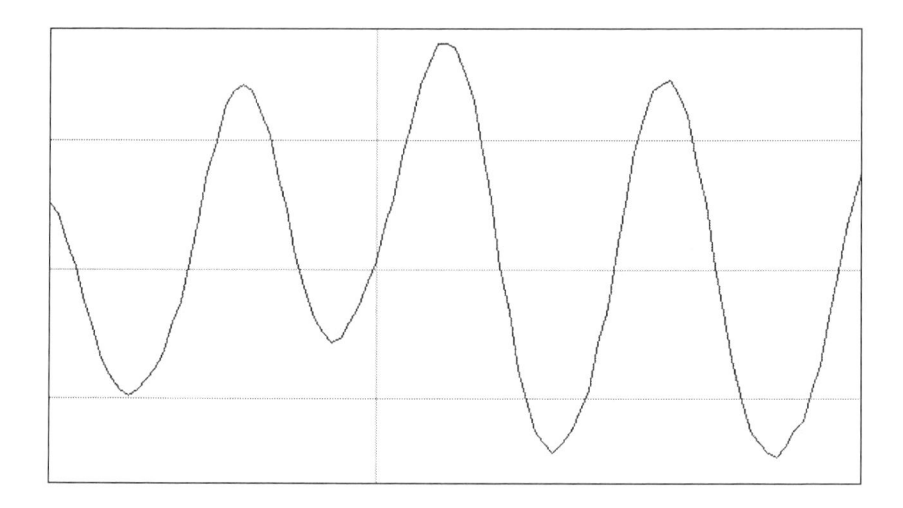

Numerous scientific studies have found that low HRV is one of the leading indicators of heart disease. They have also shown that high heart coherence is protective of the heart. Coherence acts to balance the heart, mind and emotions. It brings all the brains into resonance. When you are in a state of coherence you'll find you feel incredibly relaxed yet alert, your mind calms down and stress levels markedly decrease. It's a powerful state and one that is used for *m*BIT integration.

Resonant Breathing, Balanced Breathing

Breathing is primal and it's a powerful bridge between mind and body; the gateway between consciousness and the unconscious. In many languages the words for spirit and breath are identical. For example in Sanskrit the word is *'prana'*, in Hebrew *'ruach'*, Greek *'pneuma'*, and Latin *'spiritus'*. Numerous ancient traditions such as those of the Native American Indians, also believe life enters the body with the first breath, not at the moment of birth or conception.

Breathing has direct and intimate connections to emotional states and moods. Take a look at someone who is angry, afraid or upset and you'll see a pattern of breathing that is shallow, rapid and irregular. Conversely, think about how you breathe when you are feeling happy, calm and contented. In fact, it's almost impossible to be upset if your breathing is slow, deep, gentle and regular. And there's a reason for this…

In part it's because your breathing is connected via the '*bridge*' of the diaphragm which is co-innervated by both somatic and enteric/autonomic nervous systems. It turns out that from an evolutionary perspective, the diaphragm can be viewed as two distinct muscles, the crural and costal, one a gastro-intestinal muscle and one a respiratory muscle. These two muscles typically act in synchrony during normal respiration, but diverge during swallowing and the reverse process of emesis (a fancy term for throwing up). The value in knowing this is that the diaphragm, being effectively two muscles in one, and therefore co-innervated by both the head and gut brains, is a powerful gateway between them.

Importantly, there's also another powerful physiological mechanism at work with breathing. This mechanism involves what is known as the '*baroreceptor reflex*' found in receptors in the carotid arteries. Deep in the sinuses of the large carotid arteries in your chest and neck, lay specialized neurons called baroreceptors. These cells are stretch-sensitive mechanoreceptors and are optimized for monitoring changes in blood pressure which they relay to the brainstem and ultimately, via the ANS, back to the heart.

The result of this is that as you breathe in, your blood pressure drops and the baroreceptors detect this and cause your heart rate to speed up. As you breathe out, your blood pressure increases and your heart rate slows down accordingly. In other words, through a complex process of information coding in the ANS, this baroreflex acts to speed up your heart as you breathe in and slow down your heart as you breathe out.

Why is this important? Well... it gives you a powerful gateway for controlling your Autonomic system and bringing your Sympathetic and Parasympathetic into balance and coherence. Via controlled, balanced breathing you can control the Sympathetic and Parasympathetic arms of the ANS through the baroreflex, and put your heart into high coherence.

Simply put, by breathing for an in-breath of approximately six seconds and an out-breath of exactly the same duration, the baroreflex, along with the co-innervation of the diaphragm, leads to coherence and balance in your ANS, and in your multiple brains. It all starts through conscious control of breathing, leads to the heart coming into resonance with the calm balanced breathing and this communicates and spreads to the gut and head brains all coming together into calm, balanced resonance with the heart.

Such a simple process, yet so powerful. And now you can see why breathing is linked to thoughts and emotions. When you alter your breathing, you profoundly alter the state and mode of processing of your ANS and your head, heart and gut brains.

Note also the importance of having a balance between the in-breath and out-breath. If you breathe longer on the in-breath, you'll cause a gradual speed up of your heart and shift into Sympathetic dominance. On the other hand, if you do lots of long sighs, that is, breathe longer on the out-breath compared to the in-breath, you'll end up slowing your heart down, and putting yourself into Parasympathetic over dominance; another way of saying, you'll depress yourself.

These insights are obvious when you think about them. We've all had experiences of seeing someone panic and watching how they breathe when in that state. Similarly, you know when someone is depressed, they do lots of slow out-breath sighing. Start to notice this in yourself and others, and make sure you do balanced breathing to keep yourself in an optimal psychological and physiological state.

Generative Wisdom up the *m*BIT Roadmap

Ok, so you now know that you have three amazing brains, filled with deep intuitive intelligence, and they can be communicated with and brought into a balanced mode. You also know they can operate in what is known as their Highest Expressions and that when you do this it opens up greater levels of wisdom. But facilitating your multiple brains into alignment and getting them operating from their Highest Expressions requires a pragmatic *'how'* and some sort of suite of simple yet powerful techniques.

And this is what the field of *m*BIT is all about (and is detailed in my book *'mBraining'*), and is summarized in the diagram on the following page, known as the **mBIT Roadmap**.

In summary, the techniques and processes of *m*BIT involve getting into communication with your three brains, getting them aligned around any particular issue and then getting the brains functioning at their Highest Expression. When this is achieved, your innate intuitive wisdom emerges and the quality of your decisions and actions becomes adaptively and generatively different. The process is simple yet powerful.

The mBIT Roadmap

Wisdom

Highest Expression
Creativity (cephalic brain)
Compassion (heart brain)
Courage (enteric brain)

Congruence

Communication

Throughout the rest of this book, as appropriate, we'll be covering aspects of these steps and processes. The techniques of *m*BIT have been incorporated into the various exercises and success strategies. And if you want to learn more then I highly recommend reading *mBraining*, or going on one of the transformational *m*BIT workshops that are run by skilled trainers across the world. You can find details of workshops and trainers near you at:

www.mbraining.com

Entraining Others

One last thing to share with you is that the state of your heart and your multiple brains doesn't just impact your own mind and body. Work by numerous researchers and organizations, and in particular by the Institute of Heartmath over the last 20 or more years, has shown that the electromagnetic signal of the heart extends strongly for many meters from each individual. And the signal has the ability to resonantly entrain other people's hearts and thereby their Autonomic state and the mode their multiple brains (head, heart and gut) are operating in.

Just like when you pluck say the E string on a guitar, a nearby instrument that is tuned to the same frequency, such as another guitar, violin etc. will begin to resonate in sympathy with the plucked string. So, in a similar way when you place yourself into Autonomic coherence and come from the Highest Expressions (of Compassion, Creativity and Courage) you are able to entrain and impact those around you and help them to more easily access these same generative states in their lives. Yes, happiness is contagious, just as is depression. This is why it's so very important to learn how to generate the Highest Expressions of happiness in your mind, body and life and thereby entrain and influence the people around you that you truly care for. Your and their long-term happiness depends on it.

> *"Educating the mind without educating the heart is no education at all."*
>
> Aristotle

Neuro Linguistic Programming, Behavioral Modeling and Accelerated Learning

Over the last 35 years, Neuro Linguistic Programming (NLP) has been one of the fastest growing developments in applied psychotherapy. It is a technology of achievement and excellence, derived from studying how experts in different fields obtain their outstanding results. NLP provides models for human communication, learning and behavioral competence.

Science Digest reported that NLP, *"could be the most important synthesis of knowledge about human communication to emerge since the explosion of humanistic psychology... It may be the ultimate behavioral engineering tool."*

NLP provides a set of models, skills and techniques for thinking and acting effectively in the world, through which you can change, adopt or eliminate behaviors in yourself and others.

Another extremely powerful technology is Behavioral Modeling. This field provides processes for understanding, replicating and transferring expertise, abilities and skills. It can of course, be used to understand and codify such incredibly useful skills as creating and achieving meaning and happiness in life and avoiding the enemies to that happiness.

Accelerated Learning also presents popular and potent techniques for increased learning of new skills and knowledge. It is helping thousands of people around the world to learn more easily and effectively. Accelerated Learning reveals insights into how our memory functions and our brains best learn.

By combining and synthesizing the ideas and concepts of Positive Psychology and CBT with models from *m*BIT, NLP, Behavioral Modeling and Accelerated Learning, the Avoiding the Enemies to Happiness (AE2H) system guides you through the processes, strategies and skills for generating and amplifying happiness.

This approach is based on modeling real-world expertise combined with scientific validity. In this way Avoiding the Enemies to Happiness helps you get results, providing you with a pragmatic approach to happiness and success.

The NLP Success Strategy

The *Success Strategy* underpins NLP and is a simple yet elegant process that successful people across the world use to achieve incredible results. It has been modeled from experts around the world in many fields of endeavor, from business, communication and negotiation, to excellence in education, art and music. Fundamentally, success involves being outcome oriented, knowing exactly what it is you want, and constantly learning from feedback as you work flexibly to obtain it.

The *NLP Success Strategy* can be summarized as:

---

1. Clearly determine your **Outcome**.
2. Take **Action**.
3. Learn from **Feedback** — notice the results you are getting.
4. Be **Flexible** — change and adjust your behavior until your results match your outcome.

By systematically applying this formula, and the strategies of excellence that have been determined for each of the steps, you can support yourself with the best possible chance for success.

Purpose, Outcomes and Success

As highlighted by the NLP Success Strategy above, one of the most important and fundamental keys to human effectiveness and success is the ability to get clear about what you want and how to achieve it. Studies show that people who excel in this ability have specific procedures and strategies by which they repeatedly get results and achieve their outcomes.

One of the main components to getting clear involves how you specify and describe your purpose and your outcomes. To begin with, your purpose and outcomes need to be positive. That is, they must describe exactly what you want and desire, rather than what you don't want.

As an example, if you wanted more happiness in your life, you might describe your outcome as: *'I want to feel happier and more satisfied with myself and my life'*, (which says what you do want), rather than stating: *'I don't want to be unhappy or dissatisfied with my life'*, (which says what you don't want).

The positive statement creates a much clearer behavioral picture of the actions necessary to achieve your outcome, and it is often easier to move towards what you do want, rather than away from what you do not want.

Your purpose and outcomes should also be sensory specific. That is, they need to describe what you would see, hear and feel once they are achieved. What exactly is it you will experience once they are achieved? This is also called your *'evidence procedure'*, that is, what evidence will indicate to you that your purpose and outcomes have been met.

By describing your outcomes in this way you are directionalizing your mind towards their achievement, and by having very clear evidence procedures there can be no doubt as to whether or not you are achieving your intended results.

A further component to well formed outcomes is that they should be congruently desirable. That is, they need to be described in such a way that all of your multiple brains and the whole of your being says: '**YES!!**' This is done by linking the outcomes to your strengths and values (the things that really mean something to you), and by using words that describe the quality of how you want your purpose and outcomes to be accomplished.

For our example above, you could now describe your outcome as: *'I want to live a life that helps others and focuses on my strengths, to provide me with more happiness, joy, flow and meaning.'* This is positive, experience-able, sensory specific, measurable and emotionally impactful. Your evidence procedure could be when you can measurably experience more happiness and satisfaction, using one of the many psychological tools for measuring personal happiness, and can see that you have been enjoying flow experiences and doing actions of gratitude, savoring, appreciation and helping others.

Of course, there are a number of other components involved in making your outcomes incredibly powerful. However, we will cover these in the appropriate chapters of the book. For more information, you can visit our web site:

---

www.enemiestohappiness.com

The Cybernetic Loop

Thinking
internal processing

Feeling
internal state

Physiology
external behavior

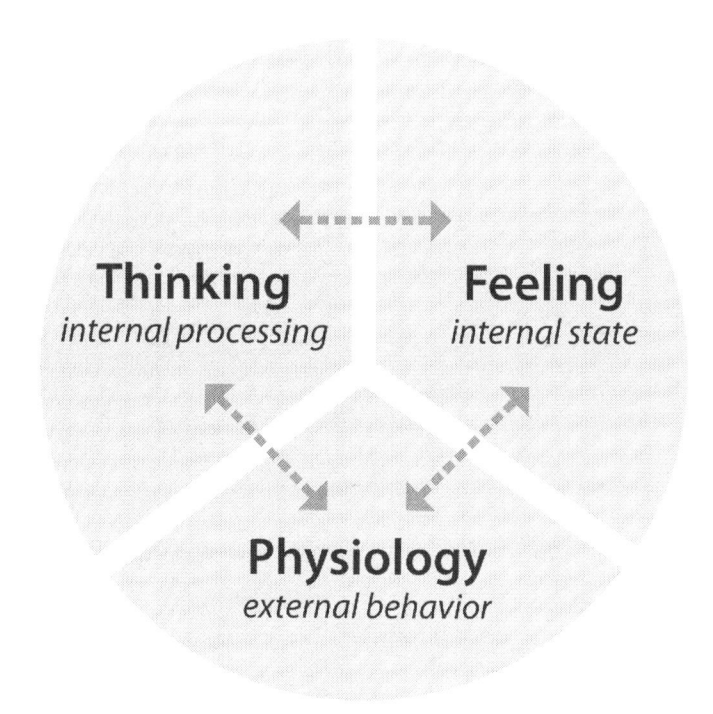

The NLP Cybernetic Loop model encapsulates the understanding that the mind and body are connected in a control loop; that the mind/brain and body interact and affect each other, they are not distinct and separate; that what affects one, affects the other. The Cybernetic Loop is summarized in the diagram on the previous page.

What this model shows is that your thoughts and thinking (your Internal Processing — thoughts, images, ideas) are connected to and both influence and are influenced by your feelings (your Internal State — your emotions). Your feelings in turn are connected to and both influence and are influenced by your physiology (your External Behavior — your body, breathing, physical state), which in turn is influenced by and influences your thinking, in a loop. The process of control runs both ways, each of the three components influencing the other.

So for example, whenever you think of something sad or picture something that makes you unhappy or depressed, you will begin to feel the emotions and feelings of sadness and depression, this in turn will cause you to hunch over, to breathe slower and lower in your chest, to tense your muscles. These changes in your physiology will lead to even more negative thinking and feeling which will amplify the negative physiological state and you will spiral into a more and more negative experience or attitude. You can see this in people who are severely depressed, they carry their depression in their stance and posture, they rarely look up, are unlikely to smile or breathe fully and deeply. They will be slow and lethargic, lacking energy and zest.

Alternately, the success spiral can function in a positive direction. If something positive happens to you, or you access a memory of a positive time or experience in your life, you will start to feel positive feelings and emotions. Your posture will change to being more upright, open, relaxed. Your muscles will relax. Breathing will be much more full and easy, bringing more oxygen to your brain and body. This in turn will support even more positive thoughts and feelings and the spiral will continue, generating positive changes in your mind and body.

Try it now. First think of something negative and depressing and notice the changes in your feelings and physiology. Notice where your eyes are looking. Odds are it will be down. You will likely stoop over or hunch your shoulders and your breathing will have decreased even if it is by a minute amount. Now, STOP! And change to thinking about something really positive. Something that thrills or excites you and makes you happy. Brighten up the image in your mind's eye and make it closer. Notice the feeling and physiology involved with these thoughts. Odds are you will be looking up, smiling and breathing fully.

According to NLP, *"Everything that happens in the mind, has a physiological effect, observable on the outside"* — the mind/brain and body are linked in a cybernetic control loop such that every thought and feeling has a demonstrable change and effect on and in the body. With training and sensory acuity you can observe these changes in yourself and others. This is what exquisite communicators do; they notice these non-verbal effects and messages that the unconscious mind is giving out, and they use these messages to influence and achieve their outcomes.

Knowing about the Cybernetic Loop and knowing how to utilize it is key in both avoiding many enemies to happiness and in achieving your own happiness and success. Throughout this book you will be learning how to utilize and facilitate your Cybernetic Loop. The first step of course is awareness and understanding, and now that you have been introduced to the concept of the Cybernetic Loop you will be able to begin to observe its operation in your life. Look for and notice times and situations where your physiology influences your thinking or vice versa; look for situations where your mood and feelings influence your thoughts. Begin to make distinctions between each of the components of your thoughts, feelings and behavior.

Staircase of Learning

There is a structure to how we gain new knowledge and skills. In NLP, we call the model of this structure the *'Staircase of Learning'*.

What's it all ABOUT?

Unconscious Competence

Conscious Competence

Conscious Incompetence

Unconscious Incompetence

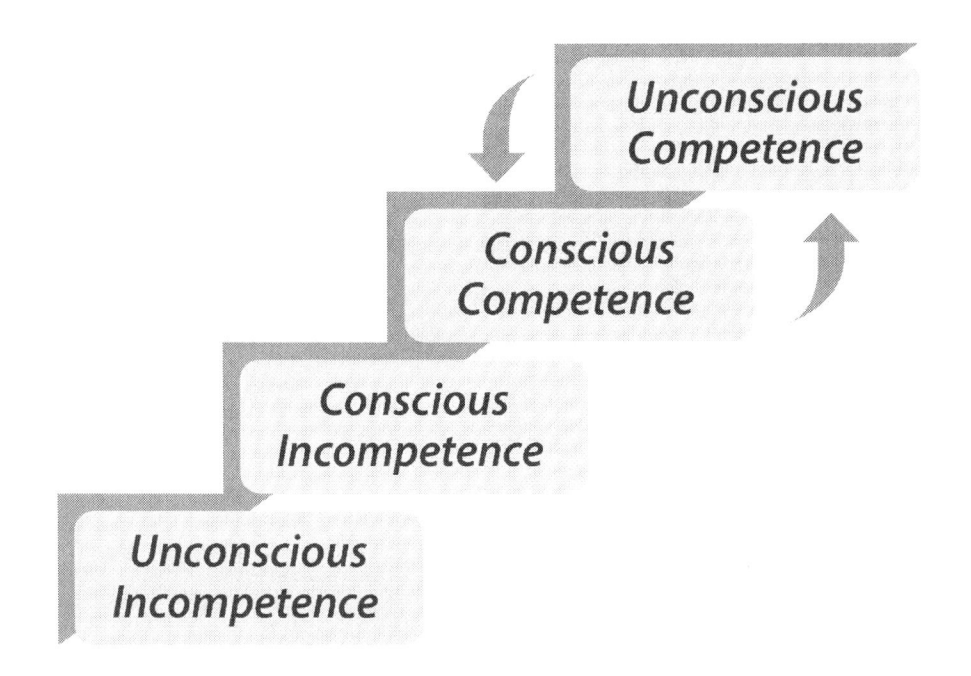

The Staircase of Learning

According to this model, we begin at a stage called '**Unconscious Incompetence**' — this is the stage where we are both not yet conscious of the skill or knowledge and aren't yet able to do it. For example, if you'd never heard about the NLP Success Strategy described earlier in this chapter, you would not be conscious of it and you would also be incompetent in its use. Through learning and awareness, by hearing about the new knowledge or skill, you have now moved to the next step in the Staircase of Learning. You are now consciously aware of the NLP Success Strategy, but not having practiced it you are still incompetent in its skill; you have moved to the stage of '**Conscious Incompetence**'.

However, by reading about and practicing the NLP Success Strategy you can move to the next stage of learning called

47

'**Conscious Competence**'. You are at the stage where, provided you consciously and assiduously focus on the skill you can demonstrate competence. Think about when you first learned to drive, or some other equivalent complex cognitive/motor skill. When you first started you had to expend ALL of your attention and consciousness on the skill. There was no room for inattention or distraction.

With practice though you move to the next stage of learning. The skill becomes relatively rote and automatic; you develop '**Unconscious Competence**'. At this stage, you can perform the skill repeatedly and usually without the need for focused conscious attention. A part of your mind/brain takes over the action. With training and practice you can develop unconscious excellence. The key to this is in '*self-reflection*', in examining your performance and in consciously practicing components of the skill. Consciously practicing to refine them, and then letting go, and allowing your unconscious mind to perform the skill at the new level of excellence.

These are simple yet profound insights into the nature of learning. For the most part, the majority of your life is lived with unconscious competence. You have learned and modeled your unconscious skills, attitudes and patterns of thinking and behavior from the experience of your life and from those around you. This provides you with both your success and failures. You have habits and patterns of happiness as well as patterns of succumbing to the various enemies to happiness. By understanding how learning occurs and how you can interrupt old patterns to generate new and supportive behaviors, you put yourself in a position of choice and control. And choice and control are major skills you will need in order to defeat the enemies to your happiness.

Conscious and Unconscious Processes

In the field of Psychology there is still an active and ongoing debate about the Unconscious mind, its role, existence and structure. In NLP however there is an accepted model of the Unconscious mind that is largely being ratified by recent research in Cognitive Psychology.

In NLP, the Unconscious mind is seen as all of those processes that occur in the brain outside of consciousness. That is, the Unconscious mind can be thought of as the '*other-than-conscious*' mind. These are the processes for example that are responsible for brain and body functioning, for performing visual processing, for unconsciously directing attention and awareness. Thousands and thousands of both simple and complex processes and patterns, operating generally outside of your conscious awareness.

The noted Neuro-physiologist and psychologist, Robert Ornstein calls these unconscious processes '*simpletons*'. He says the unconscious mind is made up of myriads of automatons; simple processes that are responsible for automatically performing small groups of tasks. Similarly, Marvin Minsky, an American Cognitive Scientist has labeled the unconscious mind a '*society of mind*'. By this he means that our unconscious mind consists largely of a society or population of relatively autonomous processes that communicate and interact with one another, much like members of society do with one another.

The insight that our mind is not unitary, not a single amorphous consciousness, is extremely important and useful. It explains why we often have conflicting parts and desires. Why we often act incongruently and undermine our own success. It's the reason why people can want and seek happiness and yet destroy this by succumbing to the very enemies of their happiness.

The nature of the brain and mind is that whenever we perform any behavior, we increase the probability that we will perform the behavior again. And through repetition of behavior, whether that behavior is an action, thought or feeling, we create a part of our brain/mind that automates the skill of the behavior. You can see this as a combination of the Cybernetic Loop and the Staircase of Learning. We create unconscious competence in a behavior and the part of our mind responsible for this skill operates automatically. It is a simpleton and automaton, often operating outside of conscious awareness.

And what applies to the brain in our head also applies to the brains in our heart and gut regions. As the field of *m*BIT shows, much of the intuitive intelligence of the heart and gut brains is processed out of our conscious awareness. And we form patterns and habits in how we communicate with and tune into the wisdom of our hearts and guts and how they respond to the world. The gut and heart neural networks also exhibit learning, memory and neuroplasticity. They are adaptive. So we can end up with unconscious competencies, habits and skills in the core competencies and prime functions of all our multiple brains (head, heart and gut).

So you need to be very careful of the thoughts and actions you take. Repeated behaviors generate *'parts'* in our unconscious mind; habits of success or failure. This is a vital and important understanding and we will return to it again and again in many parts of the book.

How this Book is Structured

Each chapter of this book follows a process and structure optimized to assist your understanding and learning of the techniques and material.

What's it all ABOUT?

There are a number of sections to each chapter, described below, that work with and complement the text of the chapter. Each chapter contains:

- You will Learn
- Chapter Material
- Deeper Understandings
- Awareness Questions
- Success Strategies
- Positive Psychology
- Thinking Tools
- Pattern-Interrupt
- Strengths and Values In Action
- Notes from the Field
- Remember This
- Extra Info

The book also operationalizes a strategy of:

1. Being able to spot an enemy to human happiness
2. Pattern-interrupt the old habits
3. Trigger new behaviors of happiness and success
4. Focus on positive results and celebrate them

Diagrammatically this can be summarized as —

The AE2H Strategy

Awareness ⇨ Pattern-Interrupt ⇨ New Behavior

Awareness — search for and beware of any of the Enemies to happiness in your life

Pattern-Interrupt — use pattern-interrupt techniques to stop any Enemy patterns, habits or behaviors you have been doing

Success Strategies — use the practical and pragmatic success strategies in the AE2H model to generate success and happiness and build positive patterns and habits in your life

> One important thing to note is that as you begin to use the AE2H strategy you will be moving yourself up the staircase of learning, so be kind and supportive with yourself through this process of positive change. Learning involves feedback and you will not always succeed at first go. Through practice, self-reflection and repetition you will improve and gain the skills and outcomes you desire. Following the AE2H model can be a brilliant and magnificent life adventure and it is definitely preferable if you approach it with this positive and flexible attitude.

So you can see a lot of thought, research and structure have been put into the design of this book. Read about each of the sections below and then go for it — get into the meat of the book and savor and digest it, and start to explore your way to greater meaning and happiness in life.

↻ Deeper Understandings

This section of each chapter provides deeper information and insights into aspects of the technology or techniques discussed in the chapter. You can skip over this section if you have no interest in furthering your understanding. However, if you really want to know more about the ideas, then this section is a must read.

⚲ Awareness Questions

Awareness Questions are questions to ask yourself in situations in which you are confronting an Enemy to happiness. Use these questions to gain more information about what's happening and to support yourself in overcoming the Enemies to your happiness.

☑ Success Strategy

A Success Strategy is a technique or strategy you use to overcome a specific enemy to happiness. You will want to practice each of the Success Strategies until you have unconscious competence and are skilled in utilizing them.

Pos Ψ Positive Psychology

This section provides information from the field of Positive Psychology. It is marked out so that you will know specifically that it is information that has been scientifically validated.

✖ Thinking Tools

This section provides sayings or maxims that are *'tools for thinking'*. By memorizing these sayings and using them to directionalize your mind and life, you will have in place the cognitive tools to support yourself in avoiding the enemies to happiness.

⚡ Pattern-Interrupt

This section provides information and strategies to interrupt any old unsupportive patterns in your life. Patterns are habitual ways of acting and responding unconsciously. Much of our behavior is habitual, instinctual and patterned. Some of these patterns support us, but many don't. Pattern-Interrupts are ways to break old habits, ways to block and change these patterns. They allow you to stop unwanted behaviors and put in place new strategies and behaviors of success.

Strengths & Values In Action

This section provides a table of Positive Psychology Values In Action (VIA) strengths. Use this table to determine which strengths, qualities and values to focus on and amplify in your life to support the processes and skills of happiness discussed in that chapter.

Notes from the Field

This section provides practical advice and tips from the real world and real people. It has been drawn from interviews and summaries of teachings from people who are experts in the field or who live demonstrably happy lives, people who in my opinion excel in living great and happy lives.

Remember This

This section provides a summary of the key learnings from the chapter and should be used for review and to assist you in remembering the ideas and strategies.

ⓘ Extra Info

This section refers you to the AvoidingTheEnemies web site for additional information, references and suggested reading on the chapter. There are numerous additional resources on the web site such as extra *'Notes from the Field'* interviews that we couldn't fit into the book and up to date information on trainings and other products to enhance your skills and learning.

Avoiding the Enemies to HAPPINESS

Chapter 1

It's YOUR world

You will learn to

- ✓ Create a fantastic self-image
- ✓ Increase your self-esteem
- ✓ Avoid self-sabotage and negative self-talk
- ✓ Use skills of freedom and flexibility
- ✓ Create a wonderful reality

It's YOUR world

It might be obvious that we all live in our own world. Whilst we do live in a shared world, we each create our own reality and version of that world. But what does *'we create our own world'* really mean? How specifically do we do that, and how can we change and enhance it to increase our happiness and avoid the enemies that detract from our success? In this chapter you will learn to create a reality focused on meaning and happiness and the skills of freedom and flexibility. It's your world and you can make it an amazing place to live in!

Enemies to your Happiness

- ✘ Poor self-image
- ✘ Low self-esteem
- ✘ Negative self-talk
- ✘ Self-sabotage
- ✘ Limiting your world — limited choice and flexibility
- ✘ Giving away freedom

Creating your model of the world

We don't operate off the world, we operate off a map or model of the world. Through our learning and experience we build an internal representation or model of the world — what we think the world is all about — and we operate unconsciously and consciously from that. This model then acts in many ways like a filter and influences what we are willing to see and do in the world. It creates stereotypes and self-fulfilling prophecies in our lives. Our map of the world can be either liberating or limiting and sometimes both.

One of the first and most important steps in creating happiness in life is to become aware of the elements that you have generated in your map of the world and selectively choose to change and enhance them. You want to remove or change any of the limitations that are the enemies to your happiness and additionally enhance and expand the elements and skills that make up your strengths in life.

"Achieving starts with Believing!"

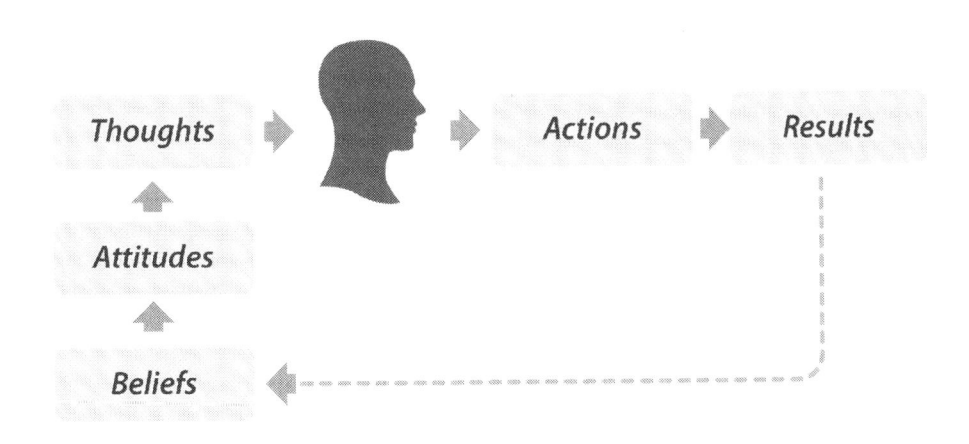

Thoughts ➡ ➡ *Actions* ➡ *Results*

⬆

Attitudes

⬆

Beliefs ⬅ ─ ─ ─ ─ ─ ─ ─ ─ ─ ─ ─ ─ ─ ─ ─ ─ ─ ┘

The diagram above shows how our model of the world influences our behavior and interacts with the world to generate experiences that reinforce the map.

For example, if you are about to undertake an activity and you believe that you can't do it or believe that you will fail at it, then you'll have a negative attitude towards the activity. This attitude can lead to negative and self-defeating thoughts as you begin the activity, which in turn can lead to incongruent and half-hearted actions, increasing the probability of negative results and possible failure. This reinforces your negative beliefs. *"See,"* you might say *"I knew I couldn't do it."* You now have a self-reinforcing, self-fulfilling prophecy in your life around that activity or context.

On the other hand, if you generate positive and supporting beliefs, you are more likely to have a positive attitude, supporting positive thoughts, resulting in congruent and positive behaviors and results. This in turn reinforces your positive beliefs. You now have a generative, positive reinforcing belief that supports more success in your life. It's not just a loop; it's like a spiral of success in your life.

Another way of looking at this is the way Henry Ford put it:

> **"Whether you think you can, or think you can't, either way you're right!"**

This saying talks about the power of beliefs and attitudes to shape behavior. If you create a reality that is filled with doubt and negative belief, then you will be constantly succeeding at failing and supporting your self-doubt. It's what is known in Organizational Psychology as *'Skilled Incompetence'*. People who fill their model with negative beliefs and attitudes, end up with a lot of unconscious competence at generating failure and negativity in their lives. It's like they succeed at failing. Which is kind of funny if it weren't so unfortunate and sad. What you want to do is the opposite, and become unconsciously competent at living and generating positive meaning and success in your life.

This is called behavioral excellence and by focusing your mind and life on building a life of positive success, you will create a reality that supports happiness in your own life and the life of those you care about.

> *"The world is a great mirror. It reflects back to you what you are. If you are loving, if you are friendly, if you are helpful, the world will prove loving and friendly and helpful to you. The world is what you are."*
>
> Thomas Dreier

Deeper Understandings — Modeling the world

There are three basic modeling processes that humans use to create their maps or models of the world. These are:

- Deletion
- Generalization
- Distortion

Deletion

The process of deletion involves focusing our attention on what we select as being important at a particular time and situation, while ignoring other information and possible experiences available to us.

The deletion process protects us from being overwhelmed and overloaded by too much information — filtering and directing our experience in a way we can cope with. Deletion restricts our present awareness to thoughts, actions and the things that are of the highest value and importance to us, removing from our attention and experience whatever is not deemed relevant to us.

For example, if you are driving along a highway and someone points out a new model of car, your attention shifts and before long you notice a number of cars of the type described. Previously these cars were being deleted from your experience as you progressed along the road.

You may also recall and become aware of your own examples of the deletion process operating in your life. Is there background noise where you are right now and that you weren't aware of until reading this sentence? What sounds and qualities of this noise are coming into your awareness now?

Notice the feeling of your body being supported where you are sitting right now. The feeling of your clothes against your skin. As you read these words, the information becomes more salient or important and your unconscious processing stops deleting this sensory information from conscious awareness and starts to bring it to your conscious attention.

Generalization

The process of generalization involves parts of our experience becoming a representation for a whole group or category of experiences.

People form and make up rules from a limited amount of information and then act on these rules as if they are a representation of the experiences all of the time and in every case.

An example of such a rule might be a person always adding extra salt to meals without first tasting the food to determine if extra salt is really needed to enhance the taste of the food.

Generalizations help us to form habits, directing our thoughts, actions and sensory experiences. We then repeat these habits on a regular basis, normally without questioning if the habit is still appropriate for our ongoing success and well-being.

Distortion

The process of distortion involves basing our experience on our own unique personal subjective interpretation, assuming the experience to be factual and true, without checking if our experience is a close representation of the reality we believe it to be.

Planning for future events, imagination and fantasy are all forms of distortion. In our mind we are creating a future experience we desire in advance of the situation arising.

These three processes of deletion, generalization and distortion allow us to expand and also limit our personal thoughts, actions and experiences of the world. By increasing our knowledge of how we create our experiences through our senses and how we communicate them to ourselves and others, we can create more empowering and effective choices.

Gaining more awareness and deeper understanding also allows you to expand your sensory experiences of the world,

> helping you gain flexibility in communicating and sharing your personal experiences with others. Knowing that the experiences of all people are truly unique to each person is vital. More importantly, realizing that how you map or model the world through the processes of deletion, generalization and distortion is an unconscious skill that you can bring to consciousness and learn to modify and change, can assist you to generate more happiness and success in life.

Awareness Questions — Questioning our Maps

Ask Yourself:

- How closely does my *'map'* fit the task, situation or conflict I'm currently in?
- What deletions, distortions or generalizations am I making that don't serve me?
- What is a more useful map that will serve me in this task or situation?

Identity

One of the key components of your map of the world is your sense of Self — your Identity. In part, your identity is made up of:

- Self-image
- Self-esteem
- Self-concept and Self-talk
- Embodied Core-self

Self-image

Fairly obviously, your Self-image is the picture you hold in your mind's eye about yourself. This image isn't static and it varies from context to context, though we tend to have an overarching image of our generalized self.

Submodalities

An important part of our Self-image is its submodalities. Submodalities are a concept from the field of NLP. They are the building blocks of the senses and as such they structure the meaningfulness of our experiences. For each of our sensory modalities (Sight, Sound, Feelings, Taste and Smell) the sub-components of the modality are its *'submodalities'*. So for sight, for example, the pictures in our mind have submodalities like size, focus, distance, position, color/black-and-white etc.

Probably the easiest way to understand this is by exploring a mental image right now. Remember the last time you went on holiday and picture it in your mind right now. As you look at this picture *'in your minds-eye'* begin to notice how far away the picture is. Is it really close or several meters/yards away? What size is it? What about color and focus? Where is it positioned, high or low in your visual field?

Research in Neuro-psychology has shown that internal imagery or visualization uses much of the same neural circuitry as used for external imagery or vision. For this reason, pictures in your mind use the same sort of submodalities as external vision. So just as objects you see in the real world have distance, focus, position, etc., so do images you see in your mind when you recall memories or when you create imagery during fantasy.

Now the most interesting and useful aspect of this is that the submodalities of the image structure the meaningfulness of the image. And when you deliberately change the submodalities it changes your subjective experience of the image.

As a graphic example, picture something you value very highly. Something that is really, really important to you. Notice where in space and how highly the image is positioned. Notice also how bright and close it is.

Now, picture something that disgusts you, that you don't value at all. Notice where in space the image is positioned. For the great majority of people, this image is lower than the highly valued image. It is often darker and further away.

As a generalization, the more valuable and salient an experience is, the higher it will be positioned in your mind-space, the closer the image will be, and the brighter it will be.

Just for a moment, try this experiment. Recall the image of the thing you value highly. Now push the image away off into the distance, making it really tiny, and dim it right down, maybe even to a sense of black-and-white. Now, as you look at this distant, small, dim image, how does it subjectively feel? For almost all people, this process will have made the memory seem much less important, much less meaningful.

Now zoom the image back in close, brighten it right up, and make it large and bold and fantastic. Just the way you like to have it. This is the power of submodalities in changing your experience and changing the meaningfulness you make of your memories and thoughts. And this process works not just for the visual modality of your experience. It works for the auditory, kinesthetic (feelings), olfactory and gustatory senses too.

But let's get back to your Self-image. Research in NLP has found that people who have a negative Self-image, use submodalities that create a subjective experience of negativity or meaninglessness. On the other hand, people who have a positive Self-image of themselves, use big, bright, bold, colorful, close submodalities. So right now, notice what sort of submodalities your Self-image is coded with. Picture yourself in your minds-eye.

What sort of submodalities are you using with unconscious competence? Could they be more positive and meaningful? Would you like to make your image of yourself one that really makes you feel great and motivates you? If so, do the following simple process to generate a positive Self-image in any context where the way you are thinking about yourself isn't as supportive as you'd like it to be.

> *"We are what we think. All that we are arises with our thoughts. With our thoughts, we make the world."*
>
> The Buddha

☑ Success Strategy — Brightening your Self-image

Use the following Success Strategy to create a bright, bold and compelling self-image:

1. Picture your Self in your minds-eye. Notice the submodalities of this image.

2. Decide on how you'd like to see the image, would you like it brighter, bigger, closer, more colorful, containing glitter and sparkle etc.

3. Zoom the image off into the distance, getting smaller and smaller, now bring it ZOOMING back in, powerfully, and as it comes back in, closer and closer, make it bigger, brighter, bolder, more colorful and any other changes you'd like to see. Make a ZOOMING or SWOOSHING sound as you zoom it back in.

4. Lock it into the new position and set of submodalities by hearing the sound of it *'Clicking'* into place. Make a sound of a solid clicking sound in your mind or even with your voice out loud.

5. Break state by looking around the room. Now repeat the above process from 3 to 5 times. As quickly as you can. Even if you have to do this whole process with an *'as if'* quality. Not everyone sees the images in their minds eye with total life-like quality, and it doesn't seem to matter for the effectiveness of this technique. You'll find it will work, even if you are just imagining all this happening.

6. Now test your work. Generate a picture of yourself in your minds-eye and notice that you are now using the new set of submodalities. Notice also how good you feel about this and your Self!

Self-esteem

Self-esteem is how we feel about or value ourselves; it's the emotional aspect of our *'self'*. The word esteem comes from the Latin *aestimare* — meaning to weigh or value. It is a process of comparison where you measure your value or self-worth by estimating yourself against some standard. For most people this process is generally done outside of their conscious awareness.

In order to support more happiness in life, it helps to feel good about yourself and your life. You need to be doing self-esteeming in a realistic positive way. To do this, you'll want to become aware of what you are comparing yourself to. There are many, many possible comparisons, for example:

- Current Self against Best Case or Ideal Self
- Current Self against Worst Case Self
- Current Self against Previous Case Self
- Current Self against Best Case Other
- Current Self against Worst Case Other
- Ideal Self against Ideal Other
- Worst Case Self against Ideal Other
- etc.

As you can see, some of these comparisons will always leave you feeling bad and negative about yourself, whilst others will leave you feeling unrealistically positive with an inflated sense of self-worth. For example, if you always compare your Best Case Self in any situation against the idea or memory of some Worst Case Other person, then you'll always come out the winner in the comparison, and end up with an unrealistic sense of positive self-esteem.

Dr. Marty Seligman, the renowned Psychologist and leader of the field of Positive Psychology suggests that Authentic Happiness comes in part from having what he calls a *'warranted'* Self-esteem. He believes the growing epidemic of depression and unhappiness sweeping the western world may be partly due to what he calls *'footless Self-esteem'* that has been promulgated since the 70's and 80's by the Californian Self-esteem Movement. In that philosophy, each person is accorded positive self-worth just for being alive and being a human, regardless of their behavior. Dr. Seligman suggests that true Self-esteem is earned through behaviors that support positive strengths, purpose and meaning in your life and your relationships with others.

NLP agrees with the findings from Positive Psychology and suggests that positive Self-esteem comes from using useful and supportive Self-esteeming comparison processes to build your model of self and the world. And these comparisons need to be aligned with your values and based on meaningful and successful behaviors.

Since the process of self-esteeming is generally done outside of conscious awareness, you'll need to begin to notice what sort of comparisons you are using in the various situations and contexts of your life. This process is actually quite simple, but because it's not something you'll likely have done a lot, it may at first be quite challenging.

Think of a specific situation or context in which you feel negatively about yourself. Now, as you think about this situation, notice the picture or pictures you have in your mind's eye. Who or what are you comparing yourself to? Do you picture some ideal sense of self in this situation and then compare yourself to that ideal? If so, this will tend to generate negative feelings that may not support you in learning and improving yourself. Or do you compare yourself to your worst-case self or some other worst-case other? That strategy tends to generate false feelings of positivity and superiority.

One of the most useful strategies is to compare your current self to your earlier self and notice how you have improved in that situation. If you haven't improved, then this can motivate you to begin learning and achieving new skills. If you have improved, you can feel good about your ability to do better. From a basis of positive feelings and Self-esteem, you can then compare yourself to your ideal self to see if you can do better still and continue to enhance and improve your life. In this way you are building a positive success spiral of warranted Self-esteem.

Nathaniel Branden, the successful author, psychologist and expert on Self-esteem says that healthy Self-esteem consists of two components:

1. **Self-efficacy** — confidence in our ability to think, learn, choose, and make appropriate decisions; and

2. **Self-respect** — confidence in our right to be happy; and in the belief that achievement, success, friendship, respect, love and fulfillment are appropriate to us.

So as you build and generate a model of your world, continuously check on how you are self-esteeming and how you compare and perceive yourself. By choosing and practicing positive and useful comparisons, you will increase your sense of self-worth and your positive regard for yourself and in that way defeat the enemy to happiness of low Self-esteem.

High Self-esteem'ing Strategies

Some other suggested strategies for generating high self-esteem — for doing high self-esteem'ing — include:

- Viewing yourself as a unique, valuable, and worthwhile person

- Believing in yourself (more on this in the following chapter)

- Loving and accepting yourself — research by Dr. Christin Neff has shown that healthy self-esteem can be generated by the use of self-compassion

- Letting go of past hurts and forgiving both yourself and others

- Believing in your dreams and persisting to make your dreams become reality

- Planning and setting attainable goals and outcomes in life.

> *"High self-esteem seeks the challenge and stimulation of worthwhile and demanding goals."*
>
> Nathaniel Branden

Pos ψ Broaden and Build Hypothesis

Research by Dr. Barbara Fredrickson on the broaden-and-build theory of positive emotion has found that positive emotions broaden the scope of attention and cognition, and initiate upward spirals of increasing emotional well-being. Her findings suggest that positive emotional experiences can lead to the building of enduring personal resources and psychological resilience.

This research links with the notion of using positive Self-esteeming strategies to induce positive emotional states, which in turn encourage positive success spirals in your life. As the skills of positive and warranted self comparison become practiced and a part of your ongoing repertoire of unconscious competence, you will find your sense of confidence and self-worth increasing. This supports you in stretching and learning new skills and increasing your levels of competence. The dance of increasing competence and confidence with the associated sense of Self-esteem and high self regard will serve you in experiencing more and more motivation and happiness in life.

The diagram on the next page summarizes these ideas.

> *"The bottom line message is that we should work to cultivate positive emotions in ourselves and in those around us not just as end states in themselves, but also as a means to achieving psychological growth and improved psychological and physical health over time."*
>
> Barbara L. Fredrickson

Building Confidence & Competence

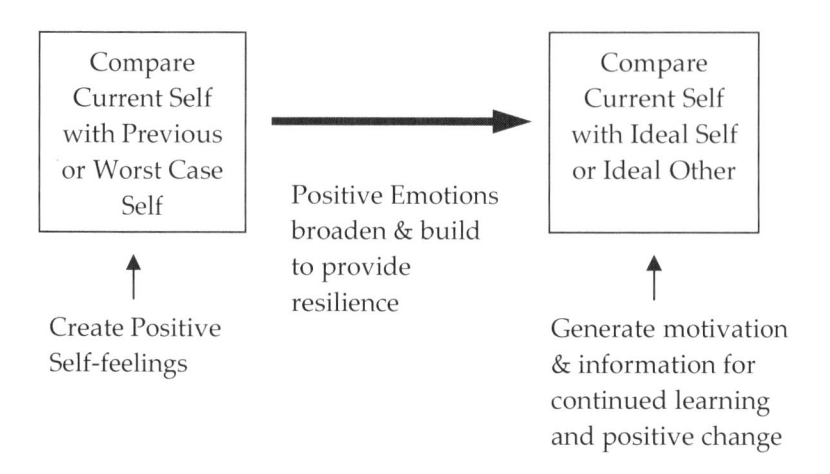

```
┌─────────────┐                           ┌─────────────┐
│  Compare    │                           │  Compare    │
│ Current Self│      ──────────▶          │ Current Self│
│with Previous│                           │with Ideal Self│
│ or Worst Case│   Positive Emotions      │ or Ideal Other│
│    Self     │   broaden & build        │             │
└─────────────┘   to provide              └─────────────┘
      ↑           resilience                    ↑
Create Positive                          Generate motivation
Self-feelings                            & information for
                                         continued learning
                                         and positive change
```

☑ Success Strategy — Building Positive Self-esteem

Use the following Success Strategy to build strong and positive self-esteem'ing:

1. Think about how you feel about yourself in a particular context or in the overall context of your life

2. Notice who or what you are comparing yourself to — call this Image A

3. To induce a state of positive emotion and empowerment, think of an example of an earlier time in your life when you weren't as able in a similar situation, or alternately, think of someone else who doesn't perform as well as you in this situation — call this Image B

4. Zoom the old comparison image (A) off into the distance,

getting smaller and smaller, now bring the new comparison image (B) ZOOMING back in, powerfully, and as it comes back in, closer and closer, make it bigger, brighter, bolder, more colorful and any other changes you'd like to see. Make a ZOOMING or SWOOSHING sound as you zoom it back in.

5. Lock it into the new position by hearing the sound of it *'Clicking'* into place. Make a sound of a solid clicking sound in your mind or even with your voice out loud. Notice how good and positive you feel about this positive comparison. Of how over time you have definitely improved and know that you can continue to do better in a positive way. Amplify these positive emotions. Really feel them and enjoy them.

6. Break state by looking around the room. Now repeat the above process from 3 to 5 times. As quickly as you can. Even if you have to do this process with an *'as if'* quality. Not everyone sees the images in their minds eye with total life-like quality, and it doesn't seem to matter for the effectiveness of this technique. You'll find it will work, even if you are just imagining all this happening.

7. Now think of an ideal image of yourself or some other exemplar in this situation. Generate a picture of yourself in your minds-eye doing even better and notice that you can feel confident, motivated and positive about increasing your competence in this situation. Notice also how good you feel about this and your Self!

Failure to Feedback

Remember the NLP Success Strategy described in Chapter 0. Operating from this success strategy you clearly know your outcome, take action, learn from feedback and then flexibly change and adjust your actions, looping until you achieve your outcome. Within this framework, there is no failure, only feedback. Every action you take either moves you closer to your outcome or further away, and provides you with information or feedback about whether what you are doing is helping you get closer to your outcome. And if what you are doing isn't working then try anything else, as it has more chance of working than an action that is providing the feedback that you are not moving toward the outcome.

It's so simple and a really powerful model for achieving success, and incredibly empowering to know that no matter what happens, you are never a failure. Instead, you are always seeking and appreciating feedback about the direction you are moving in. So when you look at the actions and results in your life and compare yourself to your values and standards, take heart that as long as you are focusing on positive outcomes and meaningful purposes, no matter what the immediate results you're achieving, you are never a failure, you are instead operating as a powerful success control master.

Thinking Tools – Feedback

No such thing as failure, only Feedback!

Self-talk

Self-talk is the auditory component of your sense of self and Self-concept. It's what you say about yourself to yourself. For some people their Self-talk is very motivational and supportive. However a lot of people, at least some of the time, use critical and judgmental Self-talk that is self-destructive and damaging to their positive sense of self. Negative Self-talk is a serious enemy to happiness.

In order to nurture your growing happiness and self-esteem, you'll need to challenge and change any negative critical messages from your inner voice. There are two key ways you can do this.

The first comes from the fields of Cognitive Behavioral Therapy and Positive Psychology and involves challenging the content of such messages. It is called the ABC model. The second method comes from NLP and involves changing the submodalities of the voice so it has less emotional impact and can be taken very light-heartedly.

By using the two methods together you can quickly turn any internal critical voice into a positive resource that will support you in your quest for increasing happiness.

One thing worth noting is that the internal critic can sometimes be seen as providing a benefit. Your internal criticizing may serve an important purpose in providing motivation and control. For example, some people use it to motivate getting out of bed, going to work, performing chores they don't like, overcoming laziness etc. You need to ask yourself what useful purposes your internal critic is serving? The strategy to use is to challenge any negative or critical internal dialogue, determine its positive intentions and then use healthier ways of achieving the critic's purpose.

Pos ψ The ABC Model

The ABC Model was originally developed in the field of Cognitive Behavioral Therapy and has been adapted and refined by Positive Psychology. Research has found that it is an effective method for challenging negative and pessimistic thoughts. In this technique you explore the thought and dispute it vigorously to come up with a more positive and useful way of thinking about it.

Adversity — the A stands for the adversity or pessimistic accusation. In this step you specifically describe and write down the negative statement you are ascribing to yourself.

Belief — in this step you explore the underlying beliefs inherent in the adversity or accusation. You need to think flexibly and accurately about the beliefs underpinning the accusation.

Consequences — here you explore the emotional and behavioral consequences of your beliefs, how you are responding to the negative beliefs and adversity.

Disputation — in this step you dispute and challenge the negative or critical beliefs and accusations. Challenge your internal criticism and pessimism by writing down and saying more reasonable, self-tolerant things about yourself. Generate new and more supportive and accurate beliefs. Gather evidence from the past to find and show yourself counterexamples to the negative beliefs or accusations.

Energization — finally, focus on the positive purpose, outcomes and beliefs you have generated in the previous steps. Find and explore new ways to achieve the positive intentions inherent in the original accusations. Energize the new ways by thinking of situations in the future where you will have applied these new beliefs and outcomes.

Celebrate a more optimistic and positive way of thinking about yourself and your world.

☑ Success Strategy — Internal Critic Tune-out

This technique uses auditory submodalities to control and tune-out any negative impact of internal critical self-talk:

1. Notice whose voice tonalities the internal criticizing is using. Are they yours or one of your parents or some significant other? This can often be important and useful information.

2. Notice also where in space the voice is coming from. Is it in both ears, or only one? Is it from in front or behind, up high or down low? Determine and notice the submodalities of this internal auditory experience.

3. Now, since it's your own internal experience, which you can control, shift the voice to coming from one of your little toes. That's right, from your smallest toe. Way down there. Notice that the voice no longer seems so serious or important when you hear it coming from your toe.

4. Now add in some circus music to the voice. And make the voice high pitched and squeaky. Speed it up and make it really low in volume. Play with the auditory submodalities so that it feels small and silly and meaningless.

5. Perform an ABC Model on that silly internal criticizing or negative self-talk to extract the positive intentions and to generate more empowering and useful ways of talking and

motivating yourself.

6. Finally, zoom the criticizing voice way off into the distance, getting smaller and smaller until it disappears. This is how you control and tune-out internal self-talk that is un-useful. In its place, zoom back in a deep and resonant, close and powerful, positive voice saying new and empowering beliefs to support your happiness and success.

Embodied Core-self

As described in Chapter 0, neuroscience has recently discovered that we have complex, adaptive and functional neural networks, or *'brains'*, in our heart and gut regions. One of the prime functions of the gut (enteric) brain is to represent and maintain a core visceral identity and a felt-sense of self. Due to its evolutionary history, the gut brain is responsible at a core level for determining what will be assimilated into self and excreted from self. It must determine what is required to maintain health and wellness in the system and decide whether molecules ingested into the stomach will be absorbed or excreted. Indeed, research has shown that more than 80 percent of our immune cells are located in the gut, and the enteric brain is intimately involved in managing immune function.

The prime functions of the gut are also around protection, self-preservation and motility. Back when evolution was at the stage of complexity of sea slugs and worms, organisms only had a neural processing system of an enteric brain. This intelligence was used to maintain a sense of self, to detect threats and food in the environment and move away from danger and towards opportunity. The gut brain in humans still provides a similar role, it maintains boundary detection, core identity and a sense of gutsy mobilization. So how you feel about yourself at a deep visceral level makes a profound difference to your happiness.

The heart brain on the other hand has prime functions around emotions, values and connection with others. How you emotionally feel about yourself is also represented and processed in the heart brain. At a heart level, do you value and love yourself? Do you love and accept your body and your inner-most you? If not then you won't be able to truly embody happiness and self-satisfaction. Feeling love and compassion for yourself is an important step in the pathway to happiness. And to do this you need to be aligned and in touch with the deep intuitive intelligence of your heart and gut brains.

At a core level you need to be integrated and whole, to fully embody your sense of self-ing. And of course the first step towards this is to begin to appreciate yourself at a heart and gut level. Once you realize that your heart and gut are not just a pump and a bunch of plumbing, but that they are places of deep intuitive intelligence, you can then start to really accept and embody your own innate wisdom. We'll discuss this more in the coming chapters, and for an in-depth look at the skills and distinctions on aligning the head, heart and gut brains, please visit www.mbraining.com or grab a copy of my book, *'mBraining'*.

Self-sabotage

Self-sabotage is another common enemy to happiness. It is the process whereby people sabotage and unconsciously undermine their own efforts to have and do the things they want in life. Fear of success is also a form of Self-sabotage.

Being aware of and overcoming any self-sabotaging behaviors is an important component of happiness-ing. The first step is to make note of situations where you are undermining your own goals and outcomes. It is vital that you develop this sort of self-awareness, to note and understand what unconscious competences you have that don't serve you and in what contexts they are triggered.

The next step is to develop strategies for interrupting any of these patterns and replacing them with new and supportive behaviors. Over time and with practice and reinforcement, the new patterns of unconscious competence will become habits that serve and support your happiness and success.

Pattern-Interrupt — Mirror Self-Awareness

Research in the neuro-sciences has shown that self-awareness is mediated by the prefrontal lobes, and that looking at yourself in a mirror and talking and reflecting on your self increases activity in the prefrontal lobes. Negative emotionality on the other hand is mediated by the limbic system and the amygdalae, which are much more primitive structures of the brain.

By looking at yourself in a mirror and reflecting positively out loud about yourself and your positive outcomes and goals, you are switching your brain into positive and creative prefrontal activity. This interrupts any negative or limiting emoting patterns.

In addition, when articulating out loud about positive emotional aspects of yourself, it is virtually impossible to do negative internal dialogue or negative self-talk at the same time. This technique ensures you are pattern-interrupting any negative or limiting patterns of self.

It's YOUR world

Interrupt any old unsupportive patterns in your life by:

- Stand in front of a mirror and look yourself in the eyes.

- With passion, positivity and conviction say positive things about yourself, your life, your goals and outcomes out loud to yourself.

- Each day, as part of your morning and nightly routine, develop a habit of looking at yourself in the mirror, repeating the following self-affirming statements —

    - I have permission to love and approve of myself

    - I deserve to take care of myself

    - It is okay to love and accept myself

    - It is okay to think well of myself

    - I am worthwhile

    - I am valuable

    - I accept and love myself

    - I do the best I can with my current awareness

    - I am courageous and accept responsibility for my thoughts, actions and feelings

    - I own my strengths

- o (Your Name) you are capable of learning

- o (Your Name) you deserve to achieve your outcomes

- o (Your Name) you can grow your awareness, skills and strengths

- o I accept where I am now and enjoy the process of achieving my outcomes

- As you say each statement, really feel it as true in your heart and deeply satisfying in your gut. Breathe evenly, approx. 6 seconds in and 6 seconds out (or whatever feels comfortable for you, as long as the in-breath and out-breath are even durations). As you say each statement and ruminate on it, breathe a sense of positive value, compassion and care for yourself into your heart on the in-breath. Then breathe that down into your gut on the out-breath. This sends strong messages from your head brain into your heart and gut neural intelligences.

- Create and repeat your own positive and encouraging scripts. Remember to include your strengths and positive character traits.

The Guy in the Glass

When you get what you want in your struggle for pelf,
    And the world makes you King for a day,
  Then go to the mirror and look at yourself,
    And see what that guy has to say.

For it isn't your Father, or Mother, or Wife,
    Who judgment upon you must pass.
The feller whose verdict counts most in your life
    Is the guy staring back from the glass.

He's the feller to please, never mind all the rest,
    For he's with you clear up to the end,
And you've passed your most dangerous, difficult test
    If the guy in the glass is your friend.

You may be like Jack Horner and "chisel" a plum,
    And think you're a wonderful guy,
But the man in the glass says you're only a bum
    If you can't look him straight in the eye.

You can fool the whole world down the pathway of years,
    And get pats on the back as you pass,
But your final reward will be heartaches and tears
    If you've cheated the guy in the glass.

The Guy in the Glass
Dale Wimbrow, 1934

Choice & Flexibility

Another serious enemy to happiness is diminishing your world through limited choice and flexibility. Freedom and choice are important values and you want to hold on to them with all your heart. There is an old Estonian proverb, full of wisdom that says *"never leave yourself with only one pair of shoes"* because if they get too tight and start to hurt, your life can end a painful misery. This maxim or learning tool refers to the idea that if you give away choice and only allow yourself one option in life, and if that option becomes problematic, you'll end up with a life of unhappiness.

There is a provable mathematical theorem from Systems Theory that supports this. Known as the '**Law of Requisite Variety**' it suggests that in any system the element that has the most choice, flexibility or requisite variety will be the controlling element. The corollary to this is that to gain more control in any system, you need to give yourself more choice or flexibility.

Remember the NLP Success Strategy. Its fourth step is about flexibility and is supported by the ideas from the Law of Requisite Variety. A simple way to remember this law is *'Choice = Control'*. Always give yourself more choice and flexibility and never give away your control. As often as possible in life always give yourself more choice (within reason) rather than less.

Of course, choice and the number of options need to be balanced. Research in psychology has shown that too many choices can also lead to stress and decreased happiness. The optimal number of choices appears to be somewhere between 3 to 6. More or less than this can be problematic.

Awareness Questions — Choice & flexibility

Ask Yourself:

- In what situations or contexts do I need more choice and control?
- In what areas of my life do I lack flexibility?
- How can I create more choice and freedom in my life?

Thinking Tools — Choice & control

Choice = Control

Thinking Tools — Power to decide

S/he is free who knows how to keep in his/her own hands the power to decide.

⚒ Thinking Tools — More freedom

Never leave yourself with only one pair of shoes!

Cognitive Dissonance

Psychological research has shown that human beings can only tolerate a certain amount of discrepancy between their thoughts and their behavior. The feeling that is generated by such discrepancy is called Cognitive Dissonance. It is a negative feeling that the unconscious mind will do its best to remove.

This process of aligning thoughts and behavior normally ensures that a person's model of the world is reasonably cohesive and self-healing. It can also lead to a reluctance to embrace change.

Knowing this however, can be very useful and empowering. By deliberately stretching and controlling your model of the world you can support your unconscious mind to bring about positive change in your behaviors and life. Fill your mind, heart and conscious thoughts with positivity and happiness, focus on your strengths and the qualities and values you want in your life, and hold strongly to these. You will find your behaviors becoming aligned and congruent with your thoughts, beliefs and values. Remember, it's your world and you can create and live a life of happiness by focusing on meaning, engagement and positive purpose.

> *"If you don't take control of your life, someone else will."*
>
> Paul McKenna, Change Your Life in 7 Days

Strengths & Values In Action

Use the following table to determine which strengths, qualities and values to focus on and amplify in your life to support the processes and skills of happiness. Also notice if you have any elements of the absence, opposite or exaggeration of these strengths and remove them from your behaviors and your life.

Enemies to happiness	VIA Strength
Identity Issues	Integrity
	Persistence
	Creativity
Choice and Control	Self-regulation
Poor Self-love	Love
	Kindness
	Forgiveness
	Humility

Notes from the Field — The Natural Bardo

Sogyal Rinpoche, in his book, *'The Tibetan Book of Living and Dying'* talks about the Natural Bardo. He says that *"If we have a habit of thinking in a particular pattern, positive or negative, then these tendencies will be triggered and provoked very easily, and recur and go on recurring. With constant repetition our inclinations and habits become steadily more entrenched, and go on continuing, increasing and gathering power, even when we sleep. This is how they come to determine our life, our death and our rebirth."*

This is why it is so important for happiness and for living a good life to notice our habitual thinking patterns and behaviors. To notice what maps we are building of our world.

Imagine your life like a bank in which happiness is deposited as imprints and habitual tendencies. The more positive tendencies and behaviors you deposit, the more happiness you'll achieve in your daily living.

☞ Remember This

✓ Track for and create a fantastic Self-image in every context of your life.

✓ Notice your Self-esteeming comparisons and strategies and use positive emotions to support yourself in increasing your self-confidence and competence. Make sure your actions are aligned with your values and your concept of your ideal self.

✓ Avoid self-sabotage and change any negative self criticizing by altering the submodalities of your inner voice, focusing on your positive intentions and embodying a core-self of compassion and self-acceptance.

✓ Always choose to give yourself choice, freedom and flexibility.

✓ You never operate directly off the world, instead you operate off a map or model of the world that contains deletions, distortions and generalizations. It's your world, so notice and actively track for what sort of reality you are creating for yourself and continue to flexibly build and generate a wonderful reality of meaning, purpose and value to yourself and others.

ⓘ Extra Info

Refer to www.enemiestohappiness.com for

- more information about the material covered in this chapter
- additional reading and references for this chapter

Avoiding the Enemies to HAPPINESS

Chapter 2

I don't BELIEVE it

You will learn to

✓ Remove negative beliefs and limitations

✓ Create empowering beliefs

✓ Embody attitudes of success

✓ Amplify beliefs to support your happiness

I don't Believe it

You'd have to be comatose not to realize your beliefs and attitudes make a huge difference to your life. Your beliefs and attitudes influence so many factors and elements of your experience. They impact and direct your unconscious mind. They setup self-fulfilling prophecies in your decisions, behaviors and the perceptions of others. Your beliefs are vital for whether or not you achieve happiness and success.

In this chapter you will learn about the structure of beliefs, how to quickly and easily transform and change them to empower and support yourself, and learn tools and techniques for challenging and overcoming fears and limitations. Remember, *'achieving starts with believing'* — so sit up, lean forward and get excited about learning some new skills — you better believe it! Cause it's both useful and true that beliefs and attitudes really do make a difference to your happiness.

Enemies to your Happiness

- ✖ Negative and disempowering beliefs
- ✖ Limiting rules and constraints
- ✖ Fear and rigidity
- ✖ Maintaining negative attitudes

The Power of Beliefs

Beliefs, attitudes and values direct most aspects of your life and your psychology. Beliefs are generalizations or rules that you've come to accept as true about yourself and the world. Beliefs also show up as stereotypes, prejudices and mindsets. A large number of your beliefs and attitudes are outside your conscious awareness. It takes work and insight to bring them to conscious consideration. There's much research to show that a large difference can exist between your espoused or conscious beliefs and your operating beliefs, your *'beliefs-in-action'*. This is the difference between what you say and what you actually do.

Given the importance and power of beliefs, you'd think it would be something you'd be taught at school, something that society would encourage and educate about. But I bet that at school you never had a class called *'Empowering Beliefs 101'*. Well, let's remedy that here and now. Beliefs are important and since knowledge is power, let's learn about the process of generating and changing beliefs; of how beliefs influence your unconscious mind and the minds of others. We'll examine your limiting and negative beliefs and mindsets and you'll install success strategies for tracking and overcoming self-imposed limitations and creating wondrous and supportive beliefs and attitudes.

> *"Belief is Power. The power to create. We create our reality simply by what we agree to believe."*
>
> Ray Dodd, The Power of Belief

Beliefs 101

One of the first things to understand about beliefs is they don't actually exist! Yes, that's right. You've never seen a belief. Ever. You've only ever seen the process or behavior of believing. Think about it.

In NLP, the word *'belief'* is what's called a nominalization. A nominalization is a verb, or doing word, that has been turned into a noun, turned into a *'thing'*. Language is powerful. It's how you do most of your thinking, your communicating. It's how you organize and make sense of your world. It's a very powerful coding and representational system. And like any powerful system, can be used appropriately or misused.

We typically use nominalizations to fix an ongoing process into a static object so we can get a handle on it, to talk about it. But in doing this, we distort our reality and if we're not careful we end up mistaking our map for the territory. This distorting can lead to un-sane (not totally sane) thinking and behavior, creating problems in our lives.

Nominalizations

Nominalizations are quite insidious. We talk about *'beliefs'* as if they are things, something you can have, something that has a reality and a life of its own. But you can't put a nominalization into a wheel barrow, you can't hold one, you can't buy one. It's not a real noun, not a real *'thing'*. Nominalizations are just handy descriptors for processes that are spread in space or time; that are ongoing.

Some examples of nominalizations are: relationship, love, decision and negotiation. Notice the suffix *'-ion'* used in many of these words, it's one of the indicators of a nominalization. But not all nominalizations have *'-ion'* in them, for example the word *'love'* is a nominalization. You can't put love in a bucket, or shop for it at the supermarket. You don't *'have'* love. It is not a true thing. It's a process, the process of loving. It's a verb, a doing word, a process.

"*So what*" you might say, they're just words… Well, here's one of the key insights from NLP, and one which is now being backed up by modern neuroscience and cognitive psychology. Words are powerful. They influence your whole Cybernetic Loop. They influence your perceptions and the inferences and decisions you make from them. They can prime and directionalize your attention. They really can make a huge difference to both your map of the world and your ongoing reality.

For example, if you think about your relating with someone you love as if it is a *'relationship'*, then the use of this nominalization and all that cognitively goes with such a concept can lead to behaviors and decisions that only make sense within that framework. Let's explain this.

If I came to you and said "*my relationship with my partner is stuffed, it's broken*" you would understand what I'm saying and you'd probably commiserate with me. Your advice might be to try and fix the broken relationship (you see *'things'* can be broken and be mended or repaired), but if the fix doesn't work, then possibly it's time to get rid of the relationship and find another one. Notice that such advice makes sense within the model of treating relating as a thing. However, this is actually un-sane (not totally sane) thinking. This is not the way the world really works. Relationships aren't things. They are the process of relating. So let's try it differently, let's language it in a way more aligned with reality and see what's different.

If I came to you and said "*my relating with my partner is stuffed*" you would understand what I'm saying and you'd probably commiserate with me and ask me how it was stuffed, that is, how am I relating so poorly. You might also ask me what my outcome is, about how I want to do relating with my partner, and what I could do differently to do better relating. The verb form of the word and the cognitive framework that goes with it has an outcome and process focus. It leads more naturally to a focus on behavior and success. We would quickly uncover the behaviors that I am doing that are causing me to undermine my relating success and open up choice about what I can do to fix and improve my loving and relating. This is a much more sane approach to thinking and communicating.

Belief versus Believing

Let's return to '*belief*'. In the case of belief, it's a nominalization for the process of believing. This is a behavior that you generally do components of outside of your conscious awareness. You have unconscious competence in believing. This is a really important distinction and one we'll now explore in more detail so that you get conscious control and choice over your believing; conscious control over your '*beliefs*'.

How Beliefs are Formed

Beliefs are formed in many ways. Two main processes are at work in the development of beliefs. Remember, beliefs are generalizations or rules that you make about life and your experience of it. They are your brain's way of taking the overwhelming confusion of information that is the world and discovering patterns in it. It's your brain's way of simplifying the data.

So the first way in which you form beliefs is by noticing patterns and creating rules and labels for these patterns. In NLP we say it typically takes a minimum of 3 instances to form a generalization.

This is called the rule of 3. If something happens to you three times in a row, your unconscious mind will label it as a pattern and will believe that it is real. You will form a belief about it, often outside of your conscious awareness. This belief or generalization will directionalize your thinking and awareness. You will now have an unconscious expectation about this.

As an example, if someone was kind to you, or alternately was rude to you, if it only occurred once, you'd not think much about it. Next time you saw the person you'd not be influenced much by that solitary experience with them. However, if they've been kind or rude to you three times in succession, then you will have a mind-set that they are nice or rude as the case may be, and the next time you saw them you'd either be warm and positive or else wary. You would believe them to be either caring or nasty respectively. That's how beliefs form. That's how stereotypes form. That's how we build the rules and concepts about our world, about our selves and the people we interact with.

The second major way we form beliefs is through modeling significant others in our lives. This is how we learn our cultural moirés and constraints. It's how we learn our social beliefs and stereotypes. It's an important and sometimes insidious way in which beliefs and generalizations creep into our minds and our lives. We absorb the generalizations and beliefs of our culture, our families, our friends, from the media and from school and work. It's a shortcut our brains use so that we don't have to form our beliefs afresh from experience. It's like gaining pre-packaged experience. But it has drawbacks and costs, especially when these beliefs limit or constrain us, and especially when we don't know how to change and modify these beliefs.

So let's first examine the effects of beliefs, of believing, and then move on to explore the components of the process of believing, the unconscious skills of believing.

> *"Think doubt and fail – think victory and succeed!"*
>
> David J Schwartz, The Magic of Thinking Big

Effects of Belief

There is a part of your nervous system, called the Reticular Activating System (RAS) that sits near the core of your brainstem. The RAS acts like a filter or way station for almost all the information that feeds into your brain from the outlaying sensory nerves. The RAS is responsible for ensuring that your brain isn't swamped by useless and unimportant data and signals. It only let's through to the higher centers of your brain the information that is deemed as important and salient.

Cocktail Party Effect

For example, the RAS is involved in what is known in psychology as the *'Cocktail Party Effect'*. This is the effect you'll have experienced when at a club, restaurant, party or bar; a noisy environment where it's difficult to hear conversations. In order to pick out just the voice of one of your companions, your RAS manages to filter out just that auditory signal from the blooming confusion of noise and voices around you. Whilst doing an excellent job of that, and without any conscious awareness on your part, your RAS is also monitoring other conversations for anything of importance or salience. This is why, if someone three tables over, mentions your name, or starts speaking about something that is of significance to you, their voice or conversation will somehow jump out and come to your awareness. This is the cocktail party effect. Your RAS manages to filter what appears to be noise from your conscious mind, but nevertheless manages to bring to your conscious awareness anything important. An amazing and necessary feat.

The key to the RAS and its operation is salience or values. It's about your beliefs, about what you believe to be important. If there's something you strongly believe, or something you believe or value highly, then your RAS will notice examples of it and will pick it out of the world. It will be incorporated into your ongoing map of the world.

This is part of what makes belief and values so powerful. They orient your unconscious mind. I'm sure you'll have had an experience of your RAS at work for you. A friend of mine told me how his wife had decided one Saturday morning that she wanted to purchase a VW convertible. He had scoffed, saying they were a relatively rare car and there would unlikely be many to choose from. That afternoon they went for a drive in the City and lo and behold, VW convertibles were everywhere. He couldn't believe how in *'normal'* circumstances he had never seen a VW convertible, yet once his RAS had been alerted to the salience and importance of them, they were now numerous. In reality, the number of VW convertibles hadn't changed; previously they were unimportant to him so his RAS blocked them out. But once his RAS was attuned to them, they jumped out at him and seemed more plentiful. I'm sure you have your own examples of this.

Self-fulfilling Prophecy Effect

An even more impactful example of the effect of belief is called the *'Self-fulfilling Prophecy'*. This effect was first scientifically documented in an experiment in 1968. Researchers informed elementary school teachers that randomly chosen students in their classes had been identified as *"late bloomers"*, intellectually gifted children who would outpace their peers in academic performance over the course of the school year. A later examination found this expectation to be confirmed. The teacher's beliefs had actually caused a change in the learning behaviors and measured IQ of the students, even though in reality the students had been picked at random. Beliefs and attitudes are incredibly powerful as shown by this and hundreds of further experiments on this effect.

Placebo Effect

The placebo effect provides another graphic example of the power of belief. People who are told a drug will have a particular result will many times experience that effect even when given a pill without those properties.

Confirmation Bias

A huge body of evidence and research shows that our brains actively seek confirmation of our beliefs. Another way of putting it is that we see what we expect to see. This can be either a positive or a negative depending on the context. When our beliefs are positive and supportive of our happiness and success, then confirmation bias will engender a positive success spiral — the positive beliefs lead to positive attitudes and thoughts, which support positive actions, producing positive results, which feed back to support those positive beliefs. On the other hand, limiting beliefs create a downward failure spiral. It's the old Henry Ford thing: *"whether you think you can, or think you can't, either way you're right"*.

Effect on Outcomes

Holding positive beliefs that you deserve and can easily achieve success helps generate the enthusiasm, power, skill and energy needed to achieve your goals and outcomes. Behavioral modeling of happy and successful people has shown that they are just ordinary people who have developed great belief in themselves. They believe they control what happens to them and that they deserve success and fulfillment. Their belief in themselves and their success creates positive self-fulfilling prophecies and orients their unconscious mind to elements that support that success.

One of the keys to achieving outcomes is to remove negative beliefs or attitudes that undermine your success and in their place install and amplify empowering and supportive beliefs. Too often people desire outcomes but don't truly believe it's possible for them to be achieved. This is a form of incongruence and is an enemy to happiness. In the following section you'll learn about the structure of believing and how to change your beliefs quickly and powerfully.

Thinking Tools — The Belief Spiral

Achieving starts with Believing!

Awareness Questions — Empowering your Outcomes

Ask Yourself:

> What are my beliefs about my outcome? Do I believe I can easily achieve my outcome?

> What are more empowering beliefs and attitudes I can emphasize to support my outcome?

> Do I have any beliefs that might limit my success in achieving my outcome?

The Structure of Believing

You will remember from Chapter 1 that submodalities are the sub-components of our sensory modalities and are the building blocks that structure the meaningfulness of our experiences. As such, they are used by our unconscious mind to code and structure our beliefs.

Think of something you believe in really strongly. Now examine the image of this belief you have in your mind to notice its submodalities. Do this right now. Look at its size, focus, distance, position, color/black-and-white etc.

Now picture something you don't believe at all. Notice the submodalities are very, very different from those of something you totally believe in. Or picture something you have a positive belief about and compare and contrast it with the submodalities of something you hold a negative belief about. You'll find some key differences in the submodalities. Take a moment and write down the submodalities of each of these belief types. You'll use this information in the exercises and Success Strategies that are coming up.

Now here's the really interesting and useful thing about submodalities. Take the image of the thing you really believe, and change its submodalities to match those of the thing you don't believe. For example, if the thing you don't believe has a picture that is small, dim and low in your visual field, then shift and change the image of what you believe so that it is small, dim and low. Notice that as you shift the submodalities, your subjective feelings about the belief change. You'll find it's no longer quite so believable. Once you've experienced this, remember to put the image back where it belongs, make it believable again by returning it to its original submodalities.

Using Submodalities

Submodalities code for how meaningful and believable your belief is (or put more accurately, how meaningful and believable your believing is). It's that simple. With unconscious competence, your brain assigns appropriate submodalities to each of the generalizations and concepts that make up your beliefs. This is how you structure your believing. What's powerful about knowing this is that you can now use this to quickly and impactfully change your beliefs.

You can take ideas and concepts and change them from something you believe to something that has a very different subjective feeling and response — to something you just don't fully believe. Equally, you can take something you don't really believe, but would like to, and make it so much more believable, just by changing its submodalities.

In the following Success Strategy you'll learn and use this

process to identify and change some limiting beliefs and replace them with empowering and supportive beliefs. By practicing and practicing this technique, you'll build a part in your mind that will automatically create positive beliefs — just like those people who are incredibly successful and happy in life.

Remember, through repeated practice you create autonomous unconscious competencies that operate to generate your reality and your world. It's your world, and you can make amazing changes and develop automatic skills of happiness and joyfulness. The key is understanding how your mind and brain works, installing new behaviors and skills and removing or interrupting the enemies to happiness.

Before we get to the Belief Change Success Strategy however, we'll explore the nature of limiting and negative beliefs so you'll have something to make awesome and magnificent changes with.

⟳ Deeper Understandings — The language of belief

As discussed in Chapter 1, there are three basic modeling processes we use to create our maps or models of the world. These are:

➢ Deletion

➢ Generalization

➢ Distortion

Each of these modeling processes has language elements that are

I don't BELIEVE it

indicators of the process. In NLP, these language distinctions are described by what is called the NLP Meta-Model. By becoming aware of and tracking for these distinctions you can become more precise in your thinking and communicating with yourself and others. You can also gain more choice and control over how you are modeling your world by choosing language that supports your outcomes.

Generalization

Fundamentally, the process of belief formation is one of creating generalizations and building rules and patterns from the information in your on-going experience. The language of generalization typically involves:

Modal Operators

Modal Operators are the rules about how you believe you *'must'* operate in the world and what you believe is possible. There are two main forms —

- Modal Operators of Necessity — these are indicated by words such as *'must'*, *'have to'*, *'need'* etc.

- Modal Operators of Possibility — these are indicated by words such as *'can'*, *'can't'*, *'won't'*, *'might'* etc.

Universal Quantifiers

Universal Quantifiers are the generalizations you have made about extent or scope. They are the beliefs you have about how universal something is. They are indicated by words such as *'all'*, *'everyone'*, *'everything'*, *'totally'* etc.

So for example, if you hear someone saying *"I can't do that!"*

you know they have formed a rule or generalization about what's possible in the world for them. Often, such beliefs and the presuppositions they are formed from, are outside of conscious awareness for the person. You can help them, or yourself, question these limiting beliefs by asking the following questions.

Modal Operators

- What will happen if you do?
- What stops you?
- Has there ever been a time when you have?

Universal Quantifiers

- All? Every? Absolutely every single one?
- Can you find a counter-example to this over-generalization?

Distortion

There are a number of distortions that can be involved in belief formation. Key of these are:

Cause Effect

Cause Effect distortions are where you believe one thing causes another. For example, if you hear someone saying *"She makes me angry"*, this is a distortion because, in reality, no one '*makes*' you feel anything. You create your own feelings, based on your perceptions and generalizations. The way to challenge and explore Cause Effect distortions is to ask *"How specifically does X cause Y?"*

Complex Equivalence

Complex Equivalence is where you believe that X is equivalent to Y, that X is connected to and an indicator of Y. Many stereotypes take this form. For example, the statement that *"Money equals happiness"* is a complex equivalent distortion. There are many rich people who are desperately unhappy. Equally there are many poor people who are happy and live meaningful lives. To explore a Complex Equivalence ask, *"How specifically does X mean Y"*.

Lost Performative

There are a number of beliefs you have absorbed from your culture and from unconsciously modeling significant others in your life. Such beliefs often get expressed as axioms, or rules. However, for a belief to be well-formed it should express who performed the creation of the belief. When you express a belief that has come from someone else, but have unconsciously deleted who created the rule, you have *'lost the performer'* and you are distorting your map of the world. You need to question your beliefs to ensure they are accurate generalizations of the world. Question beliefs and rules by asking *"According to whom is this a valid belief"*. For example, if you heard someone say *"You should always respect your elders"*, ask *"According to whom?"*, *"Where is it written that I should always respect my elders?"* You can also explore the Modal Operators and Universal Quantifiers that are often contained in such beliefs.

Universal Frighteners

An insidious form of linguistic distortion is known in CBT as Universal Frighteners. These beliefs are generalizations about FUD — Fear, Uncertainty and Doubt. Universal Frighteners are indicated by global qualifiers associated with generalizations about fear. Comments like *"It's totally shocking," "That's completely horrifying," "It's all really scary."*

Challenge these linguistic distortions by asking yourself and others questions like *"How specifically are you scaring yourself about this?"* and *"What specifically about this are you fearing?"*

Language is Powerful

You can gain power over your thinking and believing by listening for and questioning your use of linguistic distortions and generalizations. Because we are habit forming creatures, you can overcome old habits and patterns of thought by using words and expressions that presuppose possibility and hope. Language and thought is powerful, so listen to what you say and ensure you are using words that support happiness, choice and meaning in your life.

Limiting and Negative Beliefs

Limiting and negative beliefs and attitudes are an enemy to your happiness. Many of these are unconsciously installed by our culture and the micro-culture of our family. They are often so ingrained and unquestioned that at first you may not be aware of them. Have you ever travelled overseas to another culture and noticed how many strange and unusual customs there are? The inhabitants of that country think their customs and beliefs, their societal and cultural norms and practices are totally sensible and normal. To your eyes they can be crazy and non-sensical. Well, guess what, a traveler visiting your world would find your customs and beliefs equally weird and wonderful.

This is not an issue when your beliefs, values and generalizations support you and support meaning and happiness in your life. However, often your beliefs and attitudes don't fully serve you. They are habitual patterns, mostly performed outside your conscious awareness, and can undermine your happiness and peace of mind. It's vital that you become aware of these enemies, of these unnecessary self-imposed limitations and learn how to dispute and change them.

In the following sections we'll cover

- Conditional Happiness
- Happiness Sabotage
- FUD — Fear, Uncertainty & Doubt
- Automatic Negative Irrational Beliefs
- Pessimistic Attitudes
- Binary Submodalities
- Setting Limits on Others

> *"Argue for your limitations and sure enough, they're yours."*
> Richard Bach

Conditional Happiness

An insidious enemy to happiness is the negative belief that your happiness is conditional or reliant on some event or experience. *"I'll only be happy once I've got $100,000 in the bank"* or *"I can't be happy and satisfied until I've paid off my mortgage"*. *"I can't truly feel happy in myself until I have a loving romantic partner."* Rubbish! Making happiness conditional on people and things creates an artificial and self-imposed limitation.

The reality is that you can enjoy happiness and meaning in your life regardless of your life situation. Even in the midst of pain and suffering, you can still find small things to focus on that will bring happiness. After all, happiness and joy are feelings, and by focusing on learning and meaning in your life, and by performing neuro-physiological state control, something you'll learn about in the coming chapters, you can generate thoughts and feelings of happiness. Doing this in some life situations may certainly be challenging, but as Viktor Frankl proved in his experiences in the Nazi concentration camps in Auschwitz, it is absolutely possible.

Remember the Cybernetic Loop from Chapter 0. Your mind and body are connected in a cybernetic loop that controls your state and ongoing experience. By consciously modifying your posture, breathing, thoughts and their submodalities and the things you are saying to yourself, you can generate *'happiness-ing'* in your life.

It's about focus and the understanding that you do have a choice about the meaning you are making in your life. So stop making happiness conditional. Realize you can have happiness and joy right now. You can be *'in-joy-in-yourself'* whenever you choose. You can do happiness-ing in almost any situation. It's your choice, and this book will teach you the skills of how to put that choice into action.

Take a moment right now to grab a pen and paper and write

down your beliefs about your happiness and what you think it has been conditional upon in the past. Now actively and accurately dispute these erroneous beliefs. Think of times when regardless of these limitations and conditions you have actually experienced joy, happiness and meaning. Or think of someone you know who has been in a worse situation or has had less going for them and yet has still remained positive. Remember, if it's possible in the world, it's possible for you; not a question of '*if*', just a question of '*how*'.

You can also think of how it would be possible to transcend those limitations and conditionals by thinking of what you could focus on or what you could do to experience some level of happiness and satisfaction regardless of the conditions. By actively analyzing, challenging and practicing to overcome the enemy of conditional happiness, you will have created an unconscious part that continues to serve you and helps you experience more and more happiness in life.

Happiness Sabotage

Some people have an incredible skill at creating happiness in their life and then just when things are going wonderfully they crash and burn. Something happens that causes them unhappiness or misery. It's like their unconscious mind is operating from a belief that they don't really deserve to be happy and so with unconscious competence and outside of conscious awareness they undermine and sabotage their own success. Sometimes this can be from a deep sense of worthlessness, sometimes from fear of failure and sometimes it is even motivated from a fear of success. Whatever the reason, it is the underlying core beliefs about your deserving success and happiness that are the drivers for this enemy of happiness sabotage.

The key to defeating this enemy is first awareness of the pattern in your life and then in challenging and removing the self-defeating core beliefs that drive it, replacing them with new more empowering beliefs. So take a moment and examine your life and your beliefs about happiness to determine if this enemy exists in your life. Look for situations or patterns where just when you were most happy something occurred in limiting your happiness and joy.

If you've found any evidence of this enemy, write down your thoughts and beliefs about this, then actively challenge them. Once you have this list you will use the New Belief Generator Success Strategy later in this chapter to destroy the old unsupportive beliefs and replace them with empowering beliefs that will help you generate more and more meaning and joy in your life.

FUD — Celebrating Fear, Uncertainty & Doubt

The world operates on FUD! Money is made on FUD. Newspapers sell through FUD. Society and individuals celebrate the failure of FUD every single day. Fear, Uncertainty and Doubt! They're enemies to happiness and they abound around you. Most certainly you'll have culturally conditioned unconscious competencies in fearing, amplifying uncertainty and doubting.

It takes vigilance and practice to overcome these nefarious enemies. It's the nature of the evolved nervous system that we are quicker to perform fight and flight than we are to move towards food and possibilities. The negative is more salient in our patterning system of the brain/body than is the positive. Any animal that would prefer to keep eating a tasty meal rather than run away from an approaching threat, was unlikely to contribute its genes to the gene-pool, and so over the millions of years of evolution we have come to have a stronger drive towards negative focus than positive. We'll explore this in more detail in the section on *'Negation'* later in this chapter.

The take home message though is that whilst FUD is important for survival, in most normal situations of our life, there is little to fear or be really uncertain about. We live in a world of massive and accelerating change. So certainly *'uncertainty'* is going to be a given, no pun intended. No one can know everything, and with knowledge and information exploding, it's unlikely this will ever change. You can be certain that uncertainty is here to stay. You need to get comfortable with that. And in a world of ever increasing choice, you will always be able to doubt whether you've made the best choice. We'll be covering these issues and strategies for dealing with them in later chapters.

For the moment though, and with respect to negative beliefs and attitudes, it's important for you to be aware of how you deal with FUD in your life. FUD is an enemy to happiness. So you want to track for times when you are focusing on it, amplifying it or celebrating it. Yes celebrating it. You see, the process of celebrating is not just limited to positive events. Think about it.

Celebrating is the process of making a big deal about something, of getting excited about it, of announcing it and focusing on it. So anytime you make a big deal about something, you are celebrating it; and whenever you amplify your emotions about something it enhances your memory and learning about it. That's how memory works. If you make something emotionally impactful (positively or negatively, and remember, negative emotions are more biologically salient than positive ones) then you make it *'memorable'* and your unconscious mind will store it. With repeated celebratings you will build a part in your mind for this. So the more you celebrate FUD — fearing, focusing on uncertainty and doubting, the more you will create and build a part that continues to do those processes in your life. And of course the converse of this is also true!

Happiness is based in large measure on the opposite of FUD. It is rooted in feeling secure, in having knowledge, choice and control. You want to become a control master in your life, not a FUD-master. It's also worth remembering that FEAR can be thought of as False Evidence Appearing Real. Often when you closely examine the things you fear, you'll see that you had exaggerated or false impressions. Once you embrace your fears and do the thing you feared you often find there was nothing to fear at all. We'll be looking at this in more detail in later chapters.

For now, grab that pen and paper and write a list of any FUD-type behaviors and attitudes you have indulged yourself in the past. Look for patterns and write down your beliefs around these. Then actively dispute and challenge them. Again, you'll use this list with the New Belief Generator Success Strategy later in this chapter to destroy those old unsupportive beliefs and replace them with more empowering and useful beliefs.

> *"It is very obvious that we are not influenced by 'facts' but by our interpretation of the facts."*
>
> Alfred Adler

Automatic Negative Irrational Beliefs

The fields of Cognitive Behavioral Therapy (CBT) and Rational Emotive Behavioral Therapy (REBT) have done a lot of excellent research on negative irrational beliefs and how they become automatic and streamlined into unconscious strategies that limit your ability to cope with life. Such negative and pessimistic self-talk can occur when you are under stress and can cause emotional and physical reactions.

Remember CBT and REBT are based on the idea that how you emotionally respond at any moment depends on your interpretations — your views, beliefs and thoughts — of the situation. It's the things you think and say to yourself, not what actually happens to you that causes your positive or negative emotions. It's important therefore to become aware of any habitual negative beliefs and attitudes.

The following is a list of typical negative irrational beliefs. Take a look through and mark off those that you indulge in:

☐ In order to be happy, I have to be successful in whatever I undertake

☐ My happiness depends on my performance

☐ To be happy, I must be accepted (liked, approved, admired) by all people at all times

☐ I just can't be happy without love

☐ I should always be able, successful, and on top of things; if I'm not, I'm an inadequate, incompetent, hopeless failure

☐ I should be happy all of the time

☐ I should be happy I've got so many things, or conversely, I can't be happy because I don't have enough things

☐ I can't stand not knowing something, I'll be happy when I find certainty

☐ I'll be happy when I can just be myself

☐ I'll be happy when I find a purpose to my life

☐ I'll be happy when I find a more meaningful calling

Avoiding the Enemies to HAPPINESS

- ☐ Happiness is having everything I want without giving up anything!
- ☐ When things do not go the way I wanted and planned, it is terrible and I can't stand it!
- ☐ I am hopeless and worthless
- ☐ I don't deserve happiness
- ☐ I'm going to fail
- ☐ My happiness won't last
- ☐ There's too much negativity and hate in the world for me to be happy

The CBT process for overcoming such beliefs is to generate positive realistic coping statements that oppose the irrational beliefs and to repeat these to yourself often and especially whenever you notice yourself using negative beliefs. Here are a couple of examples for how to do this.

Negative Thought	Positive Coping Response
I'm going to fail.	I'll probably do ok, it's not the end of the world; I can enjoy learning from feedback.

Negative Thought	Positive Coping Response
I'm hopeless, there's no future.	This feeling is temporary, everything passes; I have survived until now and will continue to survive; there is always a future and I can learn and improve. Nothing is TOTALLY hopeless.

You can also powerfully use the *'Internal Critic Tune-out'* Success Strategy from Chapter 1 to blow away and tune-out such negative self-talk and irrational attitudes. Remember, practice makes permanent. So, support yourself by tracking for unsupportive patterns in your life, pattern-interrupting them and replacing them with new positive behaviors. That's how you create new unconscious competencies and build new skills into your life.

Pessimistic Attitudes

Research has shown that people with pessimistic attitudes are often slightly more accurate in their perceptions of the world compared to optimists. However, it's also been found that optimism and hope are correlated with high self-esteem, better resistance to depression, better work performance and better health, both physical and psychological. So whilst optimism may create a slightly distorted view of the world, it does so in a positive way that generates and supports happiness. In contrast, pessimism is an enemy to happiness and sets up a negative mindset that can lead to negative self-fulfilling prophecies. Pessimistic attitudes have a negative effect on your mind, health and success.

Research by Prof. Martin Seligman on learned helplessness has shown that people can learn from life experiences to take on an attributional style that leads either to pessimism or optimism.

Pessimism results from an attributional style that ascribes pervasiveness and permanence to negative events and conversely sees positive events as temporary and specific. When something negative happens, a person operating from a pessimistic style will believe that everything is bad and things will never change. In contrast, someone operating with an optimistic attitude uses an attributional style that sees the negative situation as temporary and specific and the positive situation as permanent and pervasive. These people refuse to make the negativity universal in their life; they believe things will soon change for the better.

Take a look at your own attributional style. When things happen in your life, how do you perceive them? Pessimistically or Optimistically?

- **Permanence** — Permanent versus Temporary

- **Pervasiveness** — Universal versus Specific

A further filter linked with pessimism and optimism is hope. Pessimistic thinkers sometimes fall into the belief traps of hopelessness and helplessness. Optimistic thinkers on the other hand operate from hopefulness and self-efficacy. They hold hope in their heart and courage in their gut. They believe they can make a difference and motivate themselves to take action to change their situation. Attitudes of helplessness and hopelessness are definite enemies to happiness and success. You will want to remove these from your emotional repertoire. The skills you want to strengthen and engender in your life are those of hope, self-efficacy, courage and optimism.

Overcoming Pessimistic Attitudes

The first step to overcoming pessimistic attitudes is to admit that pessimism and negativity is not a productive behavior and that it impacts your life in a negative way. Next, identify the irrational thinking behind the negativity and pessimism and dispute and challenge it, replacing it with more healthy thoughts and beliefs. Track for and change your attributional style so that you imagine positivity in your life as permanent and pervasive, convincing yourself that any negative experiences will be temporary and local. Finally, practice, practice, practice to build unconscious competency in positive thinking. With repetition and focus you will find it quicker and easier to interrupt pessimistic thoughts and fill your life with optimism, hope and happiness.

In an upcoming section of this chapter you will read more about Learned Optimism and strategies from Positive Psychology for enhancing optimistic attitudes.

Binary Submodalities

Some people have habits of seeing things in black and white, of simplifying their world and operating from an attitude of *'either/or'*, *'true/false'*, *'good/bad'* or *'right/wrong'*. The world is in reality rarely ever that simple. Most situations involve many shades of grey and a rainbow of possibilities. Using two-valued logic — true/false, right/wrong — can be an enemy to happiness. Over-generalizing and simplifying the world to match a binary decision system can lead to un-sane thinking and behavior.

Whenever you are operating from such binary, black and white beliefs, take a look at the pictures you are using in your mind's eye to evaluate and make your decisions, you'll often find that the submodalities of the pictures are devoid of color; they're quite simply in *'black and white'*. It's not surprising that we use the expression *'black and white thinking'* to describe the unconscious process of binary decision making. Our language is accurately describing the submodalities of the process.

So to avoid the enemy of simplistic binary thinking, make sure you use rich and colorful images. Remember, you own your own images. They exist in your mind. They are yours! You can easily change them.

Fully evaluate every situation and see the world with a multi-hued range of possibility thinking. Don't freeze your beliefs into true and false, instead actively look for the nuances in every situation and embody attitudes of flexibility and openness.

Setting Limits on Others

Setting limits on other people is an enemy to happiness. Applying one set of rules or attitudes towards your own behavior and a different set of standards or beliefs on others is a natural process we're all susceptible to. This is known in psychology as self-serving bias. It's a natural tendency and one you have to be aware of and actively remove.

Negative beliefs and attitudes about others can also act as self-fulfilling prophecies and send messages to their unconscious minds that influences them to live down to your expectations. So beware and make sure you hold positive, high expectations to support the success of those around you.

Creating Empowering Beliefs

To replace limiting and unsupportive beliefs, you can't simply get rid of them; your unconscious mind resists change that takes something away. Instead, you have to replace old beliefs with new ones. This is quite easily done using submodality shifts so that you zoom away the old beliefs, and zoom in the new ones.

First, generate new positive beliefs that you like the idea of having. Create a list of powerful supportive ideas and beliefs. Attitudes of success. Then use the following Success Strategy to install the new beliefs in place of old negative beliefs.

Here is a list of empowering beliefs to get you started:

- ☐ I am a worthwhile person and I deserve and can easily achieve happiness
- ☐ I give myself Unconditional Self Acceptance and Compassion
- ☐ Happiness is a skill that I can learn and continue improving in fun and powerful ways — I am a happiness master!
- ☐ I can wonderfully embody attitudes of happiness and success
- ☐ I am an Optimist and can easily cope with setbacks
- ☐ I see setbacks as challenges that bring new opportunities and learnings and that I can overcome
- ☐ I am a fallible human being and I forgive myself and empower myself to realize that even when I don't get what I want I can still live a worthwhile and happy life
- ☐ There is no failure, only feedback; I learn from my mistakes and get satisfaction in overcoming obstacles
- ☐ I have High Frustration Tolerance, and know I can experience happiness as a choice, even when my preferences aren't being met
- ☐ I am a worthwhile and happy person and I know it!

The real key to amplifying and owning a new belief is to make it bright and big and bold. Fill the belief with color and movement, so that it engenders fantastic juicy feelings. Add music and surround-sound to the image. Really amplify and enhance it. By repeating this process a minimum of three times you'll create a new pattern of believing in your life and your unconscious mind will continue to embody the attitude in powerful ways.

☑ Success Strategy — New Belief Generator

In this Success Strategy you will learn to install a new more empowering belief.

1. Picture and think about the belief you want to change. Elicit the submodalities of this image. Notice its size and position, distance and brightness. Is it colored, is it focused, does it have a border or is it panoramic? Is it still or a movie? Write down the submodalities to use later in the strategy.

2. Think about and picture something you really don't believe. Something you just cannot believe at all. Elicit the submodalities of this *'Don't believe it'* belief. Write them down.

3. Create a new, more empowering belief. You may not totally believe it yet, but decide on a belief you'd like to have. Write it up in bright bold colors. Refine it. Make it impactful in its wording and description.

4. Now, take the image of the belief you want to get rid of and zoom the image off into the distance, getting smaller and

smaller, then bring it back but to the size, position and other submodalities of the *'Don't believe it'* image. Repeat this process 3 to 5 times. You may have to do this whole process with an *'as if'* quality. Not everyone sees the images in their minds eye with total life-like quality, and it doesn't seem to matter for the effectiveness of this technique. You'll find it will work, even if you are just imagining all this happening.

5. Take the image of the new positive belief, and starting with it way in the distance, ZOOM it in to the submodalities of belief. Zoom it in powerfully, and as it comes in, closer and closer, make it bigger, brighter, bolder, more colorful and any other changes you'd like to see. Make a ZOOMING or SWOOSHING sound as you zoom it in. Repeat this process 3 to 5 times.

6. Put this whole process together. Take the old negative belief and zoom it away in the distance. Bring it zooming back in to the position and submodalities of *'I don't believe it'* as quickly as possible then ZOOM in the new positive belief to the position and submodalities of total belief.

7. Lock the beliefs into position by hearing the sound of them *'Clicking'* into place. Make a sound of a solid clicking sound in your mind or even with your voice out loud.

8. Break state by looking around the room. Repeat steps 6 and 7 from 3 to 5 times. As quickly as you can.

Now test your work. Think about the old belief and notice that your subjective feelings and experience have changed. Think about the new empowering belief and notice you are now using the new set of submodalities. Notice also how good you feel about this and your Self!

Pos ψ Learned Optimism

As described earlier in this chapter, Prof. Martin Seligman and colleagues have scientifically documented the effects of optimism and pessimism. The research shows that optimists respond better to adversity of all kinds, have better physical health and often live longer.

Most importantly, optimism can be learned. The key seems to be your approach and what you say to yourself when confronted with failure and disappointment. Pessimists, according to Seligman, respond with helplessness; they give up. Optimists, on the other hand, persevere. Optimism does not equal positive thinking. Optimism is about your *'Explanatory Style'*; it's about the way you interpret things that happen to you. Optimism also entails positive emotions about the future as well as the present.

Optimism

- ✓ reacting to setbacks from an attitude of personal power
- ✓ negative events are seen as temporary setbacks
- ✓ negative events are perceived as being limited to particular circumstances
- ✓ negative events can be overcome by your own effort and abilities

- ✓ focuses on hope and possibility

Pessimism

- ✗ reacting to setbacks from an attitude of personal helplessness
- ✗ negative events are imagined as lasting a long time
- ✗ negative events are seen as undermining everything you do
- ✗ negative events are perceived as your own fault
- ✗ focuses on hopelessness and negativity

Using the ABC Model

Since optimism and pessimism are skills, the message is that you can change with thoughtful, explicit practice. The main technique or skill that'll help you become more optimistic is the ABC model, described in Chapter 1. With this technique you explore negative, pessimistic thoughts and dispute them vigorously to come up with a more positive and useful way of thinking.

Adversity — the A stands for the adversity or pessimistic accusation. In this step you specifically describe and write down the negative statement.

Belief — here you explore the underlying beliefs inherent in the adversity or accusation. You need to think flexibly and accurately about the beliefs underpinning the accusation.

Consequences —explore the emotional and behavioral consequences of your beliefs, how you are responding to the negative beliefs and adversity.

Disputation — actively and vigorously dispute and challenge the negative or critical beliefs and accusations. Challenge your internal criticism and pessimism by writing down and saying more reasonable, self-tolerant things about yourself and the situation. Generate new and more supportive and accurate beliefs. Gather evidence from the past to find and show yourself counterexamples to the negative beliefs or accusations. Most importantly, shift your explanatory style to seeing things as temporary, specific to this situation and something you can definitely control and overcome.

Energization — finally, focus on the positive purpose, outcomes and beliefs you have generated in the previous steps. Find and explore new ways to achieve the positive intentions inherent in the original accusations. Energize the new ways by thinking of situations in the future where you will have applied these new beliefs and outcomes. Celebrate a more optimistic and positive way of thinking about yourself and your world.

Hope and Possibility — Opportunity Thinking

Another useful and scientifically validated exercise for combating the enemy of pessimism is the '*One Door Closes, Another Door Opens*' exercise. With this strategy, whenever you face a difficult life situation — whenever a door closes — think about the issue in terms of the opportunities and possibilities it presents. Refuse to dwell on the negative aspects of the situation and instead force yourself to find something positive you can gain from your experience. Tell yourself that as one door closes, often many more open. Encourage yourself to remember times when things worked out for the best and to focus on hope and possibility.

To enhance your ideas and attitudes to this and to build generalizations around this in your unconscious mind, grab a pen and paper and explore and answer the following questions.

Think about three doors that closed on you in the past:

1. What was one of the most important doors that closed on you? As a result of this door closing, what was the opportunity that resulted?

2. What was a door that closed on you through loss or rejection? What door opened as a result of this?

3. What door closed due to bad luck, poor timing or missed chances and what opportunity did this eventually lead to? What door opened in the place of the missed opportunity?

Write about and explore these experiences and the beliefs you formed about them. How did the doors closing make you feel at the time? What did you feel once the new opportunity opened? Did you do anything that helped open the new doors? Are there things you can do in the future to help generate new opportunities? What can you do to encourage yourself and overcome the enemy of pessimism and replace it with a focus on hope and opportunity? How can you more easily hold hope in your heart?

Most importantly, practice seeing problems as challenges and opportunities for learning and growth. By using an optimistic explanatory style you can support yourself in overcoming negativity and bring more happiness and joy to your life and the lives of those around you.

Managing Risk

One final point to note however is that according to Prof. Seligman, pessimism may sometimes be a useful skill. It can keep you from taking risky, over-optimistic actions in areas where the downside risks are unacceptable. So use optimism and pessimism wisely and in their appropriate contexts. Being overly and unrealistically optimistic can be as much an enemy to happiness as being overly pessimistic. The key is to use conscious choice in how you respond to life and to control the unconscious skills you bring to achieving happiness and success.

🛠 Thinking Tools — Optimism & Opportunity

As one door closes, many more open.

Negation and Positivity

Negation doesn't exist in experience. What does this mean? The NLP model is that the unconscious mind does not track negation, instead it only ever experiences the positive through your five senses. For example, if you were in a closed and darkened room and I turned on the light, you would experience light rather than *'not dark'*. Equally if I then turned off the light, you would be experiencing darkness rather than *'not lightness'*. You might use negation — *'not'* — in your language to describe your experience, but at the level of your unconscious, you do not experience negation.

What this means is that when you use negation in language, in order to make sense of what is being said, your unconscious mind builds a picture of what it is hearing. If someone tells you *'not'* to think of a car, and especially to definitely not think of a red sports car, you can't do it. Your unconscious mind generates a picture of the thing you are hearing about. You'll have done this right now reading this paragraph. To negate that picture you might then put a cross through the image, or zoom it away, or replace it with another picture. But just to make sense of the words, your brain pattern matches on the concepts that the words describe.

So if you went to someone and said, *"whatever you do, I don't want you to get tense, don't get stressed now"*, what do you think would happen in their cybernetic loop? Their unconscious mind, in order to make sense of what they'd heard would create a state of stress and tension in their mind-body. So if you really wanted someone not to get tense, you'd tell them to relax. You'd be best served in saying what you want and not what you don't want.

This is a very powerful understanding. It is backed up by research on hypnosis and altered states that has shown that when someone is in a trance or altered state, their response to language can be very literal. People in these states often ignore negations. If you tell someone who is drunk for example not to do something, they'll often ignore the negation and do the very thing you instructed them not to do. The take home message from this is that when communicating to your unconscious mind, and to others, you should always focus on the positive and say what you want and not what you don't want.

When it comes to beliefs this is equally important. You want your beliefs to be positive and to focus on what you want. Research in classical psychology has discovered that the more you attempt to not think about something the more you will actually focus on it. What you resist persists. In one experiment people were asked not to think of a polar bear, and the more they tried to actively not think about it, the more their unconscious mind brought it to their awareness.

So ensure your beliefs focus on the positive and direct your mind to positive outcomes. Be very aware of how you word your self-talk and use positives rather than negation to support meaning and happiness in your life and the lives of those around you.

🛠 Thinking Tools — Focus on the Positive

*Negation doesn't exist in experience.
Focus on positive outcomes*

Mind-body Loop and Attitudes

Remember the NLP Cybernetic Loop model from Chapter 0. It shows how your mind and body are connected in a loop; your thoughts, feelings and physiology are linked and whatever affects one leads to a change in the others. In terms of belief, this means your thoughts influence and are directly reflected in your physical body. You embody your attitudes.

You know this is true. You know you can take one look at someone and see if they have a positive or negative attitude. It shows in their face, in their eyes, in their physical stance. When someone is positive towards something (and notice the language here) they will lean towards it. If you are in a discussion with a friend and start talking about something they have a negative attitude to, or disagree with, you'll notice they will turn away slightly and lean away from you, even if minimally. Their head will move back marginally. They will *'look down'* on what you are saying. This is an insight from NLP and shows that your language is a representation of your unconscious experience and mapping of your world. Your language is a literal descriptor of your ongoing experience. That's why our language is expressive of our process; why we say things like "*I have a leaning towards X*" when we have a positive attitude towards it.

The main message here is that we embody our beliefs; our attitudes are connected to our physical stance towards or away from things. What's useful about knowing this is that you can use this understanding to notice your physiology and make powerful changes in how you are responding to situations. When you find yourself being negative about something, stop! Take a look at your body, your posture, your muscular tension, how you are holding your head, your mouth, the muscles around your eyes, your breathing. Then deliberately and specifically change your behavior and physiology to one of relaxation and positivity. Embody a positive attitude. Or go do some exercise; go for a run, take a long walk. Get your blood flowing and change your breathing as you think about the situation. You'll find that it makes a huge difference to your attitude.

⚒ Thinking Tools — Cybernetic Loop

Everything that happens inside a person, has a physiological effect observable on the outside. The mind and body are connected in a Cybernetic Loop.

The following Success Strategy provides an explicit method for embodying a positive attitude. Use it to escape the enemy of negative attitude'ing — yes, attitude is a nominalization, you don't '*have*' attitudes, you do attitude'ing with unconscious competence. So change your attitudes and you'll find you are supporting yourself for greater success and happiness.

☑ Success Strategy — Embodying Attitudes of Success

This technique uses your Cybernetic Loop and the NLP technique of anchoring to help you embody a physical and psychological attitude of success. Use it anytime you want to feel and act more positive and in control.

1. Perform an inventory of your body and stance. Notice how you are breathing, the patterns of stress and tension in your face, neck, shoulders, back, stomach and anywhere else that is not relaxed. How are you holding your mouth and jaw? Is there tension around or in your eyes? How are you holding your hands and arms? Track your physical attitude. Get a sense of how you are feeling.

2. Now, stop and break state. Shake yourself loose. Look around the room or your surroundings. Take some big deep even breaths, and enjoy a few great sighs. Fill your lungs with oxygen.

3. Fill yourself with positive feelings by remembering at least 3 times in your life when you were really fantastically happy.

Relive those memories. Go back and see what you saw, hear what you heard, feel what you felt at those times. Amplify the feelings of joy and happiness. Make your pictures of the memories brighter and more empowering. Bring them closer. Really enjoy experiencing your happiness.

4. Take an inventory of your body. Notice how you are now breathing, how you are holding your body. Notice where you are relaxed. Adjust and tune your physiology to make it even more positive and powerful. Check and adjust that you are centered and balanced, that you are breathing fully, evenly (same duration on the in-breath as the out-breath) and deeply, that your face is relaxed, you are smiling, that you are leaning ever so slightly forwards. Embody that positive attitude of happiness and joy.

5. Now anchor these positive states of joy, by imagining a colored circle on the ground, a nice bright colorful circle in front of you. Make it a color that delights you. Re-access the memories from Step 3 and when the feelings of happiness and joy are peaking, when they are really strong, step into the circle and say the words *"I am sooo happy"*, or make a particular sound, like a delicious positive sigh. Repeat this process at least 3 to 5 times to build the generalization and set the anchor.

6. Now test your results. Think of a time in the future when you will need to embody an attitude of happiness, positivity and success, and as you do, see your circle on the ground, step into it, say your words or sound to yourself, and adjust your body into a wonderful position of happiness. Embody your positive attitude of success.

Use this technique whenever you need to encourage and support yourself or to shift your attitude to one that embodies hope, joy and positivity. The image of the circle and the words or sounds are specific triggers to fire off your anchor.

And remember that the power of your anchor is determined by the power of the state you have anchored. So anchor truly impactful and intensely positive states. Whenever you use your anchor you will find your cybernetic loop responds and you will re-experience your positive states and a physiology that matches.

✒ Pattern-Interrupt — Stopping Negative Beliefs

The following process combines the ideas and skills described throughout this chapter. Use this to interrupt any negative or limiting belief patterns. If you find yourself at any time engaged in a negative thought or attitude, use and practice the following technique.

Interrupt any old unsupportive patterns in your life by:

- ✒ If you hear or notice yourself expressing or thinking a negative belief, say forcefully to yourself 'STOP!' (And if it helps, you can even add in a visual of a stop sign in your mind's eye, or anything else representative of this that works for you.)

- ✒ Quickly adjust your mind-body loop to a more positive and relaxed attitude.

- ✓ Perform an ABC challenge to the old negative belief, forcibly rip that unsupportive belief apart.

- ✓ Replace the belief with a more supportive and optimistic one.

- ✓ Use the New Belief Generator Success Strategy to install and amplify the empowering belief and replace the old negative one.

- ✓ Embody the belief: feel joy in your heart and truly value and savor the new belief deep in your gut — remember the heart and gut have innate intuitive intelligence, so use it positively and powerfully.

- ✓ Celebrate your new more positive attitudes, congratulate yourself and enjoy your increasing happiness and success.

Awareness Questions — Supporting Positive Attitudes

Ask Yourself:

> ➤ In what situations or contexts do I need to improve my attitudes and use a more positive orientation?

> ➤ In what areas of my life am I thinking in a negative way?

- How can I make my attitudes more positive and supportive?

- What beliefs can I choose and install that will give me more joy, happiness and success?

Identity, Values and Beliefs

NLP has a very useful model for showing how your identity, values, beliefs and behaviors are connected. It is called the Levels of Identity model and is diagrammed on the following page.

In this model, your identity influences, and is in turn influenced by your values. Your values influence your beliefs and vice versa. Your beliefs in turn are linked to your capabilities. Your capabilities impact your behaviors and finally your behaviors determine your results in the world. Equally, your results influence your behaviors and back on up the chain. In this way you can see how your sense of self interacts with your values, beliefs and eventually with your behaviors leading to results which feedback and modify your beliefs, values and identity. It's an ongoing success spiral that is either cycling in a positive or negative direction.

Levels of Identity

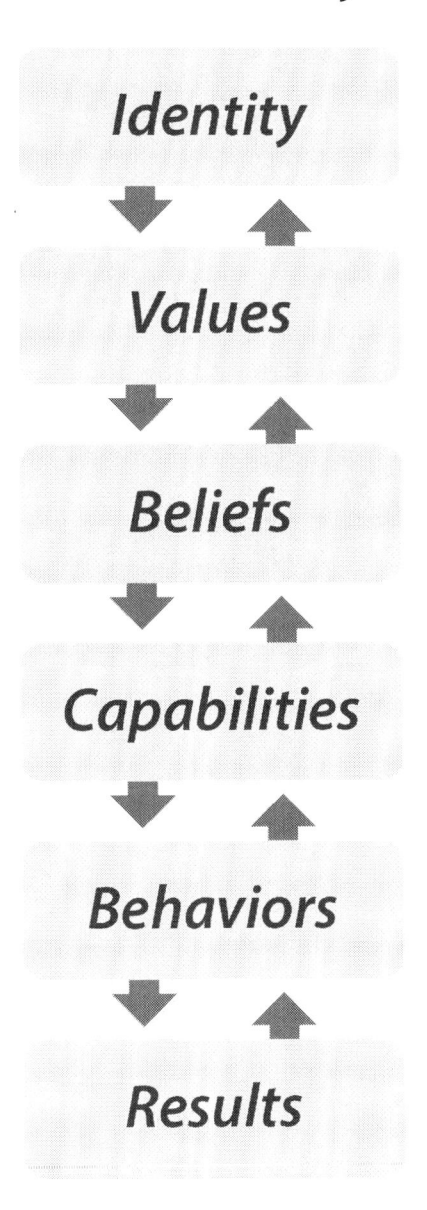

Identity
↓ ↑
Values
↓ ↑
Beliefs
↓ ↑
Capabilities
↓ ↑
Behaviors
↓ ↑
Results

When it comes to changing your beliefs it is useful to understand how beliefs are linked to other aspects of your mind and self. One of the insights from this model is that if you want to change a belief and that belief is linked to a core value or a core sense of identity — to some aspect of your self-image for example — then you will need to first modify and change the beliefs you have about your identity and values. Notice that your values and identity are really beliefs; values are what you believe is important, and identity consists of your beliefs about yourself — your self-concept and self-image.

Another important thing to understand about values and beliefs is that they are connected in a semantic web. That is, they are connected by shared meaning. This is shown in the diagram below.

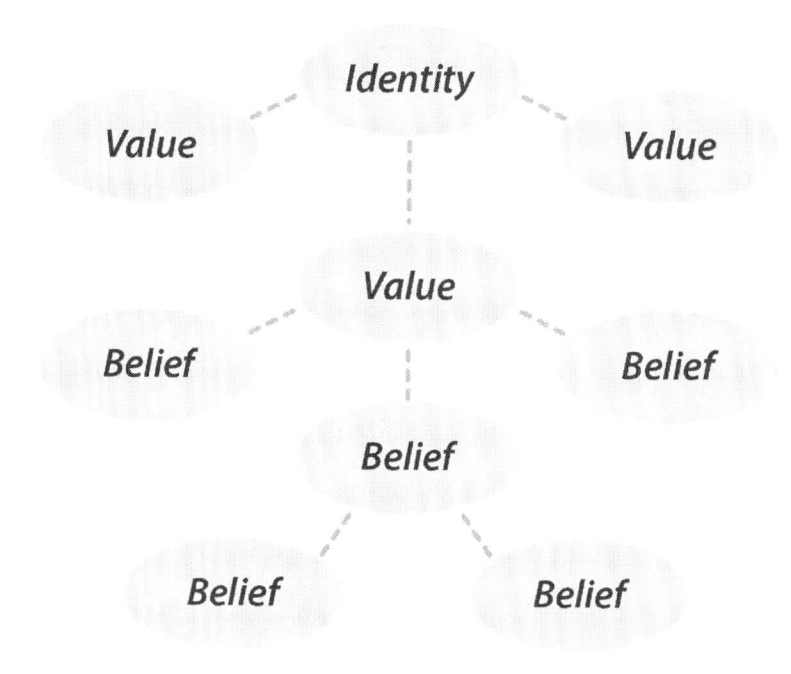

Identity

Value *Value*

Value

Belief *Belief*

Belief

Belief *Belief*

Beliefs and values do not exist in isolation of each other. When you form beliefs, you are creating a generalization, and this is linked to existing ideas and beliefs you have previously formed. In NLP these are called the *'legs'* of the belief and when you want to change an important belief you often have to change the supporting generalizations that are presupposed by that belief.

Examine each of the self-limiting beliefs you are changing and ask yourself what else you believe or what else must be true in your map of the world for you to accept the belief as true. By deeply analyzing your core beliefs and challenging the underpinning values and concepts you can quite quickly and powerfully demolish whole networks of beliefs that no longer serve you. It's like pulling out one of the cards from a *'house of cards'*, once the foundation has been demolished, the whole house comes tumbling down.

And remember always to install new networks of positive and empowering beliefs in the place of any negative beliefs and values that you remove from your life.

Putting it all together

Let's put what you've learned together now to create a concise list of the strategies and actions to use in overcoming the enemies described in this chapter. Use the following set of processes to amplify and enhance your success and happiness in life.

1. Actively search for and **challenge negative beliefs** and attitudes

2. Refuse to give in to pessimistic thoughts, **focus** instead **on the positive and on possibilities and opportunities**

3. **Create empowering beliefs** and use the New Belief Generator to install them

4. **Focus on positive outcomes** — on what you want and not on what you don't want

5. **Embody positive attitudes of success** in your heart, gut and posture to support your outcomes, create positive self-fulfilling prophecies and directionalize your RAS

6. **Use confirmation bias to support your happiness** by holding positive beliefs high in your mind and deep in your heart and actively seeking confirmation and examples in your life that **uphold your positive beliefs**

> *"To succeed, we must first believe that we can."*
>
> Michael Korda

Strengths & Values In Action

Use the following table to determine which strengths, qualities and values to focus on and amplify in your life to support the processes and skills of happiness. Also notice if you have any elements of the absence, opposite or exaggeration of these strengths and remove them from your behaviors and your life.

I don't BELIEVE it

Enemies to happiness	VIA Strength
Negative Beliefs	Perspective/Wisdom
Limitations	Social Intelligence
Pessimism	Hope
	Creativity
FUD	Bravery

📋 Notes from the Field — Believing in Happiness

Robert Dilts has been and continues to be a key developer in the field of NLP since its creation in 1975. He is a well known author, trainer and consultant, with over 20 books on NLP as well as hundreds of articles and publications. In addition, Robert has been responsible for spearheading the application of NLP to education, creativity, health, and leadership. His personal contributions to the field of NLP also include important and insightful work on the NLP techniques of Strategies, Belief Systems, and the development of what has become known as *'Systemic NLP'*.

I spoke to Robert to find out his thoughts and ideas on happiness, the enemies to happiness, and in particular, about the beliefs that support or limit happiness.

According to Robert, happiness is largely about connection, value, contribution and creativity. It's also about alignment and balance. As he points out, you won't feel happy all the time. Instead, as Milton Erickson said, happiness is about *"reacting to the good and bad and dealing with it adequately. That's the real joy in life"*.

A big part of happiness is also about stretching and growing. Challenging situations in life push you into new territory, and it's how you respond that determines whether you experience happiness and joy or misery.

Alignment and Connection

Robert's research and experience suggests that happiness comes from feeling fully connected with yourself. This connection occurs when there is alignment and congruence between the various levels of self — between your identity, values, beliefs, capabilities, behaviors and environmental results. So belief and values issues are very relevant.

The main belief issues that are related to unhappiness are:

- Hopelessness
- Helplessness
- Worthlessness

The key belief areas that support happiness are the reverse of these, namely

- Optimism/hope
- Confidence/competence
- Self-worth/self-esteem

The beliefs that support happiness can be articulated as *"it's possible for me to achieve happiness"*, *"I'm capable of achieving happiness"* and *"I deserve happiness"*.

In terms of values, certain core values contribute to happiness. These include:

- Connection to others
- A sense of contribution
- A sense of safety (internal and external)

In Robert's work, these notions of connection, contribution and safety are combined in the concept of *'Positive Sponsorship'*. This is about being truly seen and acknowledged by other people, about valuing yourself and about feeling genuine and involved.

Positive Sponsorship

Positive Self-Sponsorship consists of the experiences and understandings that:

1. I am seen, I exist
2. I am valuable, I am sufficient as I am
3. I am unique and special (not necessarily better than others)
4. I have something to contribute
5. I belong, I am part of something bigger than myself

Positive Sponsorship is about being able to create these for yourself and for others.

Negative Thought Viruses and Negative Sponsorship

Robert believes there are a number of debilitating negative beliefs that act like thought viruses. These are beliefs that people succumb to. They often involve negative sponsorship and include thoughts and ideas about not being welcome, not being valued. They are beliefs that take away from you as a person. You can hear them in negative invectives and statements like *"who do you think you are!"*

and *"nobody wants you around"*. If you hear and believe such statements as you are growing up then you become infected by these negative sponsorship thought viruses. They are enemies to happiness.

You can use various NLP techniques to remove and replace these beliefs with messages of positive sponsorship. Give yourself positive messages and give them to those you care about. Your beliefs and values make a huge difference to your success and happiness in life. As Robert says *"it's vitally important to exist to yourself and be important and valued by yourself"*. He also points out that it's difficult to be generous to others if you can't be generous to yourself.

Alignment with Meaning

Robert is also known for introducing many ideas of spirituality into NLP. In his Levels of Identity model, he has a level above that of Identity, which he calls *'Vision'*. This is the highest level, and is the level of meaning and spirituality. It's about purpose and mission. About what you believe you're purpose is for being here on this planet and in this life. You will experience the deepest levels of happiness, joy and fulfillment when you align all the levels of your life; when your vision and mission in life match. So examine your values and beliefs. Look for the positive intentions in your life and embrace the enemies to happiness in ways that allow you to transcend them. Choose empowering and supporting beliefs for both yourself and those you care about. Really make a difference in your life by believing in and sponsoring happiness in life.

NLP University

You can get more information about Robert's ideas and his

various courses and books from the NLP University web site. Check out www.nlpu.com and really start believing in happiness.

☞ Remember This

This section provides a summary of the key learnings from the chapter and should be used for review and to assist you in remembering the ideas and strategies.

- ✓ Beliefs are powerful. What and how you believe and the attitudes you embody are important to your happiness and success.

- ✓ You don't *'have'* beliefs, this is a nominalization of the process of believing. The process of believing uses submodalities (visual, auditory and feeling etc.) to code for believability. Use the New Belief Generator to shift your beliefs and install new empowering ones.

- ✓ Your RAS (Reticular Activating System) controls your unconscious attention. Directionalize your RAS by focusing on positive beliefs and values.

- ✓ Use the effects of believing — Cocktail Party Effect, Self-fulfilling Prophecy, Placebo Effect and Confirmation Bias, to support your outcomes and gain greater success and happiness.

- ✓ Track for and actively dispute any limiting negative beliefs of:
  - ➢ Conditional Happiness
  - ➢ Happiness Sabotage
  - ➢ FUD — Fear, Uncertainty & Doubt
  - ➢ Automatic Negative Irrational Beliefs
  - ➢ Pessimistic Attitudes
  - ➢ Binary Submodalities
  - ➢ Setting Limits on Others

  And install in their place new and more empowering beliefs.

- ✓ Apply Learned Optimism in your life and focus on building hope for the future. Hold hope in your heart.

- ✓ Amplify and embody positive attitudes using the Cybernetic Loop.

ⓘ Extra Info

Refer to www.enemiestohappiness.com for

- more information about the material covered in this chapter
- additional reading and references for this chapter

Avoiding the Enemies to HAPPINESS

Chapter 3

Ignorance is NOT bliss

You will learn to

- ✓ Value knowledge and learning
- ✓ Move away from ignorance and deceit
- ✓ Track for and change un-sane thinking
- ✓ Overcome and utilize cognitive dissonance
- ✓ Embody a state of wanton curiosity

Ignorance is NOT bliss

If ignorance is bliss, why aren't there more happy people? Ignorance is NOT bliss! Ignorance is risky and dangerous. Ignorance can kill you! Lack of knowledge, stupidity and deception of yourself and others are all enemies to happiness and meaning in your life. Replace them with a desire for knowledge, wanton curiosity about the world and an ever increasing store of wisdom and skill. Knowledge brings choice and control.

In this chapter you will learn the importance of overcoming the enemies of ignorance and deception. You'll explore success strategies for installing a desire for learning and a wanton curiosity for knowledge. You'll also learn how to create a saner map of the world to generate greater success and happiness.

Enemies to your Happiness

✘ Ignorance and stupidity

✘ Deception and lying

✘ Inappropriate deleting, distorting and over-generalizing

✘ Un-sane thinking and behavior

✘ Minimizing or discounting the positive

Ignorance is Dangerous

It might seem obvious, but ignorance and stupidity are dangerous. They can kill you. At the very least, they severely impact your success and happiness.

Some of the dangers of ignorance are:

➢ You can't prepare

➢ You can't see what's coming

➢ It limits your choices and power

➢ Amplifies consequences

➢ Leads to more mistakes and greater costs

Whilst most people would agree with this, nevertheless, the majority of people are largely ignorant of the most important things and processes in their life. They don't know how their mind, brain and body work. They don't know how they unconsciously generate their own reality and happiness. They don't know the enemies to their success and happiness. They can't even articulate their values and core beliefs, let alone improve and refine them for greater success in their life.

Such ignorance means they end up living average and unhappy lives. They make stupid mistakes that cost them peace of mind. They bounce from failure to failure in their relationships, finances, careers and health. This book and the skills you will have gained from it can change all of that. The first step is awareness. The next step is gaining and expanding your knowledge. Finally, through practice you'll have achieved new skills and mastery. Knowledge and choice provide power and control. By instilling in your unconscious mind a desire for learning, and a passionate move away repulsion from ignorance and deception, you will make an incredible difference to your happiness.

We don't operate off the world, we operate off a map or model of the world. Through our learning and experience we build an internal representation or model of the world — what we think the world is all about — and we operate unconsciously and consciously from that. This model then acts in many ways like a filter and influences what we are willing to see and do in the world. It creates stereotypes and self-fulfilling prophecies in our lives. Our map of the world can be either liberating or limiting and sometimes both.

> *"Most people, sometime in their lives, stumble across truth. Most jump up, brush themselves off, and hurry on about their business as if nothing had happened."*
>
> Winston Churchill

🛠 Thinking Tools — Overcoming Ignorance

Ignorance is NOT bliss. Ignorance is dangerous!

Denial of Reality

One of the most important enemies to knowledge and happiness involves denial of reality. While philosophers might argue over it, for the rest of us, reality exists and denying or ignoring any part of that reality can cause problems and issues in your life.

A great learning story that shows the futility of denial is the one about the two guys driving across the desert. They drive and drive and eventually run out of fuel and become dangerously stranded in a barren and hostile environment, miles from help. The passenger looks at the fuel gauge, which is still sitting on full, and asks the driver *"Hey, how come we're out of fuel? The gauge shows a full tank..."* The driver turns to his stranded companion and says *"Yeah, I don't understand it, I disconnected the wires from the gauge, and it's still showing a full tank. We should still have plenty of fuel!"*

What foolishness you might think. What craziness! Yet, how many people live their lives exactly like that. They delete and distort their model of the world; deliberately ignoring facts and confabulating evidence until the consequences impact their lives so painfully that they can no longer deny their reality. How many people ignore the evidence of infidelity in their relationships? Or the warning signs of failure in other areas of their lives? The indicators of ill health or financial difficulties for example.

It reminds me of another story, a very real story. One of my father's work colleagues, we'll call him *'Old Bill'* had an excavator, a large machine used for digging dirt and soil. It was a very expensive machine and was the main component of his business. One day he was servicing it. He had the side of the machine open, when the phone rang and he had to leave it and take the call. When he returned, he saw some kids running away and noticed some sand and gravel sticking to the edge of the opening into the side-case of the machine.

Now I have to explain that this particular machine is filled with very expensive and complex hydraulic motors and pumps and sand in the internals would destroy them in a matter of seconds. Well,

Old Bill decided that it would be a huge amount of work to strip down the machine and clean out any sand, if the kids had thrown it into the machine. So he figured he'd just ignore the evidence and pretend that nothing had happened. He finished the service, re-assembled the machine and started it up.

In a matter of seconds, he heard terrible noises and the machine ground to a halt. The kids had definitely filled the side-cases with sand and gravel. Now not only was Old Bill faced with having to clean out the hydraulic system, he was also faced with the incredible expense of replacing all the pumps, lines, filters and motors. The machine was a wreck. His denial of reality caused him even more cost and delay than if he'd faced up to the truth from the start. This was a valuable lesson for both Old Bill, and for me when I heard it. Never ignore the facts. The facts are our friends.

> *"Nothing in the world is more dangerous than sincere ignorance and conscientious stupidity."*
>
> Martin Luther King, Jr.

Thinking Tools — Facts

The facts are our friends!

Cognitive Dissonance

In 1956, Stanford University psychologist Leon Festinger heard about a group of doomsday cultists who were predicting that the Earth would be destroyed by aliens at midnight on December 21st of that year. Festinger and his students decided to infiltrate the group and covertly study what happens to people when their strongly held beliefs are disproved. What he discovered lead to the theory of Cognitive Dissonance.

So what did happen, in the minutes and hours after midnight, when the prophesied destruction and the predicted appearance of alien spacecraft to save the faithful didn't occur? Initially there was shock and disbelief by the members of the group; many had left jobs, colleges and spouses to prepare to leave on the flying saucer supposed to rescue them. Within hours however, people began to deny they ever believed in the doomsday prophecy. They were saying things like *"I didn't really believe it, I was just going along for the adventure."* Or, *"Because of our strong faith, the aliens chose to save the planet"*. Basically, they said and thought anything other than the truth which was that they'd all been duped.

Based on this research and thousands of subsequent laboratory and real-world studies, Festinger posited that the unconscious mind does not like what he called *'dissonance'* and will do anything to remove it. Dissonance is the disagreeable feeling we get when faced with mismatching cognitions or beliefs. Our mind likes harmony and congruence between our thoughts and beliefs and will utilize a number of unconscious strategies to remove cognitive dissonance. The tension of cognitive dissonance leads people to change either their beliefs and attitudes or their behavior.

The importance of this is that it leads people to denying reality and deleting or distorting their cognitions and perceptions.

Cognitive dissonance can be a serious enemy to happiness if it leads to denial of reality and un-sane distortions or behaviors. Of course, cognitive dissonance is like any tool or process, it can be used positively or negatively. As described in Chapter 1, you can use cognitive dissonance and the unconscious mind's response to it to assist you in positively aligning your thoughts, values and behavior. However, when cognitive dissonance occurs outside your conscious awareness to minimize your life and lead you into ignorance then it is a dangerous enemy.

The key to using cognitive dissonance constructively is to be aware of what are known as *'Dissonance Signals'* and track for them in your life. When you notice them, you need to pattern-interrupt the typical dissonance removal strategies and replace them with more useful strategies and behaviors. To do this you need to know about Dissonance Removal Strategies and your own Dissonance Signals.

Typical Dissonance Removal Strategies

There are a number of unconscious strategies that people's minds normally use to remove cognitive dissonance.

- **Avoidance** — people avoid information that is likely to lead to dissonance

- **Distortion** — people delete and distort facts and beliefs to reduce dissonance

- **Confirmation** — people are attracted to or perform selective bias on information that confirms or bolsters their cognitions

- **Reassurance** — people look for reassurance from others that their cognitions are correct and ok

➢ **Re-valuation** — people change the importance of existing and new cognitions to reduce dissonance

You should also note that research has shown that the more effort and time invested in a decision or the forming of a belief, the larger the potential dissonance created if mismatching evidence is discovered. Therefore, the more important the outcome the more likely your unconscious mind is to perform the above strategies. For example, if you purchase a low cost item, you are unlikely to experience buyer's remorse. However, for an expensive item that you spent a lot of time evaluating, you are more likely to experience buyer's remorse and therefore more likely to go seeking confirmation and reassurance after the purchase.

By being aware that your evolved animal brain doesn't like negative change, that it doesn't like things that don't match, you can begin to transcend this un-useful pattern. The facts are our friends and knowledge is power. Denying reality and ignoring facts just because the evolved patterning system of the brain desires congruence, is dangerous and crazy.

Use the following Success Strategy to learn about and track for cognitive dissonance signals and then support yourself in facing reality — in looking at all the facts and evidence. Don't let your unconscious mind seduce you into the enemy of ignorance. Instead, build patterns in your life of overcoming cognitive dissonance and using valid, valuable feedback and knowledge to gain greater happiness and meaning in your life.

🛠 Thinking Tools — Knowledge

Knowledge is Power!

☑ Success Strategy — Tracking Cognitive Dissonance

This Success Strategy will allow you to track for and overcome the process of cognitive dissonance.

1. Remember a time when you experienced cognitive dissonance. A time when you were faced with facts that challenged one of your beliefs, or a time when your behavior didn't match your values or self-concept. Role-play and re-live that situation. Fully access what you were feeling then, seeing then, hearing then and thinking then. Totally associate into re-living the experience. Once you are totally in the dissonance state, track for and note what feelings you are doing in your body. Cognitive dissonance often impacts the heart and gut brains, so pay particular not to these regions. Track all of the pressures, movements, flows, temperatures, textures etc. of the experience. Notice also the submodalities of any pictures and sounds. Write these onto a piece of paper for you to remember.

2. Pick two other cognitive dissonance experiences/times and note the dissonance signals for these. You should find that the three experiences have similar signals and components.

3. Determine what the main indicators are for the state of cognitive dissonancing. Think about how you can now remember the signals so that in the future you will know when you are doing dissonance and be able to become more aware of your own unconscious processes.

4. Think about what you can do to overcome cognitive dissonance in a positive way, without giving in to it. What can you say to yourself? What can you do to support pushing through the dissonance to face reality and not deny it?

5. One very powerful way to overcome dissonance is through humor. By laughing at the dissonance feeling, by seeing it as humorous, you can shift your cybernetic loop to one of positive feelings. Anything that helps you overcome the negative emotions of dissonance will help you push through and stop the typical dissonance strategies.

6. You can also use the Embodying Attitudes of Success strategy from Chapter 2 to overcome the negative state of dissonance.

7. Finally, by being aware of the possibility of cognitive dissonance and knowing your dissonance signals you can float above the dissonance feelings by just acknowledging them and telling yourself *"Oh, that's just cognitive dissonance — I can ignore and transcend it, it's just an animal response, I'm better than that!"*

Questioning Assumptions

So much of our model of the world is based on unquestioned assumptions absorbed from our culture, our families and friends. Unquestioned assumptions are an enemy to happiness when they limit your choices and cause you to repeat patterns that no longer serve you.

A great learning metaphor that demonstrates this is the story of a young woman cooking a roast. She's about to cut the meat into two, to put into the baking tray when she wonders why she is doing this. She decides to call her mother and ask. Her mother, perplexed by the question, says *"I don't know darling, that's just the way I was taught. You'll have to ask your Grandmother."* The girl calls her Grandmother, *"Grandma, how come when I cook a roast I have to cut it in half? Why do I do that?" "Oh darling,"* says the older woman, *"You don't have to cut it. In fact, it's better if you don't, that way the meat won't dry out as much." "It all started with your Great Great Grandmother. Back in her day, the stoves and baking dishes were very small. So to fit a roast in the tray you had to cut the meat in half. She taught her daughter that way, who taught my mother that way, who taught me. In turn, that's what I taught your mother, and she taught you. It's just the way we've always done it. But no, now that you've asked, you're right, you don't have to do it that way any more."*

This story is so typical of many habits and patterns, many assumptions, we have and do in our life. We learn things from family and society and unless we question the assumptions that these learnings and patterns are based on, we end up doomed to repeat the inefficient and unproductive patterns of the past.

Many practices from the past, especially those embedded in our culture, come from a time of scientific ignorance and superstition. Unless questioned, these practices cause you to metaphorically cut your roast in half. Leading to dried out, shriveled results in life.

Begin to question everything. All the old patterns and habits in your life. Ask yourself *"Why do I do X?"* Figure out the purpose and outcomes of your behaviors. Question the assumptions inherent in each of the patterns in your life. Then use the NLP Success Strategy described in Chapter 0. Get clear on your outcome, take new action, use your sensory acuity to learn from feedback and with requisite variety, change and adjust your behavior flexibly to keep moving closer to your explicit outcome. Throw away old patterns that are an enemy to your happiness.

Awareness Questions — Questioning Assumptions

Ask Yourself:

- What is this behavior or pattern based on? What are the assumptions this action is based on? Why am I doing this?

- What outcomes and purpose does this pattern achieve? How else can I achieve the positive intent in a more useful and productive way?

- Does this behavior still serve me? What else can I do to achieve more happiness?

> *"Honesty is the first chapter of the book of wisdom."*
>
> Thomas Jefferson

Deceit and Dishonesty

There is nothing surer, lying and deceit will create problems in your life. Deceit and dishonesty are huge enemies to happiness. They destroy trust, they distort and destroy the truth and lead down a seductive path of denial and illusion.

Remember, your mind is made up of a multitude of simple automatons — simple autonomous processes that operate with unconscious competence, usually outside of your awareness. You build new parts, new processes into your unconscious, through repeated practice.

If you lie and cheat, even if you think you are in control and only doing it in certain contexts, you are actually creating a part that does lying with unconscious competence. Such behavior, repeated enough, creates a part that will generalize and begin to do that behavior in other contexts and areas of your life. In NLP we say that in the unconscious patterning system of the brain, processes generalize across contexts. Processes get learnt in one context but eventually spread across to other contexts and aspects of your life.

You can see this in your and other people's lives. Often, if you look at how someone dresses, it's similar to how they drive, how they eat, how they walk, what their house looks like, their desk, etc. This is the cybernetic loop at work. The way they think influences the way they feel and act, which spirals around and patterns the way they think and act. So for example, you'll often see that someone who is messy has a messy house, a dirty car, they'll drive poorly, their desk will be messy, their clothes unkempt. Conversely, someone who is a neatness freak will drive neatly, walk properly, have a neat and tidy desk, a neat and tidy mind. Processes generalize across contexts. So beware what patterns and processes you put into your life.

Personal Honesty

When it comes to honesty, if you teach yourself and practice honesty, you'll build a part that generalizes across the contexts of your life to be accurate and honest and to generate maps that are accurate representations of the territory of your life. But if you lie and practice dishonesty and deceit, you'll create a part that does deceiving and that part will generalize through your life and before long, you'll lie to yourself and not even know you are doing it.

This will cause major problems. You'll no longer trust yourself — the various parts of your society of mind, your multi-mind — won't trust each other. And because we have three brains (head, heart and gut), these processes of distrust can generalize within and across your multiple brains. You can end up with for example, a *'lying heart'* and then deceive both yourself and others. You'll start undermining yourself. You'll end up with few quality friends, with no one who trusts or values you. You'll end up with a life of misery and sadness.

Instead, as often as possible, be honest with yourself and with others. The facts are our friends. Face the truth. Be accurate. Refuse to distort or deny reality. Deceit is an enemy to happiness. Focus on personal honesty and openness with others. Happiness is based on knowledge and meaning. Honesty is a friend of happiness, so embrace it and share it with others.

Deeper Understandings — Mapping the World

In 1933, Count Alfred Korzybski wrote and published a seminal book called *'Science and Sanity'* and founded a field of philosophy known as General Semantics. In his book, Korzybski showed how language influences our perceptions and actions and that incorrect use of language and thought can lead to what he called un-sane behavior. Indeed, Korzybski coined the term *'neuro-linguistics'* and created the foundation for the many fields that sprang from his original insights, including the field of NLP.

Korzybski focused on the process of abstracting, of how we as humans build and evolve concepts and generalizations. He described how we build theories and maps of the world in order to make sense of it. One of the key insights from General Semantics is that *"the map can never be the territory"*. What this means is that, given that humans can never operate off and know the full world — the territory — they must, and can only ever operate off a map of the territory. And no map can ever be a full representation of the territory; therefore we will always be operating off a deleted, distorted and generalized/abstracted map of that territory. This sounds like a very simple idea, yet it has profound implications and applications.

Most people don't realize that their five senses do not actually provide an absolute and real experience of the world. Our senses and brains evolved to efficiently track and notice difference in the world, not to provide an absolute and accurate representation. Each of our senses tracks change rather than absolute data, and our brain then takes each of these differences and changes and does its best job of making a useful map of the territory.

For example, you probably didn't know that your eyes are not like a camera. A digital camera has an array of pixels that take the amount of light focused on them and provide an absolute representation, a one-for-one representation of the image that the camera sees. Your eye however, has rods and cones for receptors, but these don't measure the absolute amount of light focused on them. Instead they only give a signal when the amount of light changes; they only measure and track change and difference. You have small muscles around your eyes called *'micro-saccades'* and these muscles keep your eyes moving and tremoring in micro-circles. These movements ensure that the image on your retina keeps changing.

When neuro-physiologists first anaesthetized these muscles, they found what was called the *'Ganzfeld effect'* — the grey field effect. When the image subtended on the retina stops moving, the eye stops sending a signal to the brain. If we anaesthetized your eye muscles and kept your head still, and if there was nothing moving in your visual field, your vision would grey out and become blank. After about 5 seconds, you would see nothing. This is because the eye and brain didn't evolve to get an absolute image of the world. It evolved to efficiently help you survive, and the best way to do this is to only notice and respond to difference and change.

All of your senses and nervous system are *'designed'* by evolution in the same way. You only track for difference and your unconscious mind builds a *'best-guess'* map of the world from integrating and summing all these little changes and differences. You see, you can never ever absolutely know the world. You don't have the sensory apparatus to experience the world absolutely.

Add to this your sensory systems only operate over small ranges of size, frequency, speed, etc. and you'll realize that your map is certainly very, very deleted, generalized and distorted. And as Korzybski pointed out *'The map is NOT the territory'*. So when it comes to knowing the world, when it comes to knowing the *'truth'* you need to be very, very careful. You can never absolutely know the *'truth'*. Your abstractions and the abstractions of your abstractions are a long way from absolute reality. That's what science is all about, it's a method for attempting to create accurate theories about the world; and any theory in science is always provisional and always an abstraction.

So what can you do with these insights? Well, Korzybski pointed out that there are certain forms of abstracting that our language and our culture encourage that are not accurate and lead to un-sane or neurotic behavior. Language influences our perceptions. By becoming aware of how your language influences your brain, your thinking and decisions, your motivations and inevitably your actions, you can begin to consciously choose more accurate and sane languaging and abstracting.

You've already been introduced to many of the General Semantics tools for sane and more rational thinking and throughout this book you'll experience and learn many more.

⚒ Thinking Tools — Mapping the World

The map is NOT the territory. It only represents the territory.

Knowledge Provides Choice and Power

As you know, knowledge and learning provide choice and power in your life. We live in a world of massive and accelerating change. Almost every aspect of our lives is advancing and changing at an increasing rate. Technology and the quest for ever increasing profits are the major drivers. This accelerating rate of technological change drives social change, economic change, environmental change and ultimately personal change. You cannot escape it. By continuing to learn and evolve and increase your skills and knowledge, you give yourself the best chance of coping with and mastering this change. We'll explore this in much more detail in Chapter 6.

By mastering the skills of learning and change you will

- Be prepared for what's coming
- Increase your choice in how to respond and benefit
- Minimize uncertainty
- Be able to intelligently choose the most useful direction
- Gain more happiness
- Support others with increased wisdom and understanding

Law of Requisite Knowing

Remember the *'Law of Requisite Variety'* from Chapter 1. This is a mathematically provable theorem from Systems Theory that says that the element that has the most requisite variety or flexibility will be the controlling element of a system. This can be summarized as the thinking tool: **Choice = Control**. What this means is that if you want more control in life, you have to have more choice and flexibility.

There is a sister theorem to this known as the *'Law of Requisite Knowledge'*. This related theorem says that as the requisite variety and complexity increases in a system, you need more knowledge about which choice to use in order to control the system. What this is saying is that in any system, to gain more control you need knowledge and flexibility. You need the choice to act along with the knowledge and skill to act appropriately.

What these theories tell you is that knowledge and skill are incredibly important for control over your life and your environment. Learning and knowledge increase your power over your life. Ignorance is dangerous and an enemy to happiness and success. Wisdom and knowledge are the keys to greater happiness, joy and meaning.

✂ Thinking Tools — Requisite Knowing

Knowledge + Choice = Control

🔍 Awareness Questions — Knowledge and Learning

Ask Yourself:

➢ What can I do to learn more about myself or this situation?

➢ What outcomes do I have about learning and knowledge?

➢ What am I doing in my life to increase my knowledge, skills and wisdom?

> *"The problem in my life and other people's lives is not the absence of knowing what to do, but the absence of doing it."*
>
> Peter Drucker

All Knowing is Doing

According to Dr. Humberto Maturana, an influential Systems Theorist, Biologist and Philosopher, all true knowing involves action. You don't really know something until you can use it. This is the difference between knowledge and information. Facts are data you have available, but don't translate into knowing and skill until you can use them. The key to wisdom and knowing is in having unconscious competence in using your knowledge to create positive change in your world.

The importance of understanding that *"all knowing is doing"* is in ensuring you stay out of the trap of thinking that data and information equals knowledge. Knowledge involves integrated understanding about using data in ecological ways. About intentions, actions and consequences of the data. Knowledge is powerful, but only when it involves successful doing. The saying *'with a little bit of knowledge we're dangerous'* is a reflection on the difference between facts versus an integrated mastery of knowing.

To support happiness and meaning in your life, ensure you put knowledge into action. Apply your learnings to your life and the lives of others. Make a positive difference and integrate your experiences through self-reflection and a focus on feedback and choice.

Thinking Tools — Knowledge & Action

All knowing is doing!

Learning from Feedback

We discussed the NLP Success Strategy earlier in the book. The NLP Success Strategy says to maximize your chance of success you need to operate the following strategy.

1. Clearly know your **Outcome**

2. Take congruent **Action**

3. Sensory Acuity — Learn from **Feedback**

4. **Behavioral Flexibility** — Change and adjust to achieve your Outcome

From this strategy comes the insight that there is no such thing as failure, there is only useful and valid feedback. If what you are doing isn't working or is moving you further from your outcome, then this is really excellent feedback and allows you to use requisite variety to change and adjust your actions until you are moving closer to your outcome. Excellent. There's no failure, only feedback. What a great thinking tool.

Too often people see negative feedback as failure. They hate hearing or seeing that something isn't working or that they are wrong. They then go into denial or distort the facts in order to delete such really useful feedback. When you understand that there is no failure, there is only fantastic feedback that you can use to support your success strategy, then you empower yourself to accept reality and make positive use of it. The facts really are our friends. They point us in the direction of our happiness and success. You really do want to know what works and what doesn't work in the world. You want an accurate and useful map of your world. So value and appreciate all feedback. Learn and grow from it.

> *"The way you think about a fact may defeat you before you ever do anything about it. You are overcome by the fact because you think you are."*
>
> Norman Vincent Peale

Thinking Tools — Feedback

No failure, only useful feedback!

Neuro-genesis

It was once thought you were born with all the brain cells you would ever have and that over time they slowly died off. Recent research from the field of Neuroscience has completely overturned that old fallacy. The science of *'neuro-genesis'* and neural plasticity, has shown that new brain cells and their dendrites and connections can grow and increase over periods of days, weeks and months. Equally, the brain and immune system can quite rapidly kill off brain cells and connections that are not being used.

This is exciting and important news. The evidence is that learning and stimulation, experiencing new and exciting things, encourages the growth and development of the brain at any age. Whereas, both stress and boredom decrease the number of brain cells and lead to cell death.

What this means is that ignorance and a refusal to learn and take on new activities really is NOT bliss. Ignorance kills. If you don't use your brain it will slowly atrophy and your brain cells will die off. It's use it, or lose it. The more you use your brain and challenge yourself with new learning, the more your brain cells grow and develop. The more knowledge you have, the more your capacity to take on and learn new knowledge. The better your brain functions, the better you can cope with change. It's a positive success spiral. Knowledge really is powerful and supports more joy and meaning in life.

Pos ψ The Strength of Wisdom

Wisdom is one of the six core virtues proposed by Positive Psychology as important to happiness. Studies have shown that it is a positive predictor of successful aging. Indeed, wisdom is more strongly linked to well-being than objective life circumstances such as health, financial well-being, and physical environment.

The strengths that make up Wisdom are:

- Creativity — originality, ingenuity
- Curiosity — interest, novelty-seeking, openness to experience
- Open-mindedness — judgment, critical thinking
- Love of learning — mastering new skills
- Perspective — wisdom, providing wise counsel

By focusing on these strengths and amplifying them in your life you'll support yourself in increasing your levels of happiness and life satisfaction. At the beginning of each day, ask yourself, *"how can I put these strengths into action during my day"*. Encourage yourself and elevate these values into actions in your life.

As you focus on and gain more knowledge and wisdom you'll need to be wary not to fall into one of the *'wisdom traps'*. According to psychologist Robert Sternberg, there are four main traps or fallacies to beware of.

1. **The Egocentrism Fallacy** — thinking that the world revolves, or should revolve, around you. Acting in ways that benefit you, regardless of how your actions affect others

2. **The Omniscience Fallacy** — believing you know all there is to know and so not listening to the advice and suggestions of others

3. **The Omnipotence Fallacy** — believing your intelligence and education make you all-powerful

4. **The Invulnerability Fallacy** — believing you can do whatever you want and that others will never be able to figure out what you've done or expose you

Dr. Ben Dean, a leading Positive Psychology Coach, suggests the following strategies for developing wisdom.

➢ Read the works of great thinkers and religious leaders such as Gandhi, Buddha, Jesus, Mother Theresa and Nelson Mandela

➢ Read classic works of literature and contemplate the '*wisdom of the ages*'

➢ Think of the wisest person you know and try to live each day as that person would live

➢ Volunteer at a nursing home and talk with residents about their lives and the lessons they have learned

Generative Change — Strategies for Learning

According to NLP there are two major models of change in the world: Remedial Change versus Generative Change.

With Remedial Change you only change something when it is broken — *"If it ain't broke, don't fix it"*. This is contrasted with the preferred model of change called Generative Change. With Generative Change you operate from a philosophy of continuous improvement. No matter how good things are, you continue to find ways to make them and yourself even more successful. You keep generating new and better ways of living.

This is a powerful attitude for success and learning. It encourages you to continue evolving and growing as a person. To take on new and improved ways of thinking and acting. To never stop learning. The Generative Change attitude supports you in developing your skills, wisdom and knowledge.

So continuously look for new and novel activities and processes to add to your life. Take up new hobbies. Stimulate yourself by reading and study. Involve yourself in volunteer activities. Help other people. Enroll in short-courses or further education. Regularly jump on the internet and search on areas that interest you. There's a world of knowledge available. Keep learning and renewing your mind and life.

Since learning is an important skill for happiness, you'll want to support yourself by learning how to learn more effectively. There are a number of strategies and techniques for enhancing learning:

- Mind-mapping

- Accelerated Learning

- Speed-reading and Photo-reading

Grab a book, go on a short-course or use the internet to learn more about these excellent learning skills.

☑ Success Strategy — Wanton Curiosity

NLP is built on an attitude of *'wanton curiosity'*, of seeing the world through a state of wide-eyed curiosity. It's an attitude of seeing things through new eyes and being intrigued by the world. The following Success Strategy will guide you in embodying a state of wanton curiosity to support and enhance your quest for knowledge and learning.

1. Think of a time when you were really, really curious about something. When something peaked your interest.

2. Relive those memories. Go back and see what you saw, hear what you heard, feel what you felt at this time. Amplify the feelings of curiosity and intrigue. Make your pictures of the memories brighter and more empowering. Bring them closer. Really enjoy experiencing wide-eyed curiosity.

3. Anchor this state of wanton curiosity by saying the words *'wanton curiosity'* with tonalities that match the state. Say them like you truly mean them. Say them with energy and passion.

4. Take an inventory of your body. Notice how you are now breathing, how you are holding your body. Adjust and tune your physiology to make the state of curiosity even more positive and powerful. Embody positive attitudes of wonder, interest and fascination. Feel the wonder and interest building. Hold them in your heart brain, breathe them down into your gut brain.

5. Repeat the process at least two more times, with other memories of times when you were incredibly curious and wantonly and insatiably fascinated.

6. Now generalize the process into your future. Imagine your future time-line, a line that extends from now into your future. Spread the state of wanton curiosity and passionate fascination through and along your future. Think of some specific times in the future when you will want to passionately embody your attitude of curiosity and say your trigger words *'wanton curiosity'* and feel those wondrous feelings of fascination coursing through your mind, your multiple brains, your body and your life.

7. Get curious about what you can do with this Success Strategy. Ask yourself *"How can I really use this?"* Enjoy the state of wanton curiosity and use it to make an amazing difference in your life.

Pattern-Interrupt — Moving Away From Ignorance

The following process combines the ideas and skills described throughout this chapter. Use this to interrupt any negative or limiting ignorance patterns. If you find yourself at any time engaged in a negative thought or attitude, use and practice the following technique.

Avoiding the Enemies to HAPPINESS

Interrupt any old unsupportive patterns of ignorance in your life by:

- If you hear or notice yourself ignoring or distorting facts, or if you feel evidence of cognitive dissonance signals, say forcefully to yourself 'STOP! Ignorance is DANGEROUS!'

- Use this as an opportunity to learn and grow by doing the following steps.

- Understand the present — do not hide from reality but see the present clearly, explore and analyze your motives and patterns, get curious about your world.

- Do not be burdened by the past — examine and challenge any irrational beliefs, generalizations and assumptions from the past that are limiting you.

- Accept the uncertainty of the future — face the future with confidence, plan for future success (values, dreams and outcomes) and live flexibly to enjoy the possibilities of change that the future can bring. Not everything about the future is within your control, so relax and practice flexibility and becoming a change master.

"There is only one good, knowledge, and one evil, ignorance."

Socrates

Ignorance is NOT bliss

Strengths & Values In Action

Use the following table to determine which strengths, qualities and values to focus on and amplify in your life to support the processes and skills of happiness. Also notice if you have any elements of the absence, opposite or exaggeration of these strengths and remove them from your behaviors and your life.

Enemies to happiness	VIA Strength
Ignorance	Perspective/Wisdom
	Curiosity
Denial of Reality	Love of Learning
	Open-mindedness
Deceit	Integrity
	Bravery

Notes from the Field — Reading Happiness

Suzanne Beecher is an amazingly diverse and dynamic person. She's studied to be an auto-mechanic, owned a restaurant, founded and published a business magazine, "*In Business*" in Madison, Wisconsin, and setup a non-profit program, "*Meals For Madison*" to feed the homeless.

Currently, Suzanne runs a number of internet based readers clubs, with over 330,000 subscribers world-wide. She started her

181

book clubs for the busiest people in the world, the employees of her software development company who were stay-at-home moms. The only books they had time to read were children's books, so she started including parts of books in the daily email she sent them each morning.

Soon they were thanking her for getting them back into reading. They were leaving their TV's off at night and discussing books with their husbands. One employee admitted she would sneak over to her computer late at night to see if Suzanne had sent the next installment early.

Now she has over 3,000 libraries, businesses, county governments, public schools and websites offering her book clubs to their members. She works with over eighty book publishers. People as far away as Moscow and China are reading with her.

You can sign up for this fantastic free service at www.DearReader.com and every day she'll email you part of a chapter from a book. The emails take about 5 minutes to read. After you've received two or three chapters from a book, you'll start a new book. Before you know it, you'll be in the reading groove. It's a great way to enhance your knowledge and learning. It's a great way to hear about new books and expand your horizons.

I spoke to Suzanne about her thoughts on happiness and learning. Happiness hasn't always come easy for Suzanne. Like most people, it's something she's had to work at. Suzanne believes happiness is a journey. It's something you have to do for yourself. You can't ignore it and expect it to happen.

Happiness and joy are something you literally have to put on your daily *to do* list. Like brushing your teeth and other myriad tasks you do for yourself on a daily basis, happiness needs to be on your everyday agenda.

According to Suzanne, everyone is in charge of their own happiness.

> *"Happiness really is a choice."*

The key to this is learning to know yourself and becoming comfortable with yourself. You have to look at yourself honestly. Learn what's really on your mind, what's really motivating you. It's like a good friendship. If you want to be friends with someone, it takes effort and time. It's the same with getting to know yourself. Examine each day. Learn from your experience.

Good and bad things happen in life; if you've gotten to know yourself then it's easier. You want to learn to love and appreciate the hurdles in your life. They teach you about yourself and about your life.

Don't compare yourself to other people. There'll always be someone better off, someone luckier, someone with more. If you catch yourself playing that game, STOP! Instead, focus on choosing to be happy in your own life, with your own experience.

Suzanne also believes strongly in helping others, in being approachable, in doing things for others. Life, learning and love are gifts to be shared.

Reading and writing are also gifts you can give to both yourself and others. Reading takes you to a place where you can learn and think about new ideas. It induces a peaceful, meditative state — a flow state. It produces good feelings. So read as often as you can. Choose to be happy by doing things that support your happiness.

Suzanne's Keys to Happiness

- Being approachable
- Doing things for others
- Understanding yourself
- Choosing to be happy

Suzanne's Enemies to Happiness

- Choosing to be unhappy
- Focusing on negativity, pessimism or complaining
- Comparing yourself to other people
- Self-ignorance

So make every day a choice for happiness. Ignorance is NOT bliss. Head on over to Suzanne's readers website and join with thousands of people in reading happiness.

☞ **Remember This**

✓ Ignorance and denial of reality are dangerous to your happiness. The facts are your friends. Install in yourself an intense need and desire for knowledge, learning and truth.

- ✓ Your unconscious mind does not like mismatching cognitions and will do anything to remove Cognitive Dissonance. Track for and beware of your cognitive dissonance signals and overcome this evolved animal process by acknowledging them and using logic rather than emotions to face the facts and the reality of your situation.

- ✓ Surface and question the old assumptions that underlay the patterns and behaviors in your life.

- ✓ Self honesty and honesty with others are vital for a happy and meaningful life. Refuse to lie, cheat or practice dishonesty.

- ✓ The Law of Requisite Knowing says that knowledge plus choice provides control and power in your life.

- ✓ All knowing is doing, so ensure you put what you learn into practice.

- ✓ Neuro-genesis — your brain will grow new cells and connections if you stimulate it with challenge and learning. Boredom and stress kill brain cells. Support yourself by continuously taking on new skills, hobbies and interests.

- ✓ Focus on generative change and wanton curiosity. Encourage yourself in gaining wisdom and meaning in your life. Move away from ignorance and stupidity in yourself or others. Celebrate a love of learning and embody open-mindedness and fascination for exploring the world. Fill your mind and life with the joy of knowing.

ⓘ Extra Info

Refer to www.enemiestohappiness.com for

- more information about the material covered in this chapter
- additional reading and references for this chapter

Avoiding the Enemies to HAPPINESS

Chapter 4

Warning: Slow Suicide will kill YOU

You will learn to

- ✓ Focus on maintaining your health and vitality
- ✓ Stop destructive habits and patterns
- ✓ Foster positive addictions and behaviors
- ✓ Use Psycho-Neuro-Immunology to amplify your well-being

Warning: Slow Suicide will kill YOU

Your health is one of the most important assets you have. Most people slowly kill themselves through negative addictions and destructive habits. Lack of exercise, too much stress, poor diet and negative thoughts and emotions wreak slow havoc on your immune system and your body. Slow suicide WILL kill you!

In this chapter you'll learn about the importance of health to happiness and well-being. You'll also learn about how to remove and avoid the enemy of destructive patterns and addictions that are the cause of slow suicide.

Enemies to your Happiness

- ✘ Unhealthy behaviors

- ✘ Destructive habits

- ✘ Laziness and lack of exercise

- ✘ Negative addictions

- ✘ Negative emotions of depression and pessimism

The Importance of Health

Over 62% of deaths in the western world are caused by heart disease, cancer and stroke. These are known as *'lifestyle'* diseases. They are largely caused by people's choices and behavior.

Statistics from the year 2010 for example, show that in the USA alone, heart disease caused close to two thirds of a million deaths per year, with cancer a close second killing over half a million people in that one year. In 2013, it was estimated that over 80 million people in the US suffered from cardiovascular disease. Over 80 MILLION! And these numbers are growing! By 2020, heart disease will be the leading cause of death throughout the world.

Analyzed from a different perspective, a study reported in the Journal of the American Medical Association found that back in the year 2000, over half a million people died in the US due to the effects of tobacco and alcohol, while another third of a million individuals died from poor diet and physical inactivity. Track forward to 2012 and approximately half of all the adults in the USA have a chronic health condition, and the data for other western nations is nearly as dire.

What we see from this is that the leading causes of death and disability in the developed world are SLOW suicide. People are literally killing themselves through bad habits and negative behaviors. Poor diet, lack of exercise and common addictions destroy your health, your well-being and ultimately your happiness. This is serious and you need to put in place skills and habits to combat this insidious enemy to your happiness.

Without health, most things become meaningless. I have a friend who for the last 30 years smoked and indulged in drinking alcohol on a daily basis. Along with lack of exercise and poor diet, he thought his habits and addictions were cool. He repeatedly told me how much he enjoyed his indulgences and that they didn't present a problem.

A year ago he suffered his first major heart attack. As he lay in the hospital, his lungs filled with fluid, drowning in his own blood, unable to breath and with his heart failing, he heard the doctor saying he would probably not survive. Through a mixture of luck and modern medical skill and technology, he did manage to survive. Now his life and happiness are severely impacted by his years of slow self-destruction. He cannot work full-time. He is often tired and lethargic. There's much he cannot do. Slow suicide nearly killed him, and has certainly impacted his well-being and ongoing quality of life.

There is nothing more certain, you absolutely must look after your health if you want to enjoy happiness and joy in life. As you'll see in the coming sections, and as you know from the NLP Cybernetic Loop model, your mind and body are connected. To feel good and think well, you need a body and physiology that supports this. You need a healthy body to have a healthy mind. Your health and wellness are vital. So let's examine what it takes to be healthy — actually, I'm sure you realize that *'health'* is a nominalization, it's a disguised verb, it's really about the process of *'health-ing'* — so let's explore the skills of healthing to support greater happiness and meaning in your life.

> *"As I see it, every day you do one of two things: build health or produce disease in yourself."*
>
> Adelle Davis

Healthing

Health is a result of a myriad of factors and processes. Our bodies are incredibly complex. To maintain optimal health you need to do behaviors of healthing — behaviors that support your brain and body; that support your immune system, digestive system and cardiovascular system amongst many others.

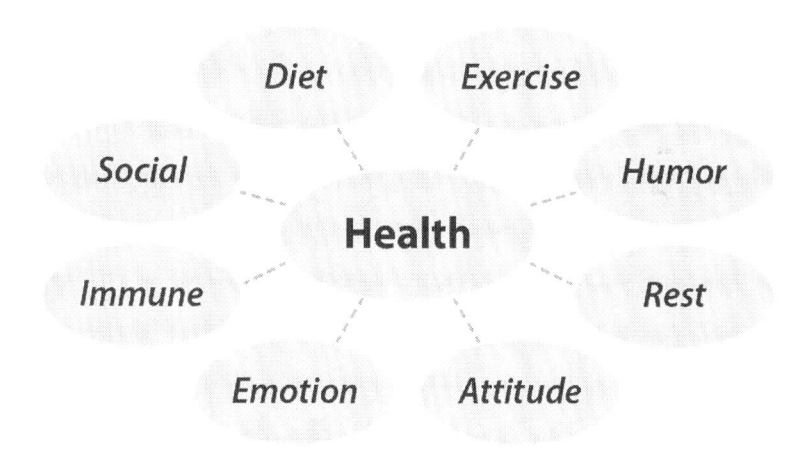

```
         Diet      Exercise
Social                      Humor
            Health
Immune                      Rest
         Emotion   Attitude
```

Healthing involves a balance between all of these aspects and processes. For a start it's vital you eat a healthy balanced diet free from toxins. As much as possible, eat organic whole foods and avoid saturated fats and sugars.

You'll also want to exercise regularly, giving your body a good cardio-vascular and aerobic work out. Additionally, do some weight-bearing exercise to build muscle and bone strength. Begin slowly and always remember to stretch. Maintaining flexibility is just as important as fitness and strength. The key is to aim for being fit for life.

See a doctor and get regular checkups before undertaking any major changes to your exercise and fitness regime. Be careful of over-stressing your body. The goal is steady gentle change and improvement.

How you cope with stress is important. You need time to relax and unwind. Meditation is a great way to build emotional and mental resilience. So take a class and learn how to relax your mind and body. Quality sleep and rest are also incredibly important for health and vitality. Tiredness and stress are definitely enemies to happiness.

Fun and humor build emotional capital. They generate flow states and as you'll see in the following sections, they fill your body with healthy neuro-chemicals and stimulate your immune system.

Your immune function is a key component to your health. So support it through vitamins, clean water, a positive mental attitude and the various success strategies that this chapter will teach you.

People with strong social networks and deep loving friendships have better health than those who are lonely and have no support. So spend time with your friends and loved ones. Join social groups and make time for helping and supporting others. The act of giving is a win-win way to make both yourself and others feel good, and positive emotions increase health. So give the gift of happiness to others by sharing your good fortune, your knowledge and your time with people you care about.

Your feelings and emotions impact your health and happiness. Beware of and refuse to indulge in negative emotions like anger, revenge, hatred, spite, fear, greed or jealousy. Instead, focus on, practice and amplify states of joy, delight, gratitude and peace. These positive emotions fill your mind and body with health.

Your long term happiness depends on having a healthy mind, a healthy heart and a healthy body. This is another way of describing the Cybernetic Loop. Happiness comes from doing healthing in how you think, how you emote and how you act. Thoughts, feelings and behavior all working in a spiral to avoid the enemies to happiness.

Remember, you don't *have* health, you *do* healthing. It's a process, not a thing. So make a commitment to yourself to start learning more about health and wellness, start doing healthy behaviors and stop old patterns of unhealthy habits and behaviors. Your happiness most certainly depends on it.

> *"The greatest wealth is health."*
>
> Virgil

Biology of Happiness

Happiness is largely a physical state of the brain and body. When you're happy your brain produces neuro-chemicals that result in positive feelings of joy and delight. When you have a smile on your face, you release more serotonin, dopamine and endorphins — happiness hormones — than you do when not smiling.

Dr. Bruce Rabin, a director at the University of Pittsburgh Medical Center found in his research that when you're stressed or anxious, there's an activation of stress areas in the brain. This alters the concentration of various hormones in the blood which then impact your health. Over time, this impairs your ability to think clearly, increases cholesterol in the heart, and changes how your immune system functions.

As you know, your mind and body are intimately linked. Neuro-hormones are an important part of that process. Neuro-hormones like serotonin for example are linked with happiness and depression. Low levels of serotonin can lead to depression and sadness. Activities like exercise and smiling have been demonstrated to increase serotonin. Correspondingly, they measurably increase levels of happiness. In one study, 20 minutes of aerobic exercise was shown to have the same effects on curing depression as anti-depressant medication.

And serotonin and dopamine are not just produced in the head brain. More than 80% of the body's serotonin is produced in the gut brain, as well as approximately 50% of the body's dopamine. So what you eat and the state of your gut health strongly influences your moods. In addition, other neuro-hormones such as oxytocin that are involved in feeling good are produced in the heart brain too.

What this tells you is that a large part of happiness is biological. Your health and happiness are entwined. Poor health and low levels of fitness are enemies to happiness. Exercise, diet, relaxation and behavior all impact on both your health and your happiness.

PNI — Psycho-Neuro-Immunology

Your thoughts and emotions can even specifically influence your immune system and vice versa. Research in the field of PsychoNeuroImmunology (PNI) over the last 40 years has shown how tightly coupled the mind and body are. There is now a huge body of published evidence documenting at the neurological and biochemical level, how states of mind such as anxiety, depression and anger affect the functioning of immune cells — T-cells, B-cells, Natural Killer cells, and macrophages.

The communication and control pathways exist both ways. For example, the nervous system directly synapses down onto immune cells in the lymph nodes. In return, there are receptors in the brain for communication chemicals such as hormones, peptides and cytokines that are released by immune cells. The brain and immune systems are an intertwined complex system. What affects one, affects the other.

To illustrate this, let's look at the results of a classic experiment on the immune effects of emotion. Researchers asked method actors to simulate either positive emotions like happiness or negative emotions like anger and depression. Immune system function was measured before, during and after short period of emotional expression. The results showed that positive emotions caused a measurable and significant increase in immune cell function and activity. More importantly however, negative emotions had both a larger and longer lasting negative effect on the immune system. Negative emotions cause a down-regulation in immune cell and system functioning that can last for many hours after the emotional event.

Other experiments have shown that the effect can also work in reverse. When the immune system is under attack from a pathogen like a flu virus or cold, it releases messenger molecules that cause a down-regulation in mood. It's your body's way of getting you to conserve energy, to remove yourself from others, to allow your immune system to get on with the job of protecting you. Whenever you are physically run-down or have a decreased immune function you are likely to find yourself feeling slightly depressed and unhappy.

There are numerous documented cases of people using a mixture of humor, visualization and meditation to overcome debilitating diseases such as cancer. Norman Cousins is a famous example. In the mid-1960's he was diagnosed with ankylosing spondylitis, a degenerative disease that causes the breakdown of the fibrous tissue binding the body's cells together. Almost completely paralyzed and given only a few months to live, Cousins checked himself out of hospital and moved into a hotel room where he began taking extremely high doses of laughter and humor. He literally laughed his way back to health, and eventually returned to full-time work and a normal life. Cousins detailed his amazing journey in his book *"Anatomy of an Illness."*

Here are some more fascinating results from recent research on the interaction between health and happiness:

- ➢ People who score high on psychological tests assessing happiness, produce about 50% more antibodies than the average person in response to flu vaccines

- ➢ Individuals that test high on scales for happiness, optimism and contentment have reduced risk of cardiovascular disease, hypertension and infections — positive emotions are healthy and protective for the heart

- ➢ Researchers found that subjects who practiced acts of happiness and gratitude had raised energy levels, improved physical health and experienced less fatigue and pain

- ➢ One important study found that optimistic individuals reduced their risk of death by 50% over the nine year period of the study.

The main message and insight from these examples and the field of PNI is that your health, thoughts and emotions are interdependent and entwined. The more happiness and joy you feel, the better your immune system will respond. The greater your health, the more positive feelings of joy and happiness you'll be able to experience.

There really is wisdom in the saying *"a healthy mind in a healthy body"*.

⚒ Thinking Tools — The Body-Mind Health Spiral

Your mind and body are connected in a loop — thoughts, feelings, beliefs and health influence each other!

🔎 Awareness Questions — Focusing on Health and Wellness

Ask Yourself:

- ➤ What are my beliefs about my health? Do I believe I can easily achieve health and wellness?

- ➤ What are the behaviors that I do that negatively impact my health? How can I stop them?

- ➤ What behaviors can I do that will improve my health and wellness? How can I support myself for greater healthing?

☑ Success Strategy — PNI: Smile, Breathe and Tap

As discussed above, the field of PNI has shown that our thoughts, feelings and immune function are all linked and contribute together to our happiness spiral.

Research has shown that smiling leads to measurable changes in nervous system and immune system function. One experiment found that simply getting people to simulate a smile by holding a pen in their mouth for 15 minutes a day lead to measurable increases in the hormones of happiness in the blood stream along with corresponding self-reported feelings of happiness.

Other research has shown that stimulating the thymus gland leads to an increase in feelings of pleasure and happiness. The thymus gland is a small gland in the center of your chest, behind the sternum. The thymus gland is responsible for a number of immune processes, including the maturation of T-cells. These immune cells are used to fight off infections and cancer and protect your body.

Breathing can also make quick and powerful changes in feelings. Deep diaphragmatic breathing, fully filling your lungs, will flood your blood with oxygen and help clear out waste gases. Breathing deeply, evenly (same in-breath duration as out-breath duration) and fully makes you feel fantastic and combined with stimulation of the thymus gland and holding a great BIG smile at the same time leads to positive changes in your mind and body.

The following technique combines all of these, with the NLP strategy of anchoring to produce a powerful method of inducing happy positive feelings.

1. Smile a really big happy smile. Really exaggerate it. Think of something or someone that makes you feel really happy.

2. At same time, breathe fully and deeply. Exhale fully. Empty all of your lungs, from the top to the bottom. Now breathe in with your diaphragm. Fill the bottom of your lungs, then the middle and finally the top of your lungs. Really get that air into and out of your lungs. Do it in a way that makes you feel good and alive. Breathe evenly with a duration of approximately 6 seconds in, 6 seconds out. And remember to keep smiling.

3. While breathing and smiling, tap your chest along the center line, from the base of your sternum, going upwards. Make sure you tap upwards. The tapping is designed to both stimulate your thymus gland, which sits behind your ribs, as well as acts as an anchor to the positive feelings associated with the experience. Repeat the tapping from the middle to the top of your chest. Every time you do this exercise, the effect will get stronger and better.

4. You can enhance the process, by imagining your immune cells spreading out from your chest, throughout your body, with every breath they are healing and cleaning and caring for your health and your body. Imagine, happy immune cells moving from the tip of your toes to the top of your head. This uses the power of visualization to send a message to your unconscious mind to do great, exquisite immuning. Make the image bright and colorful and strong.

5. Continue this exercise of smiling, breathing and tapping for at

least 20 to 30 seconds. You'll notice how good it makes you feel. Amplify these feeling and really savor and appreciate them in both your heart and deep in your gut. (Remember that the gut brain is responsible for around 80% of immune function.)

Do this exercise at least once each day, first thing in the morning. It is even more powerful if done 3 to 4 times during the day for a quick PNI top up!

> "Sow a thought and you reap an act; Sow an act and you reap a habit; sow a habit and you reap a character; Sow a character and you reap a destiny."
>
> Samuel Smiles

Habits and Patterns

The neural network of the brain is a patterning system. It takes inputs and forms patterns from them. It evolved to enable your organism to repeat learned behaviors. Every time you perform a thought or action, it increases the probability that you will perform that thought or action again. That's how the brain works (and it's just as true for head, heart and gut brains).

So you need to be very, very careful what thoughts, feelings and behaviors you do in your life. Because, without being aware, you can end up with habits and patterns that don't serve you.

Remember the staircase of learning model. Through repeated

actions, you build unconscious competence. You build an unconscious part that knows how to accurately repeat and perform the learned behavior. This might be a physical behavior, an emotional behavior or a cognitive behavior. You can end up with habits and patterns of physiology, feeling or thought.

Behaviors that were learned in one context or time of your life, may no longer be appropriate or useful in your current context or time of life. What at first appeared fun, exciting and interesting, can swiftly become something that is slowly killing you. Or put more accurately, you may be killing yourself by repeating old patterns of thinking and behaving.

That's what addiction is all about. Nobody starts off doing something they truly believe will kill them or damage them. They start off doing the behavior, believing they are getting some sort of benefit. The smoker gets stimulation, peer group acceptance, or maybe even a sense of being *cool*. The drinker gets relaxation, camaraderie and an altered state. But once the pattern of addiction has formed, once the brain and body have changed the number of chemical receptors to match the elevated levels in the bloodstream, the person is hooked. They are slowly killing themselves — performing slow suicide — and it's not so easy to stop.

Negative habits, patterns and addictions are absolute enemies to happiness. They take away from your life. They take away not just quantity, but more importantly they destroy the quality of your life.

Drugs, smoking, drinking excessively, overeating are all enemies to happiness. They might provide some small secondary gains, some side benefits, but they do so at a primary cost to your health and the quality of your mind/body.

If you want to maximize your chances for happiness and joy, you'll want to look after your health. It's that simple. If you are addicted to anything that is slowly damaging your mind or body then STOP it. Seek professional help. Do whatever it takes to stop addicting. Your long-term happiness and peace of mind depends on it.

I can't say it any simpler or more bluntly than that. The facts are our friends as we learned in Chapter 3. Negative patterns and addictions will damage your mind and body. Think carefully about what your dreams, goals and outcomes are for your life and if you decide you want to live a life of happiness and meaning, then work assiduously to stop and remove any negative addictions from your life.

Instead, clearly specify the positive outcomes you want in their place. Focus on what you want and not what you don't want in your life. Remember the power of negation. Focus on positive outcomes. Set health and wellness, and the happiness they support and engender in your life, as high values and priorities. Develop and stick to a good balanced diet. Start exercising. Look after your body. Look after your multiple brains (head, heart and gut). Keep toxic chemicals and drugs away from your precious cybernetic loop. Make an agreement with yourself to only support positive healthful actions and behaviors in your life.

The great news is, that every time you refuse to do something negative and instead replace it with a positive behavior or thought, it increases the probability of you doing that positive action again. You can create positive habits and patterns in the same way as any other habit or pattern. By choosing to sow only positive thoughts and actions in your life you will reap a destiny of happiness and meaning.

🛠 Thinking Tools — Repetition

Repetition leads to repetition. The repetition of a thought or action increases the probability of repetition.

🛠 Thinking Tools — The Wedge

Beware the thin edge of the wedge!

My father taught me many years ago the wisdom of the saying *'Beware the thin edge of the wedge!'* This thinking tool particularly applies to the issue of habits and patterns and especially the forming of addictions. The way a wedge works is that one end is very pointy and thin. If you are splitting wood for example, a wedge can be easily slipped into the thinnest of cracks. Then slowly but surely the wedge can be driven deeper and eventually, the thick end of the wedge will cause even the strongest of logs to split and fall apart. If you tried to drive the thick end in first of course, you would have great difficulty and it would not work.

It's the same with behavior and thoughts. The thin edge of the wedge is when you allow yourself or someone else to do or think something that is negative or harmful. *"It's only once"* you say. But it's the thin edge of the wedge. Before long, if you aren't careful, one drink becomes two, two drinks become four, and then you're at the thick end of the wedge, addicted to alcohol and destroying your life and happiness. So look for and beware the thin edge of the wedge in your life. It's vitally important for your long-term happiness.

> ### ✒ Pattern-Interrupt — Zooming Disease off to the Sun
>
> The following process combines the NLP and PNI ideas and skills described throughout this and earlier chapters. Use this technique to interrupt any negative or limiting health or disease patterns.
>
> I have successfully used this technique to get rid of headaches, stomach-aches, sore throats and stop the onset of colds and flu's at the early stage. The technique works by both sending a metaphorical message to your unconscious mind and through the use of submodalities. Give it a go and you'll be surprised and delighted at how such a simple process can have such amazing results.
>
> **Interrupt any pain or disease pattern by:**
>
> ✒ Make an image outside your body of the presenting complaint. For example, if you want to get rid of a sore throat or a headache then make an image just in front of you, it might be a black blob or pointy object — something that matches the pain or feeling you want to get rid of.
>
> ✒ Imagine the Sun off in the distance and then quickly zoom the image off to the Sun, way in the distance. See the object getting smaller and smaller until it disappears, burnt up in the Sun.

Warning: Slow Suicide will kill YOU

- Note that this technique works most powerfully when you place the image of the Sun in the direction of the *'past'*. To find this, point to the direction in which you feel the past is for you. You can find this by thinking of something that happened in the past and noticing where in your visual field that image comes from or is located i.e. the submodality of position/location of the image.

- Also make a zooming sound as you zoom off the object and make a sizzling, burning up sound as it disappears into the Sun. The sound really makes a positive effect to this technique, recruiting across sensory systems in the neural networks, so make sure you do it out loud.

- Repeat this process, three to five times, getting faster and faster. Don't worry if you can only do the imagery in an *'as if'* way, it will still work powerfully.

- Now just let go and get on with your day. You'll find that in a couple of minutes, or over the course of the day your problem or symptoms will decrease and disappear. Your powerful unconscious mind and immune system will now make you better.

In using this technique, be respectful of the underlying message that the symptom is attempting to communicate to you. If symptoms return or persist, then seek competent medical attention. This technique should not be used to mask symptoms of a serious disorder. It is however, very useful for stopping the beginnings of a viral infection such as a cold, or for assisting your

205

immune system and unconscious mind in helping you get over a cold or flu. By using it repeatedly throughout the course of an illness, and providing you are doing everything sensible to help yourself get better, this technique will help speed up your recovery.

You can also use it to get rid of negative thoughts, fears and pessimistic ideas. Just make an image of the thing you want to get rid of from your mind and life and zoom it off to the Sun. You can make the process even more powerful by zooming back in a replacement positive thought or feeling. Have fun with this technique and use it to replace negative healthing patterns with new behaviors of vitality and joy.

⟳ Deeper Understandings — Messages from the Unconscious

Pain and disease are signals. Disease is often a symptom of '*dis-ease*' in your system. It's your unconscious mind's way of communicating via your cybernetic loop about stress and dysfunction in your mind-body.

The unconscious mind is a patterning system. It learns to repeat and replicate patterns and behaviors. The conscious mind allows choice. It provides the means of volitional control so that you can select and change the patterns.

Disease can often be a signal or message from your unconscious mind to your conscious mind. Alerting you to processes that need attention and change. You ignore these messages at your peril.

Pain and disease are natures signal that something is wrong. Listen to the symptoms and ask them what needs changing. Maybe there's something you need to attend to in your life. Or are you deleting or blocking something from your awareness? What do you need to change? Underlying all stress is a reason or cause. It may be physical, emotional or mental.

In NLP, there is a technique called the Six-Step Reframe that is used to communicate with the unconscious part responsible for any particular process or outcome in your life. In this technique you literally talk to the part and ask what its positive intention is. You speak to it and ask what positive thing it is trying to achieve for you.

There is a presupposition in NLP that every behavior has a positive intention. By exploring and finding the underlying positive intention of the part producing the dis-ease, you can then negotiate within yourself to find a better and more generative way of achieving and satisfying the positive purpose or need that exists in your life.

Six-Step Reframe

The steps of the Six-Step Reframe technique are:

1. Identify the behavior, response or signal you want to change

2. Communicate with the part responsible for the behavior

   Literally talk to the part. Respectfully ask *"Will the part responsible for X communicate with me consciously now?"* Then carefully notice the signals or response you get. It may be words, sounds, images, feelings or physical signals.

3. **Determine the positive intention of the behavior**

   Thank the part for communicating with you and ask it *"Please tell me what your positive intention is. What are you trying to do for me?"* Notice the response you get. What intuitions or messages does the unconscious part respond with?

4. **Ask the part to work with the whole of your unconscious mind, including your creative parts and your heart and gut brains, to generate new and more generative ways of accomplishing the outcome**

   Ask the part to communicate internally with the other parts of your mind to find new behaviors and ways of achieving the positive purpose. If the part has been signaling to you that the way you are living is doing you harm, then your unconscious mind can generate new patterns of behavior that are more healing and healthful. Your conscious mind can respect this process and support the new behaviors.

5. **Ask the part if it will agree to use the new behaviors and choices rather than the old behavior to achieve its outcome**

   If you don't get a yes signal from the part, then return to step 4 until all parts of you have worked together to find behaviors and choices that work and that the part in question will support.

6. **Do an ecology check of all parts of your mind**

   Ask *"Does any other part object to my new choices?"* If you get a response that indicates there is an issue of ecology or potential negative consequences then return to step 3 and ask what positive intentions this new part is attempting to communicate about and work with it and the original part to generate behaviors and choices that work for the whole of you.

This technique can work quite powerfully. You'll be surprised at just how clearly parts can communicate. Remember, we are really a *'multi-mind'*. You need to trust your unconscious mind and work with it respectfully. It is trying to do the best it can with the knowledge and skills it has at this point in your life. You may need to support yourself with new skills and patterns, and reading and studying this book is a great step in that direction.

Do this technique in a quiet place. Relax, calm your mind and then gently talk to the parts of your mind that have a message for you. Be very positive and explicit in your communicating. With a bit of trust, you'll be surprised at how amazing this communication process can be. It's about getting in touch with your intuitions. It's about hearing the messages from your gut brain, your heart brain, your non-dominant hemisphere and other distributed intelligences around your brain and body. It's about aligning all the parts of you to support wellness in your life. By looking deeply within and explicitly communicating with the parts of your multi-mind, you can gain important insights and messages from your unconscious mind.

⚒ Thinking Tools — Positive Intent

Every behavior has a positive intention!

> *"We are what we repeatedly do. Excellence, then, is not an act, but a habit."*
>
> Aristotle

Positive versus Negative Addictions

Given that our brains are patterning systems, it's inevitable that we will form habits and patterns in our lives. So instead of fighting this, you can make good use of the process. Choose to fill your life with positive addictions that will add value to your life in an ongoing way.

Here are some positive addictions to add more joy and vitality to your life

- ➢ Moderate levels of aerobic exercise
- ➢ Meditation
- ➢ Eating healthy nutritious food
- ➢ Laughter, humor and purposively smiling
- ➢ Diaphragmatic balanced breathing

- Pursuing a fulfilling hobby
- Optimism
- Love and caring
- Compassion and understanding
- Creativity
- Courage and the desire to take action

According to psychiatrist William Glasser, in his book Positive Addiction, it can take anywhere from six months to a year of regular activity (jogging, meditating, etc.), to develop a positive, strength-giving addiction. The activity should be done with no demands, no striving for excellence and no self-criticism. Developing a positive addiction can also lead to more than just feeling better and greater happiness; it can provide you with greater self-confidence, more energy, increased creativity, and increased levels of frustration tolerance.

You get to choose. Every action you take comes from a decision, either conscious or unconscious. So decide right now to create patterns that work for you. Get clear about your goals and outcomes in life. Take action and work flexibly to achieve them. With time and practice you can change your life in amazing ways. It's all about knowledge, belief, skills and attitudes. It's your life, so make it a great one!

> *"There is nothing permanent or compulsive in your system, except what you believe to be so."*
>
> Moshe Feldenkrais

The Brain in the Body — the Heart Brain and Gut Brain

As you know from Chapter 0, and the new field of *m*BIT, there is neural tissue — brain cells and synapses — in parts of the body other than the head! Research in the last few years has uncovered this amazing fact. You have both a heart brain and a gut brain. You actually have quite large chunks of brain tissue in both your heart and your stomach.

These two additional brains are not isolated from the head brain. They have direct nervous and chemical connections with the head brain. So really, your brain is a system distributed throughout your body. This amazing discovery puts science behind the ancient wisdom that both the heart and gut are sources of insight and understanding. Such insight is indicated by sayings like *"gut instinct"*, *"gut intuition"*, *"listen to your gut"*, *"trust your heart"*, *"what does your heart tell you"*, *"the wisdom of the heart"*.

For health and happiness, it's important to look after and listen to these valuable parts of your mind/body system. For example, when you suppress feelings you can often end up experiencing symptoms such as constipation, diarrhea and flatulence. These are your gut brain speaking to you, giving you valuable feedback. Learn to tune into and communicate with your distributed brain system. Your happiness depends on it.

HeartMath

Research in the field of neuro-cardiology has established that the heart is both a sensory organ and a sophisticated information encoding and processing center. As indicated above, the heart has an extensive intrinsic nervous system sufficiently sophisticated to qualify as a *'heart brain'*. This heart brain contains around 40,000 to 120,000 neurons and has pathways directly to the head brain.

Work by Doc Childre and his colleagues at the Institute of Heartmath has shown that your heart and heart brain play a crucial role in controlling and regulating your emotions, your thoughts and your overall health and wellness. Doc developed a system called HeartMath® that can be used to decode and utilize the intelligence of your heart. What does the name HeartMath mean? Put simply, the HeartMath System provides everyday equations (the math) to live a heart-directed life, and a heart-directed life is an important step in avoiding many of the enemies to happiness.

The HeartMath system is based on concepts of Heart Rate Variability (HRV), coherence and heart-brain synchronization. It has been found that HRV is an important indicator of both physiological resilience and behavioral flexibility. It shows your capacity to adapt to stress.

The research has shown that on a second by second basis your heart rate varies considerably. When you are stressed or experiencing negative emotions, your HRV is what is called incoherent. It shows a chaotic and irregular level of change. This is an unhealthy state. When you are relaxed and your thoughts and feelings are in harmony, your HRV shows a regular, smooth level of change. This is called high coherence.

It has also been shown that through control of your breathing and a focus on positive emotions, centered around the heart region, you can increase your coherence level. This positive heart brain state communicates to the head brain, and brings your mind and body into synchronization. The key findings are that as you learn to sustain heart-focused positive feeling, your brain is brought into entrainment with your heart. This is both healthy for your heart and creates positive mind/body states of resilience.

The following Success Strategy will guide you to control your heart brain and generate high HRV coherence. You can also visit the HeartMath website located at www.hearthmath.org to obtain more information about books and bio-feedback tools to support your health and learning.

> *"Every thought and feeling, no matter how big or small, impacts our inner energy reserves."*
>
> Doc Childre, The HeartMath Solution

☑ Success Strategy — Heart-based Balanced Breathing

This strategy is a scientifically validated technique that can be used to balance your mind and body and tap into the wisdom of the heart. It works by increasing the coherence of your heart beat and bringing the Sympathetic and Parasympathetic arms of the Autonomic Nervous System into balance.

1. Shift your attention to the area of your heart and breathe slowly and deeply, with an in-breath of approximately 6 seconds in, and out-breath of the same duration. Visualize

your breath entering and leaving through the centre of your chest and heart area. You might see it as light spreading into your heart region.

2. Activate and sustain a genuine feeling of love, appreciation or care for someone or something in your life. Focus on positive feelings of love. Feel them in your heart. Remember a time or think about something that makes you feel happy and peaceful. With every breath, fill your heart with positivity, love, kindness, joy and compassion.

3. Sustain this process for at least 5 minutes or more to bring your heart beat into coherence and to relieve the mental and physical processes of stress. If you find your mind wandering, gently bring it back to thoughts and feelings of love and appreciation. Keep your attention on your heart and on slow deep breathing.

This technique is a really useful tool for quieting the mind and creating a solid connection with the heart and heart brain. It is also a great way to relieve stress and to bring your Autonomic Nervous System into balance. Your heart has wisdom, so trust its intuition and learn to connect deeply with it.

Strategies for Health

There are many strategies and behaviors that support health. We'll consider some of the most important of these. However, in one short chapter we won't be able to cover everything, so you'll want to take responsibility for your own healthing patterns and learning.

Becoming passionately interested in health, wellness and healing will help you steer clear of the enemy to happiness of slow suicide, and help you to continue growing and learning.

Replacing Negative Emotions with Positive Emoting

We've covered it before, and it's worth repeating and summarizing. Negative emotions can be destructive to health and happiness. They cause down-regulation of immune function and are implicated in heart disease, stress disorders and other causes of ill-health. Negative emotions can physically damage your heart. They also lead to negative cognitive spirals and pre-dispose you to pessimistic attitudes and mind-sets.

So throw away any old patterns of negative emoting. Track for *'drama patterns'*, *'sickness patterns'* and other negative patterns in your life. Stay away from people who wallow in these self-limiting ways of living or who celebrate disease by constantly talking about it and getting attention from it.

Instead, surround yourself with positivity and with friends who are happy and celebrate the joy of living. Your multiple brains are patterning systems, so flood them with inputs of positive emotions, thoughts and actions and you'll generate ongoing happiness in your mind and life.

Meditation

Research has recently shown that people who regularly practice meditation can make physical changes to the structure of their brains in as little as three to six months. In one experiment researchers used MRI brain scans to compare meditators with non-meditators and found increased thickness of the cortex in areas involved in attention and sensory processing, such as the prefrontal cortex and the right anterior insula.

Meditation leads to:

- A calm, peaceful, relaxed mind
- An increase in cognitive performance
- An increase in the ability to cope with stress
- A decrease in the amount of sleep necessary and better, more refreshing sleep
- Improved health and well-being.

These benefits and more have been well-proven through thousands of scientific studies. Meditation really does work and can help you overcome many of the enemies to happiness. I personally meditate every day and have done so for most of my life. Try it for yourself. Grab a book or go on a course. There are dozens of different meditation techniques. I've tried most of them and they all have positive benefits. You owe it to yourself and your own happiness to add meditation to your life.

It should be noted however that meditation may be contraindicated for people suffering from severe mental illness, particular those with a risk of psychosis. It should be supervised closely if used by anyone with mild to moderate mental illness.

Exercise

Yes, let me say it again — Regular exercise is important for health and happiness. Regular, moderate exercise is one of the best things you can do for your health and well-being. New research shows that exercise beneficially affects your genes, helps reverse the aging process at a cellular level, gives you more energy, makes you smarter, and can even help you grow new brain cells.

Once you are strong and fit you'll find that exercise feels fantastic and leaves you feeling energetic and alive. Research has proven that aerobic exercise can relieve symptoms of mild depression and can be as effective as psychotherapy. It also improves memory and increases cognitive function.

For your long-term health and happiness you need to enjoy a balanced mix of different exercise forms. Flexibility and stretching exercises are important to maintain suppleness. Weight-bearing exercise is necessary to maintain bone and muscle density. Aerobic exercise will keep your cardio-vascular system toned and healthy.

I really can't highlight how important exercise is. It's vital for your health and happiness. I know I'm being repetitive here but it's important you get the message. The cybernetic loop shows how crucial it is to have a healthy body and physiology in order to enjoy healthy feelings, thoughts and internal processing. So make a commitment to regular exercising.

If you haven't exercised for a long while, make sure you get back into it in a gentle, controlled, safe, sensible way. Go get a fitness assessment. If you need to, get a check-up first with your Doctor. Perhaps invest in a personal trainer or go to a gym and get an appropriate exercise regime designed for you and your current fitness and health level.

And make your exercising fun! To make exercise a life-long positive habit, you'll want to ensure you enjoy doing it. That way you'll look forward to it. Vary the exercise. Take up sports and physical hobbies. I love running, so I make sure I run along the beach where the scenery is stunningly beautiful. I finish my run with an invigorating swim. I love it! I so look forward to my daily exercise. I also love kayaking, so I do that once or twice a week to exercise my upper-body. Bike riding is also a lot of fun. I have a friend who has a personal trainer that takes her through boxing lessons and exercises. She has awesome fun doing her workouts. There's so many enjoyable ways to get fit and healthy. Use your creativity and imagination to find ways to make exercise entertaining.

Eating for Happiness

What, how and how much you eat are important. You know this.
I could write a whole book on the subject. However, I'll keep it short. To start with, eat to maintain an appropriate weight for your height and frame, being exceptionally over-weight or under-weight is not conducive to a happy, healthy life. Moderation and balance are the keys to eating for happiness. Don't use food and eating as a tool to overcome unhappiness or depression. Instead, eat for nutrition and health.

Eat fresh fruits, salads and vegetables. Have meat in moderation. Minimize the amount of fat and sugar in your diet. It's all obvious stuff. There are plenty of books on the subject of healthy eating. Though some of them can be confusing and contradictory. What's best for one person may not be ok for someone else. Different body types and metabolisms need different nutrient amounts. Add to this the effect of food allergies and you have a recipe for disaster. We all have our own specific requirements and these can change from situation to situation. For example, when under stress you need different amounts of nutrients to support your immune and energy requirements.

Learn to listen to your body. Your gut has a brain, as does your heart. Trust your intuitions. Augment them with appropriate advice. It's worthwhile seeing a trained Nutritionist or a skilled Natural

Therapist to get your health and diet reviewed and on track to optimal wellness.

The key to eating for happiness is self-awareness. Track for what you are putting into your precious body. Learn about food. It's really important for supporting your health and happiness.

Fun and Humor

Fun and humor stimulate the immune system. Even smiling can produce measurable changes in immune function and increase the levels of the neuro-hormones of happiness.

Research shows that laughter is a great healer. So add a healthy dose of fun, humor and laughter to every week. Schedule in trips to see humorous movies or plays. Go to Comedy Nights. Read joke books and share the jokes with your family and friends. There are even Laughter Clubs across nearly every country, in which you can practice laughing and clowning around. It's serious laughter. No seriously, it's laughter for a purpose of health and happiness. These clubs actually work, and they have scientific evidence to prove it. So why not join one?

And most importantly, don't take yourself or life too seriously. Take yourself and your challenges in life light-heartedly. Your happiness and health will be better for it. As the Broaden and Build Hypothesis of Positive Psychology has shown, positive emotions assist creativity and cognitive function. So taking your problems light-heartedly can often make them easier to cope with and easier to solve.

As much as possible, fill your life with an attitude of fun and humor. It's a great friend to happiness.

Massage

Massage has a long history. As far back as 400 BC, the great healer Hippocrates employed massage and physical manipulation in treating his patients.

Massage has many benefits, both physical and psychological. The health effects of massage extend throughout the body producing a positive healing environment. It enhances mental wellbeing by promoting relaxation, allowing time to let the stresses of the day fade away. It also reduces muscular tension, increases blood circulation and lymphatic flow and improves muscular elasticity and flexibility. Massage can help with pain management and may decrease the amount of pain relieving drugs required in certain ailments.

Overall, massage can be a great healing tool for gaining and maintaining optimal health and wellness. I highly recommend it. So pamper and look after yourself, book in for a regular massage. You'll thank yourself for the wonderful feelings of pleasure, flow and health that it evokes.

Pos Ψ Resilience

Resilience is the positive ability to adapt and cope well with adversity, threats, family and relationship problems, serious health problems, or other stressful events. It is typically characterized by patterns of positive adaptation to negative situations.

Research in Positive Psychology has shown there are a number of strategies that can help build resilience, toughness and psychological strength. Not surprisingly, since the mind and body are intrinsically linked, it has been shown that building physical toughness and resilience increases psychological and emotional resilience and strength. Even taking a cold shower, or swimming in cold water has been shown to increase mental toughness. So make sure you exercise and increase your level of physical strength and fitness.

Close relationships with family and friends can help create and support resilience. Loving, nurturing relationships help buffer against stress and can assist in overcoming adversity.

Optimism and hope also increase resilience. Seeing problems as opportunities for self discovery and personal development can really make a difference. Focusing on your strengths and values has been shown to strengthen resilience. So continue to set and achieve realistic outcomes and goals that utilize your key strengths.

One of the most powerful tools however for building resilience is the use of engagement and flow. Regularly involve yourself in activities that generate flow. This will build psychological and emotional capital and help you overcome life's challenges. Remember, the more you practice these resilience strategies, the better you'll be able to avoid the enemies to happiness in your life.

Health as Balance

Happiness and wellness require a balanced attitude and approach to health. Stressing and obsessing about health can negatively affect your life and your happiness as much as ignoring your health. It's the same with exercise, too much exercise can be as harmful as too little. You want to be *'fit for life'* not fit for beating other people or beating yourself. Think about and get clear about your health and fitness outcomes. There's no point in pushing yourself to the point where you damage your health or body.

Choose a long-term focus for your health and happiness. Don't go for short-term gratification. That will lead to problems. The occasional indulgence is probably alright. But over-indulgence will lead to eventual misery. It's all about moderation and balance. Allow yourself the occasional treat, but keep a track to ensure it doesn't become the norm. Research has shown that alcohol appears to be beneficial in moderation (less than around 4 or 5 standard drinks per week), that dark chocolate contains a powerful anti-oxidant and that tomato sauce (ketchup) is filled with beneficial chemicals (lycopenes). So enjoy these and other treats. But don't overuse them.

Your immune system also operates in a fine balance. The immune system operates as a Darwinian population system. What this means is that your body produces a population of immune cells, and that depending on the pathogens you come in contact with, the successful cells get replicated and the unused cells decrease and die off. That's why it can be quite healthy to come into contact with a certain amount of pathogens and allow your immune system to fight them off. Being ill can be healthy. It can strengthen and build up your immune system.

Recent research has also shown that living in too clean an environment can lead to immune system problems. It is now believed that the western world's focus on cleanliness has lead to the growing problem of asthma and allergies. A certain amount of dirt is good for educating the immune system. Health really is all about balance and the more you understand how your body and immune system works, the more choice and control you'll have over that aspect of your life.

Exquisite Immuning

The immune system is a very complex part of the body. It contains a myriad of different cells and components and is distributed throughout your body. The immune system is intimately connected to your nervous system and brain (and especially your gut brain) and can in some ways be thought of as an extended part of the brain/mind system. As the field of PNI has shown, your thoughts and feelings directly affect your immune function.

As discussed in the previous section, there is an optimal state of immuning that your immune system needs to do to keep you healthy. Too little immuning, and you can't fight off disease or overcome naturally occurring cancer cells. Your immune system has both a memory and the ability to track for self/not-self. The immune cells are constantly checking your body for invaders and rogue cells that don't belong. Too much immuning — an over-stimulated immune function — can lead to auto-immune problems and diseases. Too little immuning can make you susceptible to illness and pathogens.

I'd like to share a personal story with you about the optimal process of immuning. Many years ago, when first learning about NLP and Behavioral Modeling, I got interested in issues of health and wellness. So I decided to study the immune system and model the process of immuning and healing. I came across the idea of *Super-Immuning* and applied the principles of NLP to amplifying these processes and states of immuning. I used self-hypnosis and NLP techniques to communicate with my unconscious mind and install the process of Super-Immuning in myself.

A couple of weeks later, I began to notice a strange red rash on my lower left leg. The skin was raised and inflamed. I thought that I'd somehow gotten a skin mite infection from cleaning out the vacuum cleaner bag that I had accidentally dropped on my uncovered leg one morning. So I used various creams and lotions to try and remove that rash. Nothing seemed to shift or heal it. I sought medical help and also consulted with a Naturopath. Nothing seemed to help. I lived with that rash for many, many months and it was slowly spreading and getting worse.

One day, relaxing in a warm shower, I decided to use the NLP Six-Step Reframing technique to talk to my unconscious mind and find out what the symptom of the rash was trying to tell me. I knew that my unconscious mind knew the cause of the problem, even if my conscious mind didn't have a clue. So I put myself into a self-hypnotic, meditative state and gently, respectfully spoke to my unconscious, asking specifically for insight into the cause. The words *'Super-Immuning'* popped into my mind, along with the saying *'the more — the more pattern'*. This is a pattern in NLP that indicates a positive feedback loop. The more you do something, the more it causes the same process, leading to a spiral or run-away pattern. For example, the process of fearing fear leads a person into more and more fearing.

In that flash of insight my unconscious mind communicated to me, I realized I had installed in myself many months ago a runaway pattern of over-stimulating my immune function. The word *'Super'* indicates a comparative deletion. That is, something is only ever *'super'* in comparison to something else. When you call or describe something as super, without indicating what it is super compared to, you are doing what in NLP is called a comparative deletion. I had installed in myself a comparative deletion pattern of *'Super-Immuning'*. I had installed in my unconscious mind a pattern of doing more and more immuning. I had, in effect, created an over-stimulated auto-immune disorder. The rash on my leg was my own immune system attacking my skin and causing an eczema type rash.

There and then, I asked my unconscious mind for a better metaphor for the process I was trying to model. The answer came back immediately — *'Exquisite Immuning'*. What I wanted was not to do super immuning, but instead to be able to do an exquisite level of immuning appropriate to whatever was happening in my body at any point in time. Exquisite implies fitness for purpose. Exquisite implies outcome.

So I immediately removed the *'Super-Immuning'* process and changed and re-installed the unconscious immuning process as *'Exquisite-Immuning'* and within 24 hours the rash went completely away. Overnight, that angry, red, painful and itchy rash that completely covered my lower left leg disappeared and my skin returned to normal. I'd had that rash for months and months — or to put it more accurately from a neurolinguistic perspective — I'd been *'doing'* that rash for many, many months and finally I'd stopped. The rash went away. My leg healed.

The moral of the story is manifold. Firstly, NLP processes are powerful and should be used intelligently, carefully and ecologically. Secondly, always listen to your symptoms and check with your unconscious mind for the underlying message it is attempting to communicate to you. Thirdly, there is such a thing as too little and too much immuning. Balance is required. What's appropriate at one time is not appropriate at another.

For example, if you have come into contact with a pathogen such as a cold virus and have become infected, then you need to amp up your immuning to fight off the virus. Once you are well, you don't want to have too active an immune function or you'll end up developing auto-immune problems. You want and can do a balanced amount of immuning. Lastly, use the idea and metaphor of *'Exquisite-Immuning'* to track for and encourage your unconscious mind to do appropriate immuning. The unconscious mind can be influenced by belief, metaphor and symbolism, by visualization and affirmation. So be careful what you ask for, and use its power wisely.

⚲ Awareness Questions — Health and Wellness Beliefs

Ask Yourself, *"Do I support the following Beliefs?"*:

➢ My body is naturally healthy and knows what to do

➢ I have reserves of strength and resilience

➢ I can easily overcome disease

➢ Symptoms are signals that I take notice of

➢ I can learn from every illness

➢ I deserve health and wellness

➢ I only focus on health and wellbeing

➢ I am a healthy person and I look after my mind and body

➢ Examine your Health and Wellness Beliefs and install and amplify ones that are useful and supportive. Choose to do believing that gives you more joy, happiness and success.

Vital Health or Slow Suicide

The choice really is yours — Vital Health'ing or Slow Suicide. And really there's no choice. To support happiness in your life and in the lives of those you love, you have to **choose Healthing**. So, take an inventory of your patterns and behaviors. Go get a health checkup. Then use the skills and techniques from this book to make appropriate changes and build new supportive patterns in your life.

As you know, knowledge is power and learning is a key to happiness, so get some books on health and read them. Go on short-courses. Learn how to cook healthy and nutritious meals. Take a course on meditation or stress-management. Start an exercise program, and choose fun, interesting exercise activities that improve your cardio-vascular and muscular fitness. Take care of your body. Do the cybernetic loop of healthing — a healthy mind in a healthy body.

Choose life rather than slow suicide. **Choose happiness** rather than disease and misery. **Celebrate health, joy and vitality**.

> *"Health and intellect are the two blessings of life."*
>
> Menander

Strengths & Values In Action

Use the following table to determine which strengths, qualities and values to focus on and amplify in your life to support the processes and skills of happiness. Also notice if you have any elements of the absence, opposite or exaggeration of these strengths and remove them from your behaviors and your life.

Enemies to happiness	VIA Strength
Poor Health	Self-regulation
Negative Habits & Addictions	Vitality
	Forgiveness
Pessimism	Optimism & Hope
	Kindness
	Bravery

Notes from the Field — Sailing into Health and Happiness

Sailing across the crystal waters of Lake Victoria, the sun glinting off the gentle waves, the wind cooling a brilliant blue sky, I asked my sailing companion Dr. Michael (Mick) Webb, his thoughts on health and happiness. Dr. Webb is a lecturer in Chiropractic at a top Australian University where he teaches about aspects of health science and wellness.

Mick believes that lack of control and lack of order in life are the fundamental causes of unhappiness. This lack of control manifests as patterns of greed, stress, addiction and an overall lack of balance. The external pressures of unreasonable obligations of family, society and work also play a large part in this.

From a health perspective, Mick recommends a strategy of respite, recovery and balance. Using sailing as a metaphor he says you will benefit by *"seeking places of refuge and safety to shelter from the storms of life." "Where refuge is not available, reduce sail and ride out the storm, letting it take you where it will. It will eventually pass beyond."* This strategy involves adapting to conditions through a mix of knowledge, skill and awareness; along with the flexibility to change and adjust your course in life. You need to prepare for change and be willing to make the most of your current conditions through a positive attitude and mindset.

According to Dr. Mick, you can sail into health and happiness through a focus on enjoyment, laughter and humor. Don't take yourself or life too seriously. Remember to maintain a healthy balance of exercise, diet and rest. Finally and most importantly, fill your life with love for yourself, those close to you and our beautiful planet because above all, she matters most.

☞ Remember This

- ✓ Slow suicide will kill you! You absolutely need to take care of your health through eating well, appropriate nutrition, exercise, meditation and humor.

- ✓ You also need to do your best to remove stress, toxins and poisons from your life.

- ✓ Negative patterns, addictions and habits are insidious enemies to happiness and will definitely take away both the quality and quantity of your life. Replace them with positive patterns and positive addictions that add joy to your life.

- ✓ Pattern-interrupt disease and pain patterns by zooming them off to the Sun.

- ✓ Use Heart-breathing to balance your mind and body.

- ✓ Do exquisite immuning and use Psycho-Neuro-Immunology to support your immune system and your mind/body in healing and health.

- ✓ Build resilience into your life by enjoying flow activities and positive emotional experiences.

- ✓ Focus on healthing and vitality in your life in a balanced meaningful way.

ⓘ Extra Info

Refer to www.enemiestohappiness.com for

- more information about the material covered in this chapter
- additional reading and references for this chapter

Avoiding the Enemies to HAPPINESS

Chapter 5

It's all THEIR Fault

You will learn to

- ✓ Create a fantastic self-image
- ✓ Accept responsibility for your emotions
- ✓ Control and change your thoughts and expectations
- ✓ Protect yourself from the negative behavior of others
- ✓ Do appropriate and skilful trusting and relating with others
- ✓ Practice forgiveness of yourself and others

It's all THEIR Fault

Other human beings can be a source of happiness or an enemy to happiness. People and your response to them can enhance your peace of mind or destroy it. Nobody lives in total isolation. We're all dependent on our relationships with others. So the quality of your relationships is vital for your happiness.

In this chapter you will learn how to do high quality relating and how to turn negative emotions such as blame and retribution into forgiveness and acceptance.

Enemies to your Happiness

- ✖ Negative emotions of blame and retribution
- ✖ Exaggerated expectations of others
- ✖ Not protecting yourself from the harmful behaviors of others
- ✖ Misplaced and inappropriate trust
- ✖ Loneliness and social isolation
- ✖ Poor quality relating

Blaming others

Blame and retribution are absolute enemies to happiness. For peace of mind, you need to remove them from your life. How do you do this? Well for a start, you need to take responsibility for your side of every interaction and every relationship.

The emotional responses you make to other people's behavior are *'yours'*. Nobody *'makes'* you feel anything. You consciously or unconsciously choose to respond to what's happening. So no matter what's happening or has happened in your relationships — your relatings — with others, it's never *'all'* their fault. No matter what someone has done to you, at the very least, the emoting you are choosing to do in response is up to you. It's your emoting. So take responsibility for that and get clear on your outcomes in life.

Do you actually want to feel bad or fill your mind and body with emotions of fault, blame and retribution? Really? Remember that the field of Psycho-Neuro-Immunology has shown that negative emotions have a physical and lasting effect on your health. They down-regulate your immune function and make you more susceptible to disease. Negative emoting is damaging and the antithesis to happiness and joy. Long term negative emoting can even destroy brain cells and nervous system function in all your brains (head, heart and gut).

So what are your outcomes for yourself? Do you want to fill your life with joy, happiness and positivity? Yes! If so, then make an agreement with yourself right now. Make a pact with all of your multi-mind, all of the parts of yourself, that you won't support fault-finding, blame or retributive thoughts and responses. Take responsibility for your side of every relating that you do and we'll explore in this chapter the skills and understandings of how specifically to do that.

> *"All blame is a waste of time. No matter how much fault you find with another, and regardless of how much you blame them, it will not change you."*
>
> Wayne Dyer

Personal Responsibility

There are numerous '*reasons*' why you might do the process of blaming. In order to pattern-interrupt and change this process it's helpful to determine what the underlying outcomes are for your blaming. Once you know what you're trying to achieve you can then choose and practice better and more positive ways of achieving your outcome.

To start with, you need to be aware there are quite a large number of sociopaths in society and such people are likely to use, abuse and hurt you if you let them. We'll look in detail at how to identify these people and strategies to handle them. There's no point blaming such people for their behaviors. Instead, learn to track for and stay clear of them. Learn how to handle them and don't give them control over your life. Take responsibility for how you respond to sociopathic behavior. After all, that's the only side of the relationship you have any real control over. We'll explore this further later in this chapter.

Maybe you use blaming as a means of getting attention from others. There are plenty of people who celebrate failure in their lives by whining and complaining. They use this to divest themselves of responsibility and to get sympathy from others.

Look deeply at your behaviors and your motives. Who are you blaming and why? What are you really trying to get by blaming? Is it attention? Is it to take away from your own personal responsibility? Or is it perhaps to try and hide your own *'blame'*? Are you trying to find fault in others so that you don't have to look at your own life and behaviors and admit that you aren't living the way you'd really like to?

You know, you don't prove your innocence by arguing the guilt of others. This is a powerful thinking tool and one I highly recommend you memorize and use. It's useful as a rejoinder when someone tries to verbally abuse you by blaming you. It's useful to motivate yourself to stop verbally abusing others by blaming them.

🛠 Thinking Tools — No Blaming

> ### Arguing someone else's guilt does NOT prove your innocence.

Then there are the times you might do blaming of inanimate objects. You're doing something and you make a *'mistake'* and rather than taking responsibility you blame the tool. You know, it was the car's *'fault'* that it ran into the pole. I can just see it now. You're driving down the road and the car takes over and forces you off the road. Sure. Pretty humorous really.

Remember, in the NLP Success Strategy, there's no failure only feedback. You get clear about your outcome, take congruent action, learn from feedback and flexibly change and adjust until you have achieved your outcome. If what you are doing isn't working, then take that as great and useful feedback and change what you're doing. There's no fault in this model. There's no blame. It's all about outcome, feedback and flexibility. This is what success in life is all about. So track for and throw away blaming. An attitude of blaming is an enemy to happiness.

Anytime you hear or notice yourself doing blaming or faulting of yourself or others, STOP! Gently remind yourself about the usefulness of feedback. Refocus yourself on your outcomes. Then get on with happiness-ing and success-ing in your life. And congratulate yourself and feel good about your growing skills in supporting positive, useful emoting and in learning from feedback.

Thinking Tools — Feedback Excellence

There's no failure or blame,
only excellent Feedback.

Self-fulfilling Prophecies

You also need to be aware of creating self-fulfilling prophecies in your life. If you wander around sending out messages of fault and blame, you are likely to unconsciously generate the very behaviors in others that will ratify your map of the world. You'll literally create and amplify scenarios that are self-fulfilling. It becomes a blame spiral and will fill your mind, your awareness and your life with negative emotions and unhappiness.

It's all THEIR Fault

Let me share a teaching story with you. It's a joke my father often tells, and whilst it's not particularly funny, it does provide great learnings and I use it often to directionalize my thinking and ensure I do my own life very differently to this.

One fine day, a guy from the city is driving in the country. Somehow, he's gotten himself a little bit lost and finds himself travelling down a narrow country lane. An oncoming farm-truck forces him to veer off the side of the narrow dirt track. Unfortunately, the edge of the road is wet and soft and his car becomes quickly bogged. He tries and tries to drive the car out, but his efforts only make it worse. *"Damn,"* he thinks, *"I'll need to go get some help."* Across the fields he spies a farm house in the distance. *"I'll go ask the farmer for a lend of a shovel and some help to get out of the bog"* he thinks, and sets off across the paddock.

As he's walking, he begins a conversation with himself. *"I'll go up to the door and knock. The farmer will open the door. I'll say hello and he'll immediately realize from my dress and voice that I'm from the city. He'll probably say, 'What the hell do you want? You city slickers, driving down our lanes, going too fast, always expecting us country folk to get you out of trouble, ruining our roads!'. I'll try to explain. He'll just get angrier and angrier."* By this time, the driver has arrived at the farm door. Continuing his internal monologue, he knocks at the door. In no time at all, the farmer has answered the knock and opened the door. *"Yes, can I help you?"* he answers kindly. The driver stares straight into his eyes and says *"I don't want your bloody shovel or help anyway!"* turns around and storms off back to his car.

Blame-Frame

The driver's own internal expectations, stereotypes and beliefs just created a self-fulfilling prophecy. He's set himself up for a blame-frame. There's nothing the kindly farmer could do that would have changed his mind, he didn't even give him a chance.

How often in life do you do something similar? What blame-frame expectations have you setup in your life and your relationships. Have you setup your Reticular Activating System (RAS) to look for and notice fault? Is there someone that you just *'expect'* to do the *'wrong'* thing? Do you even give that person a chance anymore?

Think about this deeply and later in this chapter we'll explore an NLP pattern-interrupt technique called *'Characterological Adjectives'* that will help you break such self-fulfilling prophecy blame-frame patterns. Fault finding and blame-frames are an enemy to happiness, so work assiduously to remove them from your life.

> *"When you blame others, you give up your power to change."*
>
> Robert Anthony

Using your Emotions

Never give away your choice and control to others. Choice and control are the friends of happiness. If you let situations and people put you into a blame-frame then you are allowing them control over your emotions. Take control and responsibility for your emotions — for your emoting. Remember, you don't *'have'* emotions, instead in reality you *'do'* emoting.

One of the best ways to handle your emoting and feelings, is to think of them as helpful action signals. Use them. There's something to learn from them. An unconscious part of your multi-mind is trying to get your attention. If you find yourself feeling or doing blame or retribution, it's a valuable signal. It's focusing you, telling you that you're off track from happiness. Yes, acknowledge that you've got strong emotions, that unconsciously your doing strong emoting and learn from it. Get the gold nuggets, the life lessons from it.

Accept responsibility for your emotions. Think about your outcomes. Get clear about how you want to do yourself in life. Figure out what's underlying the emotions, what positive purpose they're serving. Then choose more useful ways to achieve this purpose. You'll be surprised at how easy it can be to let go of blaming and to use the tools we'll explore in this chapter to relate in better ways with yourself and others.

Remember also that you can use the tools from previous chapters to change your emotions and state. Exercise and meditation will immediately change your state and make you feel more relaxed and forgiving. You can also work with your Cybernetic Loop to make changes through your breathing. Doing a heartbreath or Balanced Breathing will calm your Autonomic Nervous System and help bring in the wisdom of the heart to stop the emotions of blaming firmly in their tracks. There are lots and lots of ways to take control and responsibility of your responses and your happiness. It's your mind and body, use it wisely to make a positive difference in your world.

> *"We have two choices: continue to blame the world for our stress or take responsibility for own reactions and deliberately change our emotional climate."*
>
> Doc Childre & Howard Martin, HeartMath Solution

🛠 Thinking Tools — Positive Purpose

All behavior and emotion has a positive intent.

🔍 Awareness Questions — Learning from Emotions

Ask Yourself:

➢ In what situations and what relationships do I find fault and do blaming?

➢ What is the purpose of this blaming? What am I really trying to achieve? What are my underlying positive outcomes?

➢ How can I best learn from the feedback of my emotions? What better ways can I achieve my outcomes?

Unreasonable Expectations

One of the drivers of blame and fault is having exaggerated and unreasonable expectations of either yourself or others. We've covered this in earlier chapters and it's worth repeating. There are a number of irrational beliefs and expectations that can undermine your happiness and lead to un-sane behavior in your life.

Beliefs that people and situations have to be perfect are

irrational. No one is perfect. We are all fallible. Perfection is an ideal that doesn't exist in the world. Instead of perfection, you might instead aim for excellence. Excellence implies fitness for purpose and outcome. Something can be imperfect and yet still be excellent for its intended outcome. A leaf can have a small imperfection and yet still be an excellent leaf, providing respiration and photosynthesis for the plant. Helping it to live. A car can have a scratch in its paintwork, making it imperfect, yet still provide excellent transport and enjoyment.

If you hear yourself using the words '*Should*' or '*Must*', it's a signal you are operating from a belief that is absolute. You are saying there's only one right way, and you know what that is. However, the real world doesn't operate that way. Almost nothing is that black and white. It's not about '*shoulds*', about absolute rules; it's really about preferences and values. Replace the word '*should*' with the word '*prefer*'. You'll find that it reduces the tendency to fault find and blame.

For example, if you think your friends '*should*' never hurt you or say things that cause you pain, then you're likely to go through life experiencing disappointment and suffering. You are operating from a rule that says people '*should*' be '*perfect*' friends and '*must*' never say hurtful things.

If instead, you think in terms of preferences, you'll say you prefer your friends not express anything hurtful. You'll also acknowledge that people are far from perfect in the real world, and so occasionally your good friends might not live up to your preferences. Oh well, that's ok, there are probably times when you don't live up to their preferences and values either. You can still be excellent friends; you can still do excellent friend'ing. Do you get what I'm saying here?

You can also use the feedback from situations where you or others don't achieve your preferences, to change and adjust your behaviors and communications. It's a very different mindset and leads to much more positive relating. You hold high expectations of yourself and others, but not absolute rules that are exaggerated or unreasonable. You become much more accepting of yourself and others, rather than blameful and retributive. You setup positive self-fulfilling prophecies and you become more relaxed and flexible. Now doesn't that sound good and reasonable? It certainly is part of the recipe for happiness.

⚡ Pattern-Interrupt — Stopping Unreasonable Beliefs

The following process combines the ideas and skills from NLP and Cognitive Psychology. Use this to interrupt language and thought patterns of irrational beliefs and unreasonable expectations.

Interrupt unsupportive language patterns by:

- If you hear or notice yourself using the modal operators of 'SHOULD' or 'MUST' — then stop, and replace them with the word '*prefer*'.

- If you hear or notice yourself using universal quantifiers like 'ALWAYS' in conjunction with modal operators, or with other negative beliefs — then stop, and replace them with '*mostly*'.

- If you hear or notice words or concepts of blame in your language — then stop, and replace them with words of forgiveness.

For example, REBT maintains that one of the key irrational beliefs people create misery in their lives with is:

- ✗ *"Other people MUST ALWAYS treat me how I want to be treated, or else they are no good rotten people, who deserve to suffer"*

By applying the pattern-interrupt process above, you would change this to:

- ✓ *"I prefer people to mostly treat me how I want to be treated, and if they don't I forgive them"*

This is a more balanced belief system, aligned with happiness and encourages responsibility for your emotional responses.

Deeper Understandings — Communicating Excellence

Relationships are inherently reliant upon and involve successful communication. Success in communicating in turn requires an explicit focus on outcomes. In NLP we say *"the meaning of the communication is the response that you get"*. It's not about what you think you said. It's about what the receiver thinks you've said.

With the NLP model, you don't apply *'fault'* or *'blame'* if someone doesn't understand what you've said. As a communicator, you have an outcome — something you want to achieve through the process of communicating. There is a meaning or message you want the other person to experience. Remember, the NLP Success Strategy says that for success you need to clearly know your outcome, take action, use your sensory acuity to gain feedback about whether your action is moving you closer to your outcome and then flexibly change and adjust until you have achieved your outcome.

To do successful communicating, you therefore need to use your sensory acuity to watch the other person's responses to your communication. You need to work out whether they're understanding the meaning of your communication. The meaning they are making is the response they give to your communication. It's your responsibility as a successful communicator to keep changing and adjusting till they '*get it*'.

If you understand this, then you'll never again lay blame or fault on yourself or the other person if they don't hear you properly or don't understand what you are saying. There's no blame or failure. Just keep flexibly changing and adjusting your communicating till you get the response you are after; till you achieve your communication outcomes. That's communicating excellence and that's what success and relationship happiness is based on.

✗ Thinking Tools — Communication

The meaning of your communication = the response you get!

Negative Behaviors of Others

As we've discussed, the negative behaviors of others can be a source of misery and an enemy to your happiness. Not everyone is balanced and reasonable. There are people that enjoy or gain benefit from harming others. You need to be aware of these people and stay away from them.

It is definitely important to form quality loving relationships and supporting social networks. However, you need to choose very carefully who you trust and get close to. Loving and trusting the wrong people can destroy your peace of mind and can even destroy your life.

Sociopaths and Psychopaths

Sociopaths and Psychopaths exist in surprisingly large numbers. They are found in all segments of society, all walks of life. You need to realize there are millions of them. It's estimated around one percent of the population are Psychopaths and around four percent have Antisocial Personality Disorder, leaving them with no conscience, no sense of guilt or shame.

These are people you encounter daily in your neighborhood, school, workplace, and even your family. Think about it, with up to five percent of people having sociopathic or antisocial tendencies, this means that in a room of 100 people, on average, five of them are the sort of people who will happily use and abuse you. Chances are some of the people you work with, live with or know suffer from these disorders. This makes them dangerous to your happiness. You need to learn the signs and warning signals and stay away from them.

At a conference on psychopathy I met the world leader in this field, Dr Bob Hare, and learned the shocking details about psychopathic and sociopathic behavior. Psychopaths and Sociopaths have no conscience. They are predators. They are often egocentric, callous, impulsive, excessively boastful, antagonistic and manipulative. They have a high need for risk taking, an inability to resist temptation and a grandiose sense of self-worth. Add to this the pathological lying, lack of remorse or guilt and total lack of empathy and you have the recipe for a very dangerous person. These people do not accept responsibility for their actions and are unable to form close bonds with people. Instead they connive and manipulate those around them.

Unfortunately, they are often seen as interesting and attractive. With their high need for stimulation and risk taking, their impulsivity and their shallow, changeable emotionality, they fool and lull people into their web of manipulation and lies. They cold-bloodedly take what they want and do as they please without the slightest sense of guilt or regret. They leave a trail of emotional and behavioral destruction in the lives of the people they use and abuse.

Because they love chaos and hate rules, they're often comfortable and successful in our fast-moving, modern corporations. One study found that a high percentage of CEO's and Managers are sociopathic. In the work place you'll find them as bullies and puppet-masters. They thrive in the world of high-finance, the stock-market and as promoters. They are devious conmen and women.

So how do you protect yourself from these enemies to your happiness? Start by being aware of their attributes and behaviors. Look for the signs and behaviors listed above. Track for callousness, lack of empathy, shallow emotionality, failure to accept responsibility and glib, superficial charm. If you find these traits, then steer clear of the person and certainly be very, very wary of trusting them.

Dr Bob Hare, in his excellent book *'Without Conscience'*, provides the following tips on how to protect yourself from Psychopaths and Sociopaths

- Know what you are dealing with by learning as much as possible about them

- Don't be influenced by their *'props'* and skills such as the winning smile, the captivating body language and the riveting eye contact they often use

- Don't wear blinkers — enter new relationships with your eyes wide open, looking for evidence of manipulation

- Keep your guard up in high-risk situations such as bars, clubs, resorts and airports

- Know yourself — Psychopaths and Sociopaths are skilled at detecting and exploiting your weak spots

- Be careful about power struggles — these people have a strong need for psychological and physical control over others, so don't engage them in a battle that you'll most likely lose

- Don't expect dramatic changes — the evidence is that most Psychopaths and Sociopaths can't and won't change. They may promise to change and put on an act or show of changing. But they rarely make permanent changes.

The key to handling these people is to stay away from them. Cut your losses in any relationship with them and move away. If you have one for a boss, consider moving to a new job. Certainly don't put your trust in a Psychopath or Sociopath. As we said before, other people can be a source of happiness or a source of misery. Choose very carefully who you get close to. Your peace of mind depends on it.

Psychic Vampires and Negative Influences

Some people are like *'psychic or emotional vampires'*. They thrive on the negative emotions of others. You know the sort of people I mean. They love and celebrate negativity. They're totally pessimistic and love raining on people's parade. Doom and gloom are their favorite topics. You come away from time with these people feeling washed out and drained.

Track for these damaging people and behaviors and stay away from them. There's a thinking tool I learned from an amazing man called Morris Goodman that is pertinent and useful to this topic. Morris is known as the *'Miracle Man'*. He was a leading life insurance salesmen and enjoyed incredible fortune and success, until the day he crashed his plane. With his neck broken in two places and his spinal cord crushed, Morris was no longer able to perform the most basic of bodily functions. Doctors considered his injuries too severe for him to survive. However, through a mix of courage, determination and positive thinking, Morris rebuilt his body and reclaimed his life.

According to Morris, we need to be aware of 'SNIOP' — that we are all **S**usceptible to the **N**egative **I**nfluences of **O**ther **P**eople. We are socially evolved beings and our brains are optimized for tracking and fitting in with other people. People influence us. We need to be incredibly aware of this and ensure we surround ourselves with positive people and positive influences.

So make sure you filter your life and relationships for support and positivity. Stay away from sociopaths and psychic vampires.

Focus on relating with people who hold positive values and high standards. Make all your relatings positive, nurturing and supportive. Your happiness depends on it.

⚒ Thinking Tools — SNIOP

We are all Susceptible to the Negative Influences of Other People.

Trust vs Trusting

If you are dealing with a sociopath, a psychic vampire or someone who has either a genetic or learned predisposition towards negativity, then you can hardly trust them in the normal sense of the word. What you can do however is to do *'trusting'* that they will act in ways that are self-serving and harmful to themselves and others.

This idea of trusting versus trust is a useful and important one. Trust needs to be earned. Don't just blindly give people trust. Instead, do the process of trusting in an ongoing way. When you first meet people, do a level of trusting that allows for the beginning of the relationship. Be a little wary and look for signs of manipulation and deceit. Ensure that people earn your trust. But equally, don't set up negative self-fulfilling prophecies.

As a wise man once said to me *"people are as honest as you allow them to be"*. What this means is that people generally have good intentions but are naturally fallible. So support people to be honest and to earn your trusting by not putting temptation in their way.

Don't tell people more than they need to know about your most personal secrets. Equally, don't create negative self-fulfilling prophecies by holding low expectations that people live down to. Instead, hold high expectations of others and at the same time support them to be honest by removing temptations.

For example, don't leave your car unlocked in public places and don't leave money or your wallet or purse lying around. Behaviors like that just encourage dishonest behavior. Similarly, in business relationships, ensure that all agreements are put in writing and signed by all parties. It's not about having a legal agreement that you'll use to litigate with. It's about helping people to stay honest and trustworthy by having an objective written agreement that overcomes people's fallible memories.

Trust that most but not all people will generally be thoughtful and kind. But also trust that most people will make mistakes and be a little selfish and self-serving at times. Focus on compassion, understanding and forgiveness and you'll find your relatings will benefit, as will your feelings of happiness. Friendship and trust are two way streets. So do trusting, and stay flexible about your outcomes. That way you'll avoid the enemies of misplaced trust and mistrust.

Thinking Tools — Trust & Honesty

People are as honest as you allow them to be!

Ingroup/Outgroup Bias

Research in Social Psychology has shown we all have instinctual unconscious tendencies to favor those in our ingroups and be biased against those not in our ingroups. These groupings can be quite arbitrary and situation dependent. They can vary from race, gender, family, political, religious, geographical and societal groupings, down to team membership, club grouping or even such arbitrary groupings as perceived status, hair coloring, musical preference and sporting interests.

For example, experiments have shown that group members will award one another higher payoffs even when the '*group*' they share seems as random and arbitrary as having the same birthday, the same final digit in their Social Security Number, or even from membership assigned to the same flip of a coin.

It's important and useful to be aware of this inbuilt prejudice since it can lead to negative perceptions and blame of others simply because they aren't members of your current perceived groupings. Even when you believe you aren't biased, your unconscious filtering still generates subtle ingroup/outgroup preferences. So make sure you do your best to track for ingroup/outgroup bias and that you aren't perceiving others through such negative instinctual filters.

Instead, look for and think about ways in which you and other people share some sort of common group membership. For a start, we are all members of humanity. We are all members of the group of people who are currently alive and living on this planet. There are so many things that every human shares. So look for commonality and shared membership. It will negate the enemy of ingroup/outgroup bias that can subtly destroy the quality of your relatings with others.

Pos ψ Forgiveness

The wisdom of forgiveness is highlighted in almost all spiritual traditions. Interestingly, recent research has shown that forgiveness can be accomplished regardless of religious or spiritual orientation. The process of forgiving does not require spirituality or religion.

Scientific research in Positive Psychology shows that people who forgive are healthier and happier than those who hold grudges. In one Stanford University experiment, people who learned and practiced forgiveness reported fewer backaches, headaches, muscle pains, stomach upsets and other common physical signs of stress compared to a control group. They also reported higher levels of optimism, hope and self-confidence, showing forgiveness really is both good for you and good for your happiness.

The converse is also true. People who focus on anger, injustice and who feel they have been treated unfairly suffer from a higher risk of heart disease. A study of 8,000 people by researchers at the University College London found that those with a profound sense of injustice had a 55% higher chance of suffering serious heart disease. Researchers found that the focus on injustice and unfairness engendered negative emotions which lead to biochemical changes in the body. The take home message — focus on forgiveness, your long-term health depends on it.

The funny thing about forgiveness though is that while most people know it's important, a huge percentage don't follow through and actually do it. In a recent nationwide US Gallup poll, 94% of people surveyed acknowledged it was important to forgive; but only 48% said they usually tried to forgive others.

Blame, retribution and holding grudges are all enemies to

happiness. As the research shows, the key is to learn effective strategies for forgiving and then to follow through and practice them. Forgiveness is a great friend and supporter of health and happiness.

Some people think forgiveness is a sign of weakness. Those who've studied it can tell you without qualification that forgiveness is a sign of strength. It takes strength of purpose to choose to practice forgiveness. Especially in the face of anger and bitterness.

Forgiveness doesn't mean condoning wrongful behavior, excusing thoughtlessness, or forcing reconciliation with the offender. Forgiving is not the same as condoning. Forgiving is done for yourself. To heal and support yourself. It's a gift of happiness and peace of mind that you give yourself. It's about letting go of anger and resentment. It's about moving out from under the emotional burden of bitterness and liberating yourself from negative feelings of hurt or anger.

An inability or unwillingness to forgive has also been found to be associated with persistent rumination and dwelling on revenge, while forgiving allows you to move on. When you are angry, resentful and bitter you are only hurting yourself. So it's important for your mental health and important for your physical health that you forgive.

Another important thing to note is the distinction between the inner experience of forgiving and the public expression of it. They need not both be performed to gain the health and happiness benefits of forgiving. The research suggests it can be sufficient to practice *'silent'* forgiving in the form of a softened and more sympathetic heart. This can be useful when the aggressor does not earn or merit the forgiveness.

Remember, forgiving is about healing yourself and letting go the negative responses and burden. In cases where the aggressor has apologized and made redress, a public expression of forgiveness can be appropriate and can support building better and more healthy relationships. It's up to you to decide what's appropriate for your own outcomes and happiness. The main thing to note is the inner process of forgiving is vital for building positivity and healing in your own life.

> *"Forgiveness is not an emotion, it's a decision."*
>
> Randall Worley

☑ Success Strategy — Forgiveness Letters

One scientifically validated process for letting go of anger and resentment and generating feelings of forgiveness is to write letters of forgiveness to people who have hurt or wronged you. You need not send these letters. Indeed, in some instances it is better if you don't. It's up to you and the seriousness of the situation and whether the person has shown remorse or apologized. The main purpose of these letters is for you to express in writing how the experience affected you and that you are choosing to forgive. It's about getting in touch with and expressing real feelings of forgiveness, at both a deep heart and gut level, even when the person doesn't deserve it. It's about giving yourself the experience of forgiving and the ongoing peace of letting go.

1. **Acknowledge** to yourself and focus on the idea that you are writing your letter with the intention to let go any anger, resentment, recrimination, hurt, vindictiveness or other negative emotion.

2. **Express and reveal** your feelings. Write about how the experience made you feel. Don't do this in a blaming way. Instead, focus on the feelings that the situation generated.

3. **Take responsibility** for your part of the experience. Examine how you may have hurt the other person or may have added to the situation in some small way. For healing to be complete, you eventually need to take full responsibility for your own actions and thoughts.

4. **Empathize** with the person. Step into their shoes and try to understand their point of view.

5. **Finally, do forgiving** — offer and express forgiveness in the letter. Abandon your *'right'* to resentment, anger or negative judgment toward the person who unjustly hurt you; instead offer forgiveness by focusing on the qualities of compassion, generosity, and even love toward the person.

Don't send the letter to the person unless you really think it will be well received and will make a positive difference. Remember, this letter is for you — it's for your own self-healing. Read it every day for a week or so, until you can read it with true forgiveness and warmth in your heart. Then let it go and move on with living your life with joy and happiness.

> *"Forgiveness is the most powerful thing you can do for yourself. If you can't learn to forgive, you can forget about achieving true success in your life."*
>
> Dr. Wayne Dyer

☑ Success Strategy — Multiple Brain Forgiving

Both Buddhist philosophy and scientific research from Positive Psychology have shown that compassion, forgiveness and loving-kindness are key components to health and happiness. The evidence is in. Practicing forgiveness is an important daily activity for living a happy and fulfilled life.

And of course, there's no such thing as *'forgiveness'* — it's a nominalization (a disguised verb) for the ongoing process of forgiving. You don't *'have'* forgiveness for yourself or someone, you do forgiving of them. It's an active process.

So how do you do forgiving? Well, it actually comes from both the heart and gut...

As you know we have more than one brain. We actually have 3 brains in our body. Neuroscience has found that as well as a head brain, we actually have fully functioning *'brains'* filled with complex and functional neural tissue in our hearts and our guts — a heart brain and an enteric (gut) brain.

So expressions like *"follow the wisdom of your heart"* and *"listen to your gut instinct"* are quite accurate and deep reflections of our unconscious knowing of the existence of these distributed brain functions. It's wonderful how complex and powerful our mind/bodies really are!

It's all THEIR Fault

So how do you do loving-kindness and forgiving? Well, it's really quite easy. Create and hold those feelings in your heart and swallow them deep into your gut and then apply them to the situation or context that you feel needs forgiving. Most people think that forgiving only really requires being convinced at a head level or maybe bringing that forgiveness down into the heart. But action research from the field of *m*BIT (multiple Brain Integration Techniques) has found that true forgiveness requires integration at a gut level. (For more information on this go to www.mbraining.com or read my book '*mBraining*'.)

1. **Start by getting in balance** through Balanced Breathing for several minutes to bring balance and coherence to your Autonomic Nervous System. As indicated in Chapter 0, this involves breathing through your heart, with an even in-breath and out-breath duration of approximately 6 seconds each.

2. **Begin thinking** of memories and experiences that fill your heart with loving-kindness, with compassion and forgiveness. Then really focus on those feelings, amplify the heartfelt sense of forgiving. Get in touch with these warm loving feelings. Build them up and out and around your heart and body. As you breathe in and out, feel them expand and grow, until your whole chest, your whole torso, your whole body is filled with deep feelings of loving-kindness. Breathe this sense of compassion and forgiveness up into your head, and add in a sense of creativity, then breathe that back down to your heart and on deep into your gut, where you now add in a deep sense of gutsy courage. Cycle this back to the heart and loop around again, building a strong state of Highest Expression (Compassion, Creativity and Courage).

3. **Now start to** think of the person or the situation or behavior that needs and wants forgiving. Continue to breathe and amplify the heart feelings of forgiving and compassion as you recall the situation. This focuses your heart brain on loving feelings and allows it to learn and apply forgiving to the situation. With each breath, create and hold these feelings of pure forgiving and loving in your heart. As you breathe in and out, amplify the feelings with each breath. Make sure you expand them from your heart to your head and then back through the heart down deeply to your gut, deep inside your torso and stomach. This will send important messages from your heart brain to your head and gut brains. This will align your three brains together around deep and total forgiveness. Keep expanding these pure feelings of forgiving and loving until they fill your entire body and way of being.

4. **Say the words** *"I forgive myself, I forgive the world and I certainly forgive the person who hurt me. I forgive totally and completely. I am a worthwhile person who deserves my love, kindness and support and so I do forgiving with compassion and loving-kindness."* Say these over and over, with warm, loving tonalities. Hug yourself both physically and in your imagination. And all the while keep breathing love and forgiveness into your heart, head, gut and mind. As you breathe your forgiving and compassion into your mind, notice how your thoughts, perceptions and meaning of what happened begins to change and soften. Notice your openness to new ways of understanding the person or situation from a place of compassion, loving-kindness, and a generosity of spirit.

5. **Now swallow the deep sense of forgiving** down into your gut. Feel your gut take in and assimilate these new learnings. Feel your gut relax and *'let go'* of any tensions related to defensiveness, protection, or aggression. Feel how your gut welcomes and responds to this with a sense of ease, peace and security. As your gut lets go of the old ways of being, feel how it and you are becoming increasingly ready to move on in life. Feel how letting go of this past *'baggage'* makes you feel lighter, freer, and makes it easier to focus on moving forward from now on in. Experience the sensations of your gut updating its learned responses, releasing what is no longer useful to hold onto, and mobilizing you toward acting from a new, freer identity.

6. **Do all this** for a number of minutes, and then repeat it again for at least 3 to 5 times. Each time you practice the *'doing'* of forgiveness and compassion you'll find it gets stronger and easier. Your heart, head and gut brains will learn and remember.

Remember, forgiveness is not something you have, it's a process you do. So continue to do it often. One really useful idea is to do a quick form of this every night before you go to sleep. When you rest your head on the pillow, give yourself a metaphorical hug and tell yourself that you forgive yourself and love yourself, that you forgive any and all people who have hurt you and that you forgive the world for not being perfect and really build and feel the loving-kindness in your heart and letting go deep in your gut. It's a great way to love, nurture and support your inner self and generate more happiness and joy in your life.

Thinking Tools — Behavior

People are NOT their behaviors.

Identity and Behavior

An incredibly useful and powerful presupposition from NLP is that *'people are NOT their behaviors'*. This is a great thinking tool that helps you dissociate people from their behaviors. Just because someone makes a mistake doesn't mean they *'are'* a failure. Just the same as telling a lie doesn't make a person a liar at the level of their identity.

By realizing and recognizing that people are not their behaviors, you allow yourself to more easily forgive them as a person and also allow them to move on from their behaviors and mistakes. In this way you can separate the person from the behavior. You can also be kind and supportive to the person while being firm about not accepting the behavior. In terms of doing high quality relating with people, this thinking tool is a very useful attitude to operate from.

> *"Love one another and you will be happy. It's as simple and as difficult as that."*
>
> Michael Leunig

Building Strong Relationships

We are social animals whose brains are highly specialized and adapted for thinking about and caring for others. We need strong social bonds and friendships to remain healthy and balanced.

Research on loneliness has found that it is linked to an increased risk of cancer, stroke, high blood pressure and cardiovascular disease. Loneliness down-regulates immune function and doubles the risk of Alzheimer's disease. It is also associated with depression, stress, suicide risk and other psychological problems. Loneliness can be a killer and really is an enemy to your happiness.

One recent study found that loneliness actually changes how the body functions at a molecular level. The research shows that feelings of social isolation lead to an alteration in the activity of specific genes that put lonely people at higher risk of serious disease. Interestingly, the study suggested that it's the perception of loneliness that triggers the adverse health conditions, independent of how much social interaction the person actually has.

So one of the important keys to happiness and health is to form and build strong relationships, friendships and social bonds. You need to connect with people in meaningful and supportive ways. It's not just about being around people. You actually have to bond with people and share emotional connections.

So make an effort to join clubs, dances, workshops and community and social groups. Share yourself with people. Build rapport. Engage people in friendly and meaningful conversation. Nurture your friendships and build on them. Really focus on surrounding yourself with positive people, relationships and environments.

Most importantly, do what you can to help other people. As the great motivational and personal development teacher Zig Ziggler said, *"If you go looking for a friend, you're going to find they're very scarce. If you go out to be a friend, you'll find them everywhere"*.

> "You can have anything you want in life, if you just help enough other people get what they want in life."
>
> Zig Ziggler

Loving Happiness

There are a number of enemies that hurt high quality loving and equally there are a number of behaviors and skills that support loving happiness.

One of the leading researchers in this field is psychologist Professor John Gottman from the University of Washington. In over 30 years of behavioral research, Prof. Gottman has examined what he calls the *'masters and disasters of relationships'*. These are people who are exemplars of what to do and what not to do to keep love positive and alive. From this research Gottman has been able to distil out the key factors that make relationships either succeed or fail. His findings are so powerful that he is able, by observing couples behaviors, to predict with more than 90% accuracy which couples will make it, and which will not.

So what are the enemies to loving happiness?

✘ **Contempt**

Contempt involves behaviors like insults, sarcasm and feeling and acting like you're better than your partner. Indeed the research shows that an air of superiority is, by itself, the best predictor of divorce or break up.

Antidote: create a culture of appreciation and support, refuse to accept or give contempt, ban sarcasm and replace it with encouragement.

- ✖ **Criticism**

    Criticizing and being overly negative or judgmental is another serious indicator of a toxic relationship.

    Antidote: use constructive complaining rather than criticism — tell your partner what you think the challenge or issue is and how you feel about it rather than attacking them.

- ✖ **Defensiveness**

    Defensiveness is where you respond to a complaint with righteous indignation as though you are the innocent victim in the situation or relationship. If you behave this way, you don't take any share of the responsibility for the problem.

    Antidote: accept responsibility for your part of every situation, even if it's just for a small part of it.

- ✖ **Stonewalling**

    Stonewalling involves not listening, shutting down and emotionally withdrawing from the interaction. With stonewalling you don't give the usual non-verbal responses to your partner — looking away or down and not responding.

    Antidote: self-soothing — learn to let go of any anger or negative emoting and to sooth your responses so you can stay constructively involved together in the interaction.

Look for and actively remove any of these enemies in your relatings. Remember, these four key behaviors are able to predict relationship failure with over 90% accuracy. So they are very harmful enemies and need to be removed and replaced in your relationships.

Replace these four enemies with the following success behaviors, found in Gottman's research to be major factors in high quality relating:

✓ **Shared Meaning**

Create shared understanding and meaning in your relationships. Spend time learning each other's strengths, values, passions and interests. Talk about these things with one another, and do activities and projects together that build on your shared interests and meaning.

✓ **Positive Sentiment Overriding**

Allow an enduring sense of positive sentiment and a forgiving attitude to override any negative experience. Foster and focus on loving-kindness and forgiveness.

✓ **High Relationship Standards**

Successful happy couples have high standards for themselves, each other and the way they relate. They expect and demand loving supportive behavior in the relating and don't tolerate negative or hurtful patterns. So set high standards and then live up to them.

✓ **Perform Argument Repair**

Successful couples are skilful at exiting arguments. They know how to let go of and repair any emotional damage that may have occurred in an argument or disagreement. They also know that it's important to start an argument or disagreement slowly. The research indicates that it's the first 3 minutes of the argument that set the final outcomes.

So be gentle and slow in how you approach disagreements and then ensure you do emotional repair at the end. Leave the person feeling ok about themselves, you and the relationship. End a disagreement with an apology, a positive statement of caring about the person, with some humor to diffuse the situation or some sort of caring, positive remark.

Willingly accept repair attempts by your partner, even if the attempt isn't quite what you'd like; meet them half-way and work together to repair the argument and come back to positive loving happiness together.

✓ **Focus on the Bright Side**

Focus on the positives in the person and the relationship. Look for ways to compliment each other and to build the relationship up. Successful couples give each other at least 5 positive messages for each negative message. So always look for the bright side of your partner and the situations you are in and communicate this to each other.

Relationships really can be either an ongoing source of happiness or a source of misery in your life. And since you don't *have* relationships but instead *do* relating, you can use the tools and concepts from this chapter to build the skills of high quality relating. By relating in a positive, happy, loving, forgiving and supportive way with the people in your work and life you will build an enduring network of happiness in your life. High quality and loving relatings will help buffer you from the turmoil and stress of life and bring you many gifts of meaning and joy.

⚒ Thinking Tools — Changing Patterns

If you continue to do what you've always done — you'll continue to get what you've always gotten.

⚡ Pattern-Interrupt — Characterological Adjectives

The following process is used to break negative behavioral loops in relationships and replace them with more useful, loving and supportive behaviors. It is based on the idea that all relationship patterns are created and sustained in the loop of the behavioral interactions between the people in the relationship.

'Characterological adjectives' are words that describe fundamental perceived characteristics of any relationship. What's important and useful about these adjectives is that whilst they typically describe the perception of the problem or issue in the relationship, they also necessarily imply the underlying loop that supports the behavior. For example, if a person is described as *"defensive"* in the relationship, then this implies there is some sort of aggression occurring that generates and supports the defensive behavior.

By consciously examining the characterological adjectives in your relationships and then working out new behavioral patterns that negate the pattern, you can interrupt the old unsupportive loops and create much more generative and useful ways of

It's all THEIR Fault

loving and relating with the people you interact with and care about.

Interrupt any old unsupportive patterns in your relationships by:

- Think of someone you have problems with or that you have a difficult time communicating with. Think of any counterproductive patterns that don't bring out the best in you or the other person. Look for situations in which you feel stuck and uncreative or relationship interactions that are limiting or negative.

- Now picture yourself in a theatre. Imagine yourself sitting comfortably watching either a stage or screen. Up on the stage or screen, begin to see the other person and yourself and watch as the problem behavior unfolds. Watch the other person behaving in the way that they typically behave.

- Think of a word that best describes the person's behavior. For example: *"aggressive"*, *"pushy"*, *"selfish"* etc.

- Now take a deep breath. Relax. It's just words and information. Do Balanced Breathing, 6 seconds in, 6 seconds out. Breathe peace into your heart, up into your head, and calmness down into your gut.

- Begin to look at yourself on the screen or stage and watch how your character on the screen typically responds and interacts in a loop with the other person. What is the word that you would use to best describe your own behavior?

Avoiding the Enemies to HAPPINESS

- For example, if the other person was acting *"pushy"* you might find yourself acting *"defensive"*; and notice that the more defensive you act, the more pushy the other person becomes. It's like a dance or connection. The two behaviors reinforce and feed each other. Notice that the characterological adjectives describe both sides of the communication loop.

- Once again, keep breathing in a calm and balanced way. Now ask yourself *"what way of acting or behaving would completely change this loop?"* What could you do that would stop the pattern in its track? What could you do that would no longer support the old pattern? What would be a more Compassionate, Creative and Courageous way to respond that would completely break the old pattern? Name the new behavior. Then re-run the movie on the screen or stage and see the other person doing the old behavior, then see yourself doing the new behavior and see the resulting change in the loop. See the other person stop the old behavior and do a new more positive response.

- Now step into the shoes of yourself up on the stage. See the whole new pattern through your own eyes rather than from the perspective of a member of an audience. In NLP parlance this is seeing it from '*First Position*' rather than from '*Third Position*' i.e. see if from a first person perspective — your own. Rerun the experience and really see and feel the positive change.

> ✏ Next time you meet the person and interact with them, you'll find yourself responding in the new way. Your unconscious mind will follow the new more creative and useful pattern. It will happen naturally and you'll now have more choice and control in the relationship. The old pattern will be broken and your relating will be improved and enhanced.

Strengths & Values In Action

Use the following table to determine which strengths, qualities and values to focus on and amplify in your life to support the processes and skills of happiness. Also notice if you have any elements of the absence, opposite or exaggeration of these strengths and remove them from your behaviors and your life.

Enemies to happiness	VIA Strength
Manipulative People Blaming Others Loneliness Poor Quality Relating	Social Intelligence Forgiveness & Mercy Citizenship/Loyalty Gratitude Fairness & Justice Love & Kindness Forgiveness Open-mindedness

📋 Notes from the Field — Connecting with Happiness

Judith DeLozier is a trainer and one of the key developers of NLP. She holds a Masters Degree (MA) in Religious Studies and a Bachelors Degree (BA) in Anthropology from the University of California, Santa Cruz, where she met and worked with the founders of NLP — Dr. John Grinder and Dr. Richard Bandler. Judy has taught NLP across the world, has co-authored a number of successful books on NLP, was president of Grinder, DeLozier, and Associates for many years, and is presently an associate of NLP University with Robert Dilts.

Judy's numerous contributions to the field include the development and application of Systemic NLP to the modeling of leadership, to health care, models of social change and cross-cultural competence.

I spoke with Judy about happiness, its enemies and the insights from Systemic NLP for creating happiness in relationships and life.

"Happiness is a frame you choose to organize your experience around — it is an act of will. Choose to set happiness as an intention in your life. This doesn't mean you won't feel grief, pain or other negative emotions. Happiness is a nominalization; it's a strategy, a process. So take the filter called happiness and breathe it into your life. Ask yourself 'what's the one thing I can do each day that will bring more happiness and joy into life'. By choosing to do happiness you directionalize your attention, focus your quality of movement and frame your states and perspectives."

As Judy points out, happiness is an on-going strategy for generating and directing your state of mind and being. It's about finding grace in your life; about wholeness and integration and entering into a state of grace and then choosing to live in that space.

Key to this is the notion of responsibility. Take responsibility for creating states of happiness in yourself, in your work space and in the larger community and systems in which you live. Embrace a passion for life and a commitment to something larger than yourself. Inspire yourself to take action towards changing your environment in positive and healthy ways.

For Judy, the process of generating happiness also involves creativity and wisdom. *"It's about changing perspectives so that multiple distinctions can come about."* Part of this skill involves the ability to hear/see/feel through the eyes and ears of other people — to step into their shoes. It's also about comfort in the state of not-knowing; being open to learning and change.

In terms of your relationships with others and building happiness into these, Judy notes that humor, compassion and strength are keys. *"Humor, compassion and strength awaken us and are ways to pattern-interrupt the enemies of blame, fear and negativity"*. It's important to operate from a *'Personal Responsibility Frame'* versus a *'Blame-Frame'* in dealing with people. You can do this by taking responsibility for using humor to pattern-interrupt blaming. Also remember to separate people from their behavior — *"people are not their behavior"*. Take a step back, reflect and then use humor to shift your state of relating.

So what are the main enemies to happiness according to Judy?

- **Unuseful states** of being that you get yourself into — be patient and supportive of yourself and choose states of creativity, passion and strength instead.

- **Self importance and ego** — release the greed of the "*I am*" state and allow creativity to emerge; connect instead with the larger system of others.

- **Negative internal dialog** battering the crap out of yourself — let go of the tension, blame and fear and instead take responsibility for stepping up to a state of grace in which you resolve any inner conflict between the parts of yourself generating the inner dialog.

Note that if there's something you can't do with yourself then you usually can't do it with others. For example if you can't accept some part of yourself then you are unlikely to accept it in others. So focus on integrating and building good relationships and grace within the various aspects of your self.

Choose to set happiness as an intention and frame for yourself, your life and your relationships with others. Then use creativity, humor, wisdom and grace to awaken your life and build a connection to the larger system in which you live.

☞ Remember This

✓ Blame and retribution are enemies to happiness. Replace them by getting clear about your outcomes and taking personal responsibility and control of your side of every interaction and relationship.

- ✓ Beware of creating unreasonable expectations and negative self-fulfilling prophecies in your relatings with others. Instead, hold realistic and positive expectations of others to support them in positive behavior.

- ✓ Protect yourself from the negative behavior of others — track for and stay away from sociopaths and psychic vampires.

- ✓ Do intelligent trusting of others and help them to be honest in their relating with you.

- ✓ Actively practice forgiveness and heartmind loving-kindness.

- ✓ Seek out and form strong bonds and friendships to buffer against loneliness.

- ✓ Use the pattern-interrupt technique of Characterological Adjectives to transform any negative patterns and behaviors in less than optimal relatings.

- ✓ Beware of the relationship enemies of Contempt, Criticism, Defensiveness and Stonewalling and replace them with the strategies of high quality relating.

ⓘ Extra Info

Refer to www.enemiestohappiness.com for

- more information about the material covered in this chapter
- additional reading and references for this chapter

Avoiding the Enemies to HAPPINESS

Chapter 6

Too much, too SOON!

You will learn to

- ✓ Understand and handle stress
- ✓ Prioritize your values and time
- ✓ Learn how to make effective decisions
- ✓ Build resilience
- ✓ Master change

Too much, too SOON!

We live in a world of massive and accelerating change. This can lead to overload, pressure and stress — too much, too soon. Stress, confusion and overwhelm are enemies of happiness. They sap your energy, health and peace of mind.

To cope with a world of massive change you need to master change and know how to bolster resilience and strength. In this chapter you'll learn strategies for understanding and coping with stress and building resilience to buffer against it. You'll learn about the importance of clearly identifying your values and prioritizing them. You'll also learn how to make effective decisions. Using the tools and skills from this chapter you can achieve focus and balance and ensure that too much, too soon doesn't destroy the happiness you deserve.

Enemies to your Happiness

- ✘ Stress and overload
- ✘ Confusion and overwhelm
- ✘ Unclear priorities and values
- ✘ Not coping with change

Too much, too SOON!

Massive and Accelerating World Change

The world is changing, and changing at a massive and accelerating rate. More information, more stimulus, new ways of doing things, faster ways of doing things in an ongoing race that touches us in every way. Technological change is driving business change, societal change, environmental change and even personal change. It can be a struggle to just keep up.

To understand how massive this change is and how it's accelerating at an ever growing rate, you need to see a few graphs. Let's start by looking at the amount of invention in the world. Technological invention drives change in our lives. New ways of doing things change the way we work, the way we live and just about every aspect of our lives.

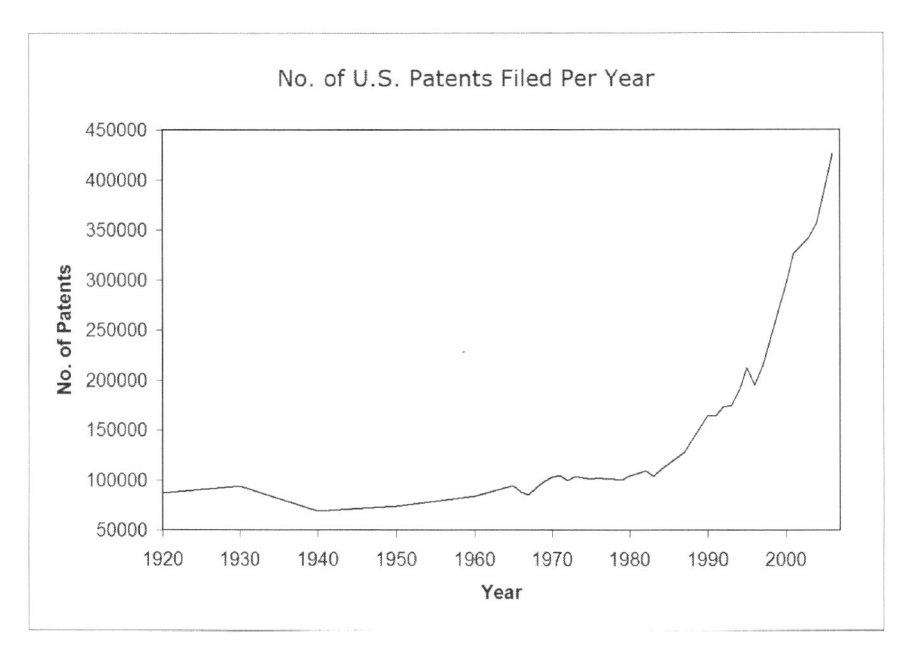

[Source: U.S. Patent and Trademark Office (http://www.uspto.gov)]

279

Above is a graph of the number of patents filed in the United States per year. You can see that the graph starts relatively flat, with a small rate of growth over the last 100 years. Indeed, the amount of invention over the last couple of thousand years has been relatively small compared to recent growth. But look what happens from about 1980 onwards. The graph starts to rise and rise at a sharper and sharper rate.

The shape of this graph is known as an exponential curve. This shape comes about due to a process of growth in which the size increases by a fixed multiple over time. For example, in computing there is a law known as '*Moore's Law*', coined by Gordon Moore, one of the inventors of the Microprocessor. Moore's Law predicts that the power of computing will double approximately every 18 months. To get a sense of this, imagine that we start off with 1 unit of computing power. In 18 months time this will have doubled to 2 units. In a further 18 months, we will have 4 units of computing power. Eighteen months later this will double to 8 units, then 16 units, 32 units, 64 units and so on. You can see from this that at first things appear to be growing slowly, but as the size increases, the doublings really start to make a powerful difference. This is the power of exponential growth. Once you reach the turning point, the graph just takes off and explodes upwards.

Importantly, it turns out that exponential growth — that is massively accelerating growth and change — is not just happening in the price/performance of computing. As you've seen from the previous graph, the number of patents for inventions is changing at an exponential rate and it's now at the near vertical rate of growth. This accelerating rate of invention is in part what is driving Moore's Law in the area of electronics and computing. And these massive changes in computing have led to the growth and uptake of the

Too much, too SOON!

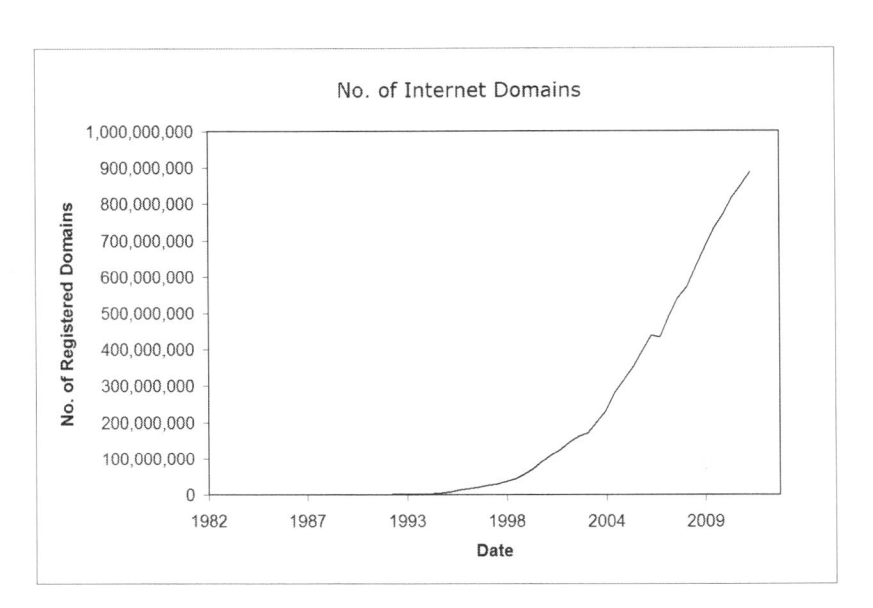

internet. Let's take a look at what its growth looks like.

No. of Internet Domains

[A line graph showing No. of Registered Domains (y-axis, 0 to 1,000,000,000) versus Date (x-axis, 1982 to 2009), displaying exponential growth reaching nearly 900,000,000 by the end.]

[Source: Internet Systems Consortium, Inc. (http://www.isc.org/)]

You can see from this graph that it's the same sort of curve and that the rate of growth of the internet is now getting close to the near vertical part of the curve. So what does this mean? It means that the rate at which the internet is growing and changing is massively accelerating. More change and quicker change. Incredible.

The rate of invention development is also feeding other diverse areas such as:

☐ Genetic Engineering: Number of genes mapped per year

☐ Medical Technology: Resolution of brain scanning devices

☐ Industry: Manufacturing productivity rates

☐ Economics: World Economic Growth in GDP.

When graphed, these all show exponential growth and are now in the near vertical parts of their growth curves. Science Philosophers have been examining these trends and have shown that these growth curves are all due to an underlying accelerating growth in world knowledge. If we take each unit of knowledge in the world, whether you consider it to be an invention, an idea, a book or a web page and we graph the number of these over time, we find... yes you guessed it, an exponential curve.

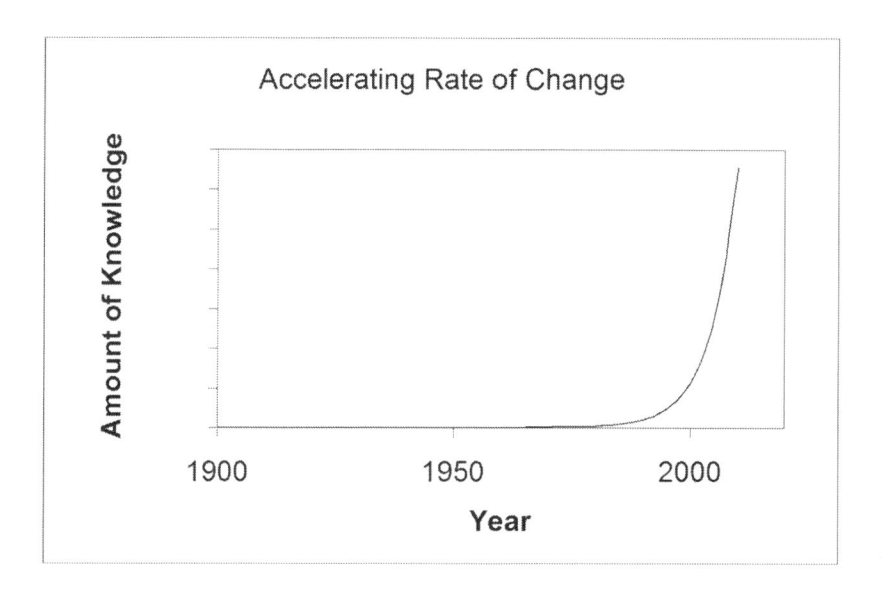

Accelerating Rate of Change

(Graph: Amount of Knowledge vs. Year, 1900–2000, showing exponential curve)

> *"If you don't like change, you're going to like irrelevance even less."*
>
> General Eric Shinseki

You can clearly see that the world is now at a point where the exponential change is producing massively accelerating growth. We are on the steep point of the curve and it's only going to get bigger and steeper from here. You see, the limits now are not going to be human limits. We are creating intelligent automated systems that are designed to create and generate ideas and knowledge themselves. For example, we now have millions of web pages created each day by *'know-bots'* (knowledge robots) — automated systems that crawl the web and synthesize, integrate and generate new web pages. Add in Moore's Law to this and you'll see that these bots are going to get faster and more powerful and more plentiful.

So what does this mean to you? Well, as one cool YouTube video created by Dr. Scott McLeod and Karl Fisch puts it:

"Shift happens"

[See https://www.youtube.com/watch?v=XVQ1ULfQawk or go to shifthappens.wikispaces.com for the latest version of this presentation.]

Yes, your world is going to continue to change in massively accelerating ways. Society is changing and changing massively. Work is going to change immensely. Economics is going to change in accelerating ways. And all this change increases the complexity of life. You'll have to keep up. If you don't you'll get run over. In order to stay economically viable, you'll have to continue to learn and adapt. Or like the dinosaur you'll become extinct. There's no ignoring it. There's no escaping it.

This massively accelerating change means there will always be *'too much, too soon'* in our lives. Unless you become a change master and learn to ride the wave of change, your happiness will suffer. The stress and overwhelm of *'too much, too soon'* are enemies to happiness. The good news is that there are skills, attitudes and strategies you can use to increase your resilience and embrace change and complexity so that it enhances your life. If you fight change, it will literally kill you. The stress of massive change can impact your mental, emotional and importantly your physical health.

In this chapter you'll learn the skills of change mastery. So take a slow deep breath, feel a calm centre point, and rather than quick quick quick!!!, let's calmly get into it. ☺

> *"Worry and stress affects the circulation, the heart, the glands, the whole nervous system, and profoundly affects heart action."*
>
> Charles W. Mayo, M.D.

Pos ψ Stress

The majority of people experience stress when faced with large amounts of change or overwhelming quantities of information, demands and stimuli. So in order to cope with and control *'too much, too soon'* it makes sense to learn about stress and how to overcome it.

To begin with, it's important to know what the effects of stress are and how crucial it is you learn skills and techniques to diffuse them.

Stress is a killer! The American Institute of Stress and The U.S. Centers for Disease Control have both estimated that up to 90% of all illnesses are due to the effects of stress. While small amounts of stress can actually increase productivity and focus, more than that causes long term damage. When repeatedly invoked, stress contributes to hypertension, stroke, heart attack, diabetes, ulcers, back pain and numerous other diseases. Stress down-regulates the immune system, kills off brain cells and causes depression and other psychological disorders. In other words, stress is a major enemy of happiness.

The thing about stress is that it's insidious. It creeps up on you. You can generally cope with small amounts of it. But like boiling a frog... slow increases in stress can be unnoticeable until it's too late. By the time you realize you're experiencing chronic stress, the damages to your health and happiness have already taken their toll.

Early Warning Signs of Stress

Look for and be aware of any of the following early warning signs of chronic stress in your life:

- Headache
- Sleep disturbance
- Difficulty in concentrating
- Short temper and irritability
- Upset stomach
- Life dissatisfaction
- Low morale
- Depression

- ☒ Loss of energy and well-being

Stress related issues can be quick to develop. The best strategy however is to build resilience and buffer yourself against stress.

The Undo Effect

As highlighted above, when you experience stress, you show increased heart rate, higher blood sugar, immune suppression, and other biological adaptations optimized for fight and flight. And as also indicated, if you don't counteract these changes over time they'll lead to illness, heart disease, and a higher risk of death.

The good news is that research has shown that positive emotions undo the damaging cardiovascular after-effects of stress and negative emotions. This is known in Positive Psychology as the *Undo effect*. Both lab and survey research indicate that positive emotions help people who were previously under stress relax back to a healthy physiological baseline.

For example, in one study by Prof. Barbara Fredrickson, participants were placed into a stress inducing situation and then shown either a short film that elicited positive emotions, neutrality, or a negative emotion such as sadness. The results showed that even short (one minute duration) positive and amusing films produced much faster cardiovascular recovery than neutral or sad films did, with recovery times nearly 50% faster.

Broaden-and-Build

Numerous studies from Prof. Barbara Fredrickson's Positive Psychology Lab have also shown that people who experience positive emotions show heightened levels of creativity, inventiveness, and broadened perceptual focus. They are more able to cope with the stressors of life. In addition, longitudinal studies confirm that positive emotions play an important role in the development of long-term resources such as psychological resilience and flourishing. Positive emotions help buffer against stress, both psychologically and physically.

So the message is really very obvious. To increase your ability to cope with and transcend the effects of change and stress, you need to give yourself regular doses of positive emoting.

This means that on a daily and weekly basis you absolutely have to schedule time for pleasurable and fun activities. I know, when life gets busy and hectic, the positive fun activities are often the first to get cancelled. But this is vitally important. In order to transcend stress and flourish in the hectic lives we live, in times of massive and accelerating change, you absolutely have to make time for positive emotional experiences.

Spend time with friends seeing an uplifting movie. Enjoy entertaining conversation over a good dinner with those you love. Laugh. Listen to comedy. Read a good book. Schedule in a massage or pampering. Do things daily that make you feel happy.

And remember to focus on gratitude and appreciation. Here's a simple technique to help you focus on gratitude. Grab a rock or a shell on your next trip to the country or beach and keep it somewhere handy. Then every time you see your *'gratitude'* rock or shell, use it as a trigger, an anchor, to remember and focus on things and people in your life that you truly appreciate.

Make gratitude, love and positive emoting an ongoing way of life. It will help to broaden and build your strength and resilience and allow you to easily cope with the massive and accelerating changes in your world.

> *"We have two choices: continue to blame the world for our stress or take responsibility for own reactions and deliberately change our emotional climate."*
>
> Doc Childre & Howard Martin, HeartMath Solution

> *"Stress is not only created by how we see a situation, but also how we react to it. We do, in fact, control our own stress."*
>
> Catherine Pulsifer

Choice and Control

We now have more choice than we've ever had before. As the world changes and expands we end up with a huge range of options and opportunities. Research shows that paradoxically this increase in choice is making people:

- Not choose
- Regret their choices
- Feel depressed
- Feel overwhelmed

There are a couple of issues and insights from these findings.

Firstly, recognize that stress is an unconscious personal reaction to what's happening to you. If a wide range of choice is stressing you or overwhelming you, notice that it is you who is stressing yourself over having to do the choosing. You create the stress, not the situation. Sure, you don't do it consciously or deliberately. Nevertheless, it's your brain (head-brain, heart-brain and gut-brain) that's generating the stressing response.

What this tells you is that you need to learn new strategies for coping with choice and control. That's what this book is about. Helping you learn and practice new skills for gaining more appropriate and wiser choice and control in life. That's what happiness-ing is all about.

Secondly, stressing over a large range of choices is indicative of a poor decision making strategy. It's a signal that you aren't clear about your values and outcomes and how to make a useful choice to satisfy them. We'll deal with this in the Success Strategy section.

Before getting into decision strategies and values however, I really want you to understand the insight that you don't *'have'* stress. Stress is another of those nominalizations — a verb disguised as a noun. There's no such *'thing'* as stress. Instead there's just the process of stressing.

The benefit of understanding this is that stressing is an action, it's a process. It's something you are doing. You have control over it. Or more to the point, you can learn to have control over how you are stressing and how you are relaxing. It's your choice.

As Dr. Hans Selye, the father of modern stress research points out *"Adopting the right attitude can convert a negative stress into a positive one."* We'll be exploring this in more detail shortly.

Once you understand that the process of stressing is something you can learn to control and build unconscious competencies in, you are firmly at a point of choice in your life. Now you can begin to gather the knowledge and skills you need to control how you respond to what happens in life. Remember the Law of Requisite Variety we discussed in earlier chapters?

🛠 Thinking Tools — Law of Requisite Variety

Choice = Control

It says that the more choice and flexibility you give yourself, the more control you get over life. There is a sister law from Cybernetics that goes hand in hand with this law, and it says that for true control you need knowledge. So the formula can be written as:

Choice + Knowledge = Control

This explains in part why people who are given lots of choice end up in *'overwhelm'* rather than feeling in control. They've got lots of choice, but they don't have the right knowledge about how to do excellence in choosing. We'll remedy that in this chapter by learning about values and decision strategies.

The formula also shows why it's important for you to understand that stressing is a process you can learn (*knowledge*) about how you are choosing to respond to what is happening to you in life (*choice*). Get it! You are now on the road to controlling stress in your life because you are learning both of these skills.

Yes we live in a time of massive and accelerating change. Instead of being a victim of that change, you can learn to master change and lead it rather than being run over by it. You can learn to become energized by the sea of information and change rather than being swamped and overwhelmed by the waves of change. I personally find this fantastic and something to be very happy about. We live in an amazing time on this planet and by using appropriate skills and attitudes we can live an awesome life of adventure, learning and happiness-ing. Now how cool is that! ☺

☑ Success Strategy — Building Resilience

Savoring good experiences and then storing them as memories builds resilience — you create a treasure trove of great memories to use when life gets tough. In this way, your wonderful memories become a valuable resource tool for creating emotional strength and resilience.

This technique uses the *'broaden and build'* effect of positive emotions to undo the effects of stress and to generate resilience in your body and mind. Use it as often as possible and certainly anytime you want to feel and act more positively and in control of your life.

1. Think of at least 5 or 6 times in your life that were great experiences — times when you were at your best, that made you feel fantastic, that really fill you with positive feelings when you recall them.

2. Now, one by one, relive each one, step back into each memory, associate into it totally, brighten up the picture, hear the sounds in surround-sound, intensify the feelings and really amplify the experience now. Savor and bask in the positive feelings each memory brings.

3. As you really, truly and deeply relive each memory make sure you go back fully and see what you saw, hear what you heard,

feel what you felt at the time and as you do so, amplify your feelings of joy and happiness in your heart and gut. Make your picture of the experience brighter and more empowering. Bring it closer. Really get into experiencing your happiness and the positive emotions your memories bring.

4. Use this technique on a daily basis. The more you use it and relive your key resilience memories, the more you will build emotional capital and resilience. Doing this does more than just make you feel good in the moment. The technique will create enduring effects and over time will shift your attitude to one that embodies more hope, joy and positivity.

Physical Resilience

Research has also shown that people who build physical resilience and strength enhance their ability to cope emotionally and psychologically with stress. Physical resilience leads to emotional resilience. Exercise for example has been found to correlate with stronger levels of resilience. This is probably due in part to the effects of exercise on immune function and physical health and the links between this and mental health. It's also possibly due to the effects of endorphins induced by exercise on mood and positive emotion. Whatever the reasons, it tells you that exercise is a key ingredient in building resilience and in learning to master change.

Other activities that build physical resilience such as swimming in cold water and enduring hot saunas also increase psychological endurance. So it's worthwhile doing things that toughen you up. Your life and happiness will benefit from them.

It's also good to remember that laughter and humor have physical effects on health and immunity and that these in turn increase both physical and emotional resilience. Indeed, all of the positive health behaviors mentioned in Chapter 4 will enhance your ability to cope with and master stress and change. So now you've got even more encouragement to make exercise, meditation and laughter an ongoing part of your life.

Finally, let's talk about the importance of the heart to stress and resilience. The heart is massively affected by stress and in turn is a key part of the trigger and cause of the stressing response. By focusing on your heart and by communicating with your heart-brain you can learn to control your nervous system in a way that allows you to function more powerfully and cope with change and the stressors of our fast paced world.

> *"The point of balance is the heart. It's the foundation on which to build. Activating heart frequencies by loving and caring will balance your system, bringing in peace in the moment. It's the best antidote for restoring balance and alleviating stress."*
>
> Doc Childre & Sara Paddison

( ) Deeper Understandings — Heart Coherence

The effects of stress are largely due to the Sympathetic Nervous System's response to perceived threat. Our Autonomic Nervous System is comprised of two sub-systems — the Sympathetic system which is responsible for the fight and flight response; and the Parasympathetic system whose role is to bring your brain and body back into homeostasis, into balance.

As you know, your gut and heart both have a brain. Each has a large independent chunk of neural tissue that acts like a little brain, taking in and processing information from your environment and responding to protect you. When the heart and enteric (gut) brains perceive a threat, they kick the Sympathetic system into action and your heart starts beating faster, adrenalin and cortisol are released and all the physical stress responses fire up. It's nature's way of helping you get ready to fight or run.

You'll remember from Chapter 4 that you can learn to bring your Sympathetic and Parasympathetic systems into balance and to calm your head, heart and enteric brains down through a technique called the *'Balanced Breathing'*. This way of focusing and breathing sends powerful messages to your whole cybernetic loop and increases your heart coherence so that your heart, body and mind remain healthy and resilient. Given the usefulness and importance of this technique we are going to repeat it in this chapter as a way to pattern-interrupt the process of stressing and as a mechanism to control your mind/body in a very powerful way.

Also remember that you can buy a fantastic bio-feedback tool from the Heartmath.com organization that helps you learn and reinforce your skills in heart-based balanced breathing and quickly allows you to see just how much heart rate coherence you are generating. I highly recommended owning and using these tools to enhance your life and happiness.

(And no, in case you are wondering, I have no shares or ownership in the Heartmath organization whatsoever, I simply think their tools and systems are Life Enhancing Devices and I've been using and recommending them for a number of years now. Their tools are powerful and in my experience really do work to help you quickly learn to control your Autonomic Nervous System responses.)

Pattern-Interrupt — Heart-based Balanced Breathing

Use the following technique to interrupt any negative or stressful behaviors or patterns. If you find yourself at any time feeling stressed or anxious, use and practice the technique.

It is a scientifically validated technique that can be used to balance your mind and body and tap into the wisdom of the heart. It works by increasing the coherence of your heart beat and bringing the Sympathetic and Parasympathetic arms of the Autonomic Nervous System into balance.

Interrupt any stressing by:

- Shift your attention to the area of your heart and breathe slowly and deeply, with an in-breath of approximately 6 seconds in, and out-breath of the same duration. Visualize your breath entering and leaving through the centre of your chest and heart area. You might see it as light or a color spreading into your heart and chest region. And remember, it is important to make each in and out-breath the same duration.

- ✒ Activate and sustain a genuine feeling of love, compassion, appreciation or care for someone or something in your life. Focus on positive feelings of love. Feel them in your heart. Remember a time or think about something that makes you feel happy and peaceful. With every breath, fill your heart with positivity, love, kindness, joy and compassion.

- ✒ Sustain this process for at least 5 — 10 minutes or more to bring your heart beat into balance and coherence and to relieve the mental and physical processes of stress. If you find your mind wandering, gently bring it back to thoughts and feelings of love and appreciation. Keep your attention on your heart and on slow deep balanced breathing.

- ✒ Add appreciation into the mix by celebrating your new more positive heart feeling and enjoying your increasing resilience, joy and happiness.

- ✒ You can also breathe the positive feelings of joy and love in your heart up into your head, and then breathe them down deep into your gut where you experience them as calm and peace. This is a form of *'calm-abiding'* where you breathe uplifting feelings of calm joy into your heart and peace down into your gut brain.

This technique is a useful tool for quieting the mind and creating a solid connection with your heart and gut brains. Your heart and gut have much intuitive wisdom that you can access only when in a state of calm autonomic coherence, so breathe in a balanced way and trust your deep intuitions as you learn to connect to your wiser self.

> *"Adopting the right attitude can convert a negative stress into a positive one."*
>
> Dr. Hans Selye

Attitudes and Beliefs

In part, stress from change and overwhelm is a result of how you think about and respond to change. If you embody an attitude that change is negative and stressful, then surely enough you'll experience the effects of stress.

If on the other hand, you embrace an attitude that change is a wonderful opportunity to learn and grow, you'll find yourself enlivened by change. Rather than being overwhelmed by new information, you'll be thrilled and excited by it.

Positive Psychology has shown that resilience to stress and change is fostered by approaching change as a meaningful challenge rather than detaching and giving up. Resilience and hardiness are bolstered through embracing the positive attitudes of commitment, control and courage.

According to Dr. Salvatore Maddi, a Professor of Psychology at the University of California and the founder of the Hardiness Institute, "*People who are high in hardiness enjoy ongoing changes and difficulties. They find themselves more involved in their work when it gets tougher and more complicated. They tend to think of stress as a normal part of life, rather than as something that's unfair.*"

So make a decision right now to live with an attitude that change is a fantastic opportunity for new learning and development. Resilient people really do view life's difficulties as challenges and respond with action, rather than with fear, self-pity or blame.

Yes, in this time of massive accelerating change, surrounded by *'too much, too soon'*, life can seem challenging. But through the use of the right attitude, by strengthening yourself mentally and physically and through buffering with positive emotional experiences, you really can choose to thrive and excel in the opportunities that massive change always brings.

Remember too, the important points from earlier chapters. For example, a positive step in becoming more resilient is to use lots of positive self-talk and continually remind yourself that you are strong and can grow stronger and wiser as you overcome life's challenges and turn them into wonderful opportunities.

And remember to cultivate optimism. Developing a more optimistic world view can help you become more resilient. Focus on your strengths and celebrate your accomplishments. Continue to look on the bright side of every single situation. Build positive beliefs in yourself and your ability to cope and thrive. Your happiness depends on it.

Attitude is a powerful tool that gets stronger and more effective the more you use it. Embrace an attitude of Change Mastery right now and use it to overcome the enemy of *'too much, too soon'*!

> *"You can look at challenges as opportunities to do your best, or you can allow challenges to create stress in your life."*
>
> Catherine Pulsifer

Awareness Questions — Embracing Change

Ask Yourself:

> ➢ What are my attitudes and beliefs about change? Do I believe I can easily embrace change and benefit from it?

> ➢ What are more empowering beliefs and attitudes I can emphasize to support myself as a Change Master?

> ➢ Do I have any beliefs that might limit my success in embracing change? How can I turn them around?

"To anticipate the future we need to invent it."

Alan Kay

Mastering Change

As we've discussed, you can either be a victim of change or a master of change. I prefer to embrace change and live in such a way that change enlivens and enriches my life. You can too. It just depends on a shift of attitude as discussed in the previous section and in a set of skills you are learning from this chapter and other parts of this book.

By thinking and acting in appropriate ways you can master and be a leader of change in your life. Change is about learning, and as you've seen in Chapter 3, learning is a wondrous friend to happiness. I really can't repeat and encourage you enough with this. Embrace learning and embrace change. Your life will spiral upwards as you do.

Changing to Stay the Same — Clinging to the Past

Have you ever noticed those people who seem to be mired in the past? At one of the organizations I've consulted to for over 20 years there's an individual who is exactly the same today as he was when I first met him. He dresses the same, talks the same, acts the same and has the same haircut. It's amazing. In a world of massive change, he has managed to remain as if he is locked in a time-warp.

Now think about this. In the last 20 years, the world has changed massively. In my short lifetime I've seen milk and bread being delivered to our door via horse and cart when I was a child, through to the dying off of home delivery of those commodities and processes. Now we have racing cars that can do 0 — 100 mph in less than 3.6 seconds. And I can order my weekly organic groceries via the internet and have them delivered free of charge to my door by courier. All in less than half a human lifetime. It's a world of amazing and accelerating change.

And with all this amazing change, the individual referred to above has managed to *change to stay the same*. Yes, that's right. For him to be able to stay locked in the past, in a world of massive change, he has to actively (though unconsciously) change to stay the same. It's an incredible skill!

Really, he is in some senses a change master. ☺ The only thing is… he doesn't realize his incredible skills at changing to stay the same. What's more, he uses his unconscious competence in change mastery to stay locked in to a past that is no longer relevant. The truth is, where once he was a key player in the organization, now he commands little respect. He is sidelined in a dead-end role and has

Too much, too SOON!

spiraled down in self-respect. He is bored and is given no opportunities for change and advancement because he has made it obvious to management that he is not someone who embraces change and growth.

Yet, he is capable of making amazing changes in order to stay the same. It's like an old guy I saw the other day in the centre of the City. He was a wizened little fellow in his 70's, attired in an old suit, with his hair slicked back with hair-oil. Now, when I was a young child, back in the 1960's, it was the fashion for men to use hair-oil to slick back their hair. It was the cool thing to do. This guy has continued to follow the same fashion and pattern for the last 50 or so years. Incredible. I didn't even think you could buy hair-oil anymore. Think of the skill this old guy needs to be able to continue to source and use the same product for all those decades. All so he can stay the same.

For me these are more than funny stories. I use them to remind myself to keep changing, evolving and moving forward.

Rather than using your skills as a change master to stay stuck in the past, how about using them to lead the changes that are happening in your world! Change is going to happen, so anticipate those changes by leading them in the directions you want them to go. Whether it's at work, in the clubs and organizations you are a member of, in your circle of friends or at home, continue to lead positive, generative change. It's an orientation and attitude that reaps many, many rewards.

Beginner's Mind

Have you noticed how kids assimilate new technologies and take on board changes so easily and with so much gusto? Kids love new things. In NLP we have an expression we use to describe a powerful way of looking at the world. It's called *'seeing the world through the wide eyed curiosity of a child'*. It's so true. Children are filled with an insatiable curiosity and passion for learning and trying new things. They love to play and make a game out of change.

In the philosophy of Zen Buddhism, there is a technique called *'Beginner's Mind'*. This is a technique that allows you to open your mind and see things anew — to return to that wide eyed curiosity state. The idea of beginner's mind is to temporarily set aside all your opinions, ideas, cherished beliefs and mindsets and explore the world with a fresh awareness.

Through a state of *"I don't know"* — that is, by actively doing *'not- knowing'* — you are able to see and try things that you would otherwise have missed. You open yourself to new possibilities. You open yourself to change more easily.

The message from this Zen wisdom is to use beginner's mind in times of change. Look at changes that are thrust upon you with a fresh mind, rather than through pre-conceived prejudices. This will support you in finding the opportunities hidden in the challenges of change.

> *"In the beginner's mind there are many possibilities, but in the expert's there are few."*
>
> Shunryu Suzuki-Roshi

🛠 Thinking Tools — Beginner's Mind

See the world through the wide eyed curiosity of a child.

Success as Failure

Finally, let's look at another reason why people stop embracing change. It's success. Yes, success. Success can make you complacent and lazy. Once you've figured out how to achieve success in some area of life, you tend to repeat your behaviors. If it works, why change it? Well, your success can become your failure. It seduces you and mires you into doing the same thing in the same way again and again. It stops you from trying new things. Success in one area of life can also place other areas of your life out of balance.

The NLP Generative Model of Change says that regardless of how good or successful things are, you can always improve and evolve. This is an important idea and one worth thinking deeply about. Make sure your success doesn't become your failure. Continue to try new ways and do things differently. It will keep you fresh and alive. A Master of Change always continues to evolve, change and adjust. Remember, true success involves choice and learning. So make sure you continue to make the most of your life by changing in new generative ways.

🛠 Thinking Tools — Success and Failure

Your success can become your failure.
So continue to learn, change and evolve.

Simplifying and Valuing your Life

In times of overload and with so much happening in our lives, we need to learn to simplify where we can. Yes, you need to embrace change but that doesn't mean you have to fill your life with noise, chaos and clutter.

In fact, one of the keys to coping with *'too much, too soon'* is to prioritize your life, get clear about your values and what's most important to you and focus your energies and time there.

The majority of people don't know explicitly and specifically what's most important to them. They don't know their hierarchy of values. Values are those things you'll spend time, energy, resources and money to move towards or away from. Most people cannot consciously tell you their top 10 values in life.

Think about this. Your values determine what you'll focus on and what you'll do in life. Values help you make decisions. They direct your life. Yet can you tell me right now what your top values are, and in what order they lay in terms of importance?

You obviously can't easily prioritize your time, energy and life if you haven't decided what the most important qualities and things you want in life are. Priorities imply values. To be able to simplify your life and get the most beneficial use of your limited time, money, attention and resources you absolutely need to *'value your life'*. You need to get clear about your values and what the hierarchy is for them. Decide what's the most important value, the second most important and so on.

The clearer your values are to you, the more conscious you are of them and the more able you are to articulate them, the more power they'll bring to your life. In modeling successful people, NLP found they are incredibly clear on their values and the order of importance of them. Clarity of values directionalizes your unconscious mind and leads to what appears to be magical effects. It's not voodoo or magic. It's the power of the Reticular Activating System — your mind's attentional filtering system — to directionalize your energies and resources in achieving your values and outcomes. It's the secret of *'the secret'* and it's also the power and effect of self-fulfilling prophecies. Many, many books have been written about the power of clarity and focus on values and outcomes. So make use of this to help yourself remove the clutter and overload from your life.

It's really very simple:

- ☑ Identify what's most important to you
- ☑ Eliminate everything else

Start right now!

Eliciting Your Values

Grab a pen and some paper, and write out what you think and feel are the most important things in life for you. Is it health? Love? Adventure? Learning? What are the things that make life worthwhile for you? What's important to your heart? Get them on paper. Make a mindmap. Write them in whatever order they come to you. Or put them on sticky notes so you can move them around.

Note the difference between Content Values and Process Values. Content Values are the *'things'* you want in life, like love, health, friends, family, wealth, adventure etc. They are the *'whats'* of life.

Process Values are the qualities by which you want to achieve the *'whats'*. They are the *'hows'* of life. For example, honesty, integrity, courage, flexibility are all *'hows'*. They are the qualities you want to bring to the way you live your life.

I like to make two separate lists. One for the Content Values and a separate one for the Process Values. Once you have your list(s) it's time to prioritize your values in a hierarchy. Ask yourself:

"If I could only have one thing in life, what would it be?" Circle it on the list as number one. Then ask, *"If I could have 2 and only 2 things, what would the second value be?"*

Continue till you've prioritized your list(s). Then re-write the lists so that the number one value is at the top, and so on.

Now memorize your hierarchy of values. Put your list(s) up high on a wall somewhere in your house or office. Make them bright and bold and colorful. Refer to them often and keep them updated as you grow, learn and evolve through life. Hold them deep in your heart and clear in your mind.

And most importantly, use your values hierarchy to organize your life and make decisions. If health is on your list as one of your highest values, and adventure is a lower value, then make sure that none of your adventures do damage to your health. Use your values as a filter to decide where to place your time, skills, behaviors, attention and energies.

Tips for Simplifying Life

Based on values, here's some tips for simplifying your life:

1. **Remove clutter from your life**

    It takes time and energy to keep possessions in working order, dusted and looked after, so get rid of stuff you don't really need or doesn't align with your key values.

2. **Evaluate your commitments**

    Learn to say *"no"*. Don't overload your schedule. Use your values to decide what's important to do and what you can say no to.

3. **Use entertainment media wisely**

    Turn off your TV and limit the amount of wasted time aimlessly listening to radio, mobile phone texting or surfing the web. Before indulging in mind-numbing media, check your values and see if there's something of higher value that you may not have done. For example, are your kids or family more important? Is your health of higher value than entertainment? If so, go share some valued time doing an outdoor activity with the people you love.

4. **Make time for yourself**

    Commit to yourself. Make time to relax, exercise, meditate and re-vitalize yourself. To cope with the stressful pace of life and change, you need some quiet space. So make time to read books that uplift you and make sure you give yourself regular peace and solitude.

5. **Automate repetitive tasks**

    Automate the ongoing repetitive tasks of life. For example, setup automatic bill payments so you don't have to waste time on these boring mechanical tasks. Simplify as many tasks as you can. There are a lot of amazing tools and devices that make jobs quicker and easier. Make use of them.

6. **Live a low-footprint life**

    Live within and beneath your means. Studies show that the majority of self-made millionaires are frugal. Choose lower cost options as often as possible and save as much as you can. That way you won't waste a huge amount of your life working to pay for things you can't afford.

7. **Listen to your heart**

    Your heart-mind has wisdom. Talk to it, ask it for guidance and listen to what it tells you. When you are clear about your values, the whole of your mind/body will work to help you live up to them. Simplify and value your life and you'll find that *'too much, too soon'* will become a thing of the past.

> "Besides the noble art of getting things done, there is the noble art of leaving things undone. The wisdom of life consists in the elimination of non-essentials."
>
> Lin Yutang

☑ Success Strategy — Halving the Crap

This great success strategy comes from Jonar C. Nadar in his entertainingly named book '*How to Lose Friends & Infuriate People*'. It's a useful and easy to implement strategy for eliminating things that don't add value to your life:

1. Assess your time and how you expend it. Start by halving and removing everything that doesn't add value to your life. By halving the things and processes you know are unproductive or negative, you'll better manage your time. By ridding yourself of time-consuming life-wasters, you'll have more time to do the things you really want to do. The key to this process is that it's easier to halve something than to give it up completely in one big step.

2. Time-wasters are life-wasters. Anyone or anything that wastes your time is wasting your life. Give no time to life wasters. Start by halving and then halving again the time used with the things and processes that don't add value. Continue to halve them till you've removed them completely from your life.

Making Effective Decisions

One of the challenges of our massively expanding and accelerating world is that we are provided with growing amounts of choice and possibility. We are bombarded with increasing levels of information and opportunities. This is great, but the more choices there are, the more confusion and overwhelm they can generate unless you have effective strategies for filtering the information from the noise and making good decisions.

Even a visit to the local supermarket can become a recipe for overwhelm. With over 80 different varieties and brands of breakfast cereal, 160 types of cookies, 125 varieties of fruit juice drinks and too many dairy products to count, it's almost impossible to choose what to buy. The same is true for nearly every other type of purchase we make. Have you been to a shoe store lately? So many different types and styles. Each with new and improved features. And the internet now allows you to shop 24 hours a day from around the world and from the comfort of your home, with purchased items shipped quickly to your door. Do a search on any item, no matter how unusual or arcane and you'll find hundreds to choose from. So with so much choice, how do you decide?

Satisficing versus Maximizing

Positive Psychology researcher Dr. Barry Schwartz and his colleagues have examined the effects of too much choice on happiness. They found that boundless choice can lead to paralysis and misery. They also discovered a very effective strategy for evading the stress and problems of excessive choice.

When making decisions, most people do what is called *'maximizing'*. This is a rational decision process where you attempt to maximize the fit with your required criteria and outcomes. For example, if you were buying tires for your car, you would attempt to get the best tires according to your requirements. If price is a major factor, along with longevity, you'd do your best to get the cheapest tire that will provide the longest mileage. On the other hand, if you want a tire that has the best grip and price is no concern, then you'd look for the stickiest tire on the market and buy that.

The problem is, there are so many tires on the market, with so many overlapping features, yet with so much individual difference amongst them, it's virtually impossible to get a single absolute best. Typically you end up with three or four potential candidates and then agonize over which one to choose.

In the case of tires, it's a relatively trivial situation. But what about all the important decisions in life. Where and what you'll do for work? Who to live your life with? What to invest in? Where you'll live? What education to choose for yourself or your kids? There's so many choices, so much opportunity. You'll never manage to maximize those decisions. There's just too many overlapping possibilities, and you'll never have all the information you require. Indeed, if you take too long to make some decisions, the world will change and the decisions will no longer be relevant.

In his research, Barry Schwartz found that some people use a very effective decision strategy that he called *'satisficing'*. These people were more able to make decisions in the face of increased choice and were more likely to be satisfied and happy with the results of their choices. People who did *'maximizing'* on the other hand had much more difficulty in making choices, were more stressed and much more likely to suffer regret and depression over their choices.

The following Success Strategy will tell you about satisficing, what it is, and how to use it to cope in a world of growing choice.

> *"Nothing is so exhausting as indecision, and nothing so futile."*
>
> Bertrand Russell

☑ Success Strategy — Satisficing versus Maximizing

This technique, based on the work of psychologist Dr. Barry Schwartz, and detailed in his excellent book *'The Paradox of Choice: Why More Is Less'*, will help you make decisions without being overwhelmed by the huge number of choices we are faced with in our modern lives.

1. In any situation where you need to make a choice or decision, start by identifying the desired values, outcomes and features you require in the sought item (e.g. a computer, a car, a house, a spouse, etc).

2. Next, look for a choice that fulfils these criteria and values.

3. Finally, when you find an option that fulfils your criteria, choose it and end the search. In other words, satisfice rather than maximize your choice.

4. The idea is to control your expectations by removing excessively high expectations. This will make the process of choosing easier and still meet your minimum requirements.

5. The process is also designed to prevent regret and disappointment resulting from focusing on trying to choose the *'absolute best'*. You will never find perfection, so resolve to be satisfied once you've found a choice that fulfils your minimum required outcomes and criteria. In this way you'll attain everything you want, make the decision less stressful and easier and not do regretting of foregone attractive features.

6. Lastly, focus your attention on the benefits of the choice and feel happy about your great decision. In this continually changing world, satisficing really is the smart choice.

Strengths & Values In Action

Use the following table to determine which strengths, qualities and values to focus on and amplify in your life to support the processes and skills of happiness. Also notice if you have any elements of the absence, opposite or exaggeration of these strengths and remove them from your behaviors and your life.

Enemies to happiness	VIA Strength
Stressing	Vitality
	Self-regulation
Unclear Values	Perspective/Wisdom
Confusion	Judgment
Inflexibility	Creativity

📋 Notes from the Field — Happiness in the Skye

Perched on a cliff top, nestled amongst magnificent gardens overlooking the deep azure blue of the Pacific Ocean, I asked Ellie, what the Enemies to Happiness are in her experience:

- *Being driven by the desire for material objects*
- *Lack of sensitivity*
- *A need for too much control and scheduling*
- *Lack of perspective — not asking yourself "does it really matter".*

Ellie runs a Boutique B&B called Skyescape. The property is located atop Table Cape in Tasmania, Australia's southern most island state. The vista from her Japanese inspired property is magnificent. It's beautiful, peaceful and awe inspiring. People come from all around the world to visit and enjoy the delightful and luxurious experience of Skyescape.

Ellie and her partner Brian chose to escape from high-profile hectic jobs, to build and live an alternative life-style. Away from the hype and pressure. They also get to see a lot of people, both the happy and the sad, who come to relax, unwind and enjoy. So they've a lot of life experience to draw from when they share their ideas on happiness. And what's most important they've put actions to their words. They live the philosophies and ideas that they describe.

So, in Ellie's words, what's the secret to achieving more happiness in your life?

- *Contemplate what 'IS' — smell the roses and revel in each step of the way*
- *Make time for all those people you care about*
- *Embody 'compassion with dispassion' — help others without becoming bound up in the ego trip of being the helper*
- *Always do new and interesting things — live your creativity and passion.*

☞ Remember This

✓ We live in a world of massively accelerating change. Support yourself to cope with this and buffer yourself against stress by using positive emotions to build resilience.

✓ Pattern-interrupt unconscious stressing and tap into the wisdom of your heart and gut brains by practicing Balanced Breathing to bring your body and mind back into a relaxed balance.

✓ Become a Change Master and embody attitudes that embrace change as a challenge and opportunity.

✓ Simplify your life by getting clear about your values and using them to remove clutter from your life and directionalize your outcomes and decisions.

✓ Make effective decisions by satisficing rather than maximizing.

ⓘ Extra Info

Refer to www.enemiestohappiness.com for

- more information about the material covered in this chapter
- additional reading and references for this chapter

Avoiding the Enemies to HAPPINESS

Chapter 7

Piss me off, pay the PRICE

☺ *You will learn to*

- ✓ Overcome anger and aggression and respond more generatively

- ✓ Accept responsibility for your emotions and control your emotional state

- ✓ Resolve conflict

- ✓ Achieve your outcomes in a more positive way

Piss me off, pay the PRICE

Conflict is inevitable in life. However, anger, aggression and retribution are dysfunctional responses that lead to a cycle of increasing violence and damaging behavior. These negative emotions and responses are absolute enemies to happiness. You cannot experience joy and happiness while in a state of anger, hate or intolerance.

There are much better ways to resolve conflict and achieve your outcomes in life. In this chapter you'll explore how to control your emotional state and how to respond generatively so that you dissolve conflict, anger and revenge before they *'happen'*.

Enemies to your Happiness

✘ Anger, hostility, aggression and violence

✘ Intolerance and inflexibility

✘ Negative emotions of revenge and retribution

✘ Lack of state control

Angering Yourself

Anger can be a normal, healthy emotion when it helps you respond appropriately to danger. The problem is, we are seldom in real danger and when anger is used as a response or motivation to perceived injustice it can lead to an escalation between yourself and others. This hostility can spiral into rage, violence and retribution. As one anger management expert put it *"the problem is not anger, the problem is the mismanagement and misuse of anger."*

Research shows that anger is rarely a useful way of responding and is more likely to damage your relationships. It's not an effective way of achieving interpersonal outcomes or motivating yourself or others. In most cases, anger is dysfunctional and does more harm than good.

Effects of Anger

Anger, like the emotions of stress, fear and anxiety discussed in previous chapters, triggers the body's autonomic *'fight or flight'* response. This leads to a flooding of your system with stress hormones such as adrenalin and cortisol. It elevates your heart rate, blood pressure and respiration. Initially it focuses your attention, but very quickly it has a negative effect and down-regulates many processes such as attention, memory, immune response and ultimately health. The long term effects of anger include depression, heart disease, cancer, gastro-intestinal disorders, insomnia, stroke and a range of other debilitating health problems.

In one study at Harvard Medical School, researchers found that anger literally breaks your heart — *'a hostile heart is a vulnerable heart.'* In the study of over 1000 men, results revealed that the angriest men were three times more likely to develop heart disease and have heart attacks than those who were calm and relaxed.

Uncontrolled anger can lead to arguments, physical fights, abuse, assault and even self-harm. Controlled anger can be equally destructive. Anger causes resentment, undermines relationships and increases the likelihood of further negative emotion.

It's obvious that anger and feelings of retribution are complete enemies to happiness. There's just no way to fill your life with joy and happiness when you are feeling angry and pissed off with either yourself, with others or with the world.

> *"Resentment, anger, frustration, worry, disappointment— negative emotional states, justified or not, take a toll on your heart, brain and body. Don't let justified emotions rob your health and well-being."*
>
> Doc Childre and Howard Martin, HeartMath Solution

Causes of Anger

It's really helpful to understand the causes of anger.

Anger is an evolved survival emotion that is a response to threat, frustration, hurt, loss or pain. Typically it's produced by your unconscious mind when you feel your boundaries have been transgressed or violated. These boundaries can be physical, emotional or psychological.

Anger is also sometimes used as a motivation to make positive changes — to get yourself to shift or fight back against real injustice. We'll examine this in more detail when we look at how you can use more generative responses to achieving your outcomes. The fact is however, anger rarely achieves positive outcomes.

Anger, like all negative emotions, shuts down your higher

cortical functions. It minimizes your creativity and locks you into restricted, aggressive patterns of thinking and acting. Positive emoting on the other hand broadens and builds creativity and enhances problem solving ability. So anger is unlikely to help you achieve successful outcomes, whereas happiness helps you cope with problems, helps bring into play the most adaptive wisdom of your heart and gut intelligences and enhances your chances of sorting things out.

> *"Anger is a killing thing: it kills the man who angers, for each rage leaves him less than he had been before — it takes something from him."*
>
> Louis L'Armour

Denominalizing Anger

As you know, words are tools you use to think and make sense of the world. So it's vitally important to use them carefully and wisely. The first step in doing this is understanding and being aware of their neuro-linguistic effects — the impacts they have on your mind and body.

Anger is of course a nominalization — a verb disguised as a noun. You don't *'have'* anger. It's not a *'thing'*, like a cup or a coat. It's a process. You don't have anger, you do angering. Whenever something happens to you that *'makes'* you feel angry, what is really happening is that you are doing the process of angering. It's an active process and requires thoughts, feelings and actions to support.

Most people don't think about anger in this way. They don't

realize it's an unconscious competence and a set of ongoing behaviors. They don't perceive there is an internal locus of control. Instead, they vest control in the external element that *'made them angry'*. They prefer to give their control over to someone else or something else — to an external locus of control.

There is power in understanding that all your emotions — your emotings — are generated by your conscious and unconscious minds. Your distributed head/heart/gut brains work together to make sense of the world and generate emotions. These emotings are their best attempt at helping you cope with the world and preparing you to respond.

So it's not accurate or useful to think that certain people or situations *'make you angry'*. What's really occurring is you are doing *angering* with unconscious competence. And once you accept and understand this, you are finally at choice. You can now learn to master the skills necessary to decide what emoting you want to do and what responses will serve you best. This is a key distinction and one you'll come across again and again in this book.

Success is powerfully linked to purpose and outcomes. The clearer you are about your outcomes and the more you take congruent action towards them, the better your chances are of getting the happiness you want from life. The power is in awareness, then interrupting old patterns, followed by learning new competencies, both conscious and unconscious.

Purpose and Outcomes

Overcoming anger really is about purpose and outcomes — about what and how you want to '*do*' yourself. Stop, self-reflect, and get clear about how you want to think, act and feel in your life, on a moment by moment basis.

Any time you find yourself doing angering, STOP! And ask

yourself:

"What is my purpose and outcome here?"

Do you really want to experience the negative feelings of anger? Will anger really serve your purpose? Is anger the best way to achieve your outcome?

Think about a situation from your recent past where you got angry and retributive — a situation where you were pissed off and wanted someone to pay the price for it. What was your real outcome?

Let's explore a couple of examples. I was driving in the City on a busy street, in the middle of peak hour traffic, when a guy in a truck suddenly cut me off and forced me to take evasive action. Obviously, this transgressed my physical boundaries and my cognitive boundaries. Not only was it physically dangerous, it also violated my thoughts and values for safety and courteous driving. I started to do angering. All the fight and flight mechanisms kicked in, my heart started racing, adrenalin flowed and my body tensed.

Now, this could have easily escalated to a road-rage situation. However, overcoming the initial survival response of angering, I paused a moment and examined my outcomes and purpose.

What are my outcomes whilst driving?

- ☑ To travel safely and calmly, with a minimum of stress

- ☑ To enjoy the trip as much as possible

- ☑ To travel as quickly as is reasonable

Given these outcomes, would it serve me to do angering and

raging? No! If I did angering, I'd feel upset and negative. The angry feelings and their effects on my psycho-neuro-immunology would stay with me for hours after the event. Negative emoting would also down-regulate my cognitive and sensory abilities and make the rest of the drive slightly more risky as I'd be less likely to see and react quickly to my environment. Also, if I got into an altercation with the other driver, it would delay my trip and could escalate into a serious and life threatening offence.

So, knowing my outcomes and purpose are to do happiness-ing and to calmly and safely enjoy my driving, I shrugged off the minor annoyance of the other driver's transgression. I had a chuckle at the natural human stupidity that caused the other driver to put his vehicle and happiness at risk. And I stopped the angering in its place, replacing it with a more generative response.

Here's another example. I was talking with a friend when he said something that offended me and made me feel a little angry. Now stop a moment, and re-read that last sentence. *"I was talking with a friend when he said something that offended me and made me feel a little angry."* Notice firstly that my friend didn't offend me, instead I unconsciously did offending of myself over something I heard him say. Secondly, no one makes you angry, rather you do angering of yourself. Let's make sure we put the locus of control where it belongs — within ourselves. Let's give ourselves the choice and control that serves our happiness best.

So, what's my purpose and outcomes for conversing with friends? Well… in part, it's to do high quality relating and to enjoy positive emotional experiences with them. Does angering my self support these outcomes and purpose? Definitely not. It's not high quality relating to do angering with a friend.

By staying focused on outcomes and purpose, and figuring out what the angering is really about, you get more choice and get to respond in ways that align your behavior with your outcomes.

> *"Anger is a signal, and one worth listening to."*
>
> Harriet Lerner

Angering as a Signal

Anger is a signal. It's a useful emotional indicator that your outcomes are not being achieved. Rather than embroiling yourself in the emotional responses of angering and retributing — of pissing yourself off and then paying the price — look at the emotion as a useful information signal. Your unconscious mind is telling you something. Listen to it. Then get focused on your real outcomes and do a more generative response that helps you achieve them.

In the example above, does it serve me to do angering with my friend? No. Instead, I can recognize that people don't always share the same values as me and I can feel happy that my friend is a unique person with the right to his opinion. If what he's said upsets me too much, I can talk openly and honestly about my feelings and we can explore together the underlying issue that is causing the difference between us. In this way the friendship grows stronger. That's my real purpose and outcome. To do wonderful friending. In this way, the initial feeling of anger becomes a valuable signal that triggers the thoughts, feelings and responses for creating more happiness in life.

> *"Revenge does not long remain unrevenged."*
>
> Proverb

The Danger of Vengeance

Vengeance is a seductive enemy to happiness. Anger and retribution are evolved animal responses that come easily and naturally. They seem like sweet paybacks towards those who have thwarted or crossed you, yet they rarely achieve more than either escalating the problem or causing damage to your own health and peace of mind.

Added to this, friends are empowering and add to your happiness while enemies are disempowering and take away from your happiness. The danger of vengeance and retribution is that they create hostility, adversaries and enemies. And every antagonist becomes a negative influence in your life. Even if you never see the person again, they can be working against you.

Most certainly, when you invest time, energy and emotion on anger and vengeance, you create negative unconscious patterns of hatred and negativity that diminish you and influence you unconsciously. Research on the effects of unconscious emotion has found that negative emotional responses can remain active in your unconscious mind and have lasting effects on behavior, mood and preference judgments.

> *"Revenge is the sword that wounds the one who wields it!"*
>
> E. C. McKenzie

The neural networks of our brains are patterning systems. They take inputs and form patterns from them. They evolved to enable your organism to repeat learned behaviors. Every time you perform a thought, feeling or action, it increases the probability that you will perform that thought, feeling or action again. That's how your multiple brains work.

🛠 Thinking Tools — Repetition

Repetition leads to repetition. The repetition of a thought or action increases the probability of repetition.

Think about it this way… when you do retributing and vengeance-ing, you are practicing and building neural circuits and unconscious competencies in strong negative emoting. As you've seen, negative emotions are damaging to long term health and have ongoing negative influences on your emotional and cognitive well-being. So you really don't want to build patterns and skills of angering or retributing in your life.

The very real danger of vengeance is that it damages your own peace of mind and happiness. Do you really want to amplify the processes and skills of these harmful emotions?

In the heat of the moment, vengeance and retribution may appear sweet, but they do more harm to you than to the other person. When you act out *'piss me off, pay the price'* you damage your health and happiness and end up being the one that pays the real and ongoing price.

I hope you are now convinced that anger and retribution are horrible enemies to happiness. Shun them with all your heart and mind. In their place, focus on positive emotions and responses. Find more useful ways to achieve your interpersonal outcomes. Refuse to pay the price of these dangerous negative emotions and instead make your life and feelings flourish through a commitment to forgiveness, patience, calm-abiding and positivity.

Control and Choice

As you've read many times in this book... never ever give away your choice and control. Giving away control is an enemy to happiness.

> *"He who angers you conquers you."*
>
> Elizabeth Kenny

When you let someone anger you — when you do angering of yourself — you've let them conquer you and given away your control to them. What's more, if you let them anger you so much that you respond with violence or aggression, then you've truly shown how incompetent you are as a person.

There's a great thinking tool I learned many years ago from the famous writer Isaac Asimov. Isaac said that *"violence is the last refuge of the incompetent"* and he is right. Violence shows that you have allowed your emotions to master you rather than the other way around. Violence is a base animal survival instinct that is mediated by the lower regions of your brain. Our head-brain is made up of three functional brain regions, each with their own structures that evolved over time.

Central to the core of the brain, lying in the stem, is the reptilian brain. This part of the brain evolved first, and we share it with reptiles like lizards and snakes. It's the part of the brain that regulates our survival processes such as breathing and heartbeat.

Surrounding the reptilian brain is the mammalian brain. This is the emotional brain and is responsible for the fight and flight response. It mediates and controls our emotional responses to the world.

On top of these two brains, and most recent in evolutionary terms, is the neo-cortex. This is the grey matter of the brain that is the source of our higher thinking processes. It's responsible for language and cognition.

Whenever you get stressed or angry, your brain down-regulates and switches off the newer cortical processes, kicking down to the mammalian and reptilian responses. So violence really is an incompetent response. It's a primitive response from the evolutionarily primitive parts of your brain.

I use Asimov's thinking tool to help me remember to stop and search for more intelligent, creative and generative responses to the negative situations of life. Violence just begets more violence. Anger encourages retribution. Hate more often leads to hate. On the other hand, compassion and forgiveness generate their likeness. Kindness leads to kindness in return. Happiness in life is served by positive emotions. So use Asimov's thinking tool to help you live more intelligently and competently.

🛠 Thinking Tools — Responding Generatively

Violence is the last refuge of the incompetent.

Self-Reflection and Meta-Emoting

Meta-cognition is cognition about cognition. It's thinking about your thinking. It's an important part of self-reflection. Self-reflection also involves feeling an emotion, experiencing it and taking the time to think about and understand it. Thinking about your feelings and thoughts, reflecting on your behaviors and emotions and deciding whether you support them or want to change and improve them are keys to life intelligence. You can produce amazing results in your life by thinking positively and generatively about your emotions and behaviors and then using the NLP Success Strategy to change and adjust.

You literally can also create hell on earth in your own life in the same way. It's the same process, just different content. For example, if you feel angry about something, (that is, if you do angering of yourself over something), and then you get angry about the anger, you set yourself up to spiral out of control. The angering about anger is a meta-emotion — an emotion about an emotion. You need to be very careful about what meta-states you are generating in your mind and body. On the other hand, if you were to feel entertained by the anger, you would find the anger dissipating and not so impactful on your mind, body and behavior. It's a much more useful meta-state to be in and to be doing.

As highlighted earlier, it's all about your outcome and purpose.

What and how do you want to '*do*' yourself? Stop, self-reflect, and get clear about how you want to think and feel in your life, on a moment by moment basis.

The capacity to do meta-cognition is vital for success and deep happiness-ing. Going '*meta*' to yourself and observing your behavior, observing the patterns and quality of your thinking and emoting, is a skill you want to practice and practice and hold as a high process value. Really value this and make it salient in your life. Make the time and space in your life to think about your thinking and feeling. It's a key strategy for overcoming all the enemies to happiness.

> *"Forgiveness is the most powerful thing you can do for yourself. If you can't learn to forgive, you can forget about achieving true success in your life."*
>
> Dr. Wayne Dyer

Pos Ψ Forgiveness and Kindness

Research from Positive Psychology has shown that people who practice forgiveness suffer less anger, depression and hostility. Forgiveness increases happiness. So actively practicing forgiving and living with a spirit and attitude of forgiving is a proven strategy for overcoming the enemies to happiness of anger and retribution.

Kindness has also been shown to reliably increase positive emotion. So next time someone does something that pisses you off, do the kind thing and forgive them. Let it go. You'll not only be kind to them, more importantly you'll be giving yourself the gift of the positive emotions that kindness brings. And remember, as the famous American humorist Josh Billings said *"There is no revenge so complete as forgiveness."* ☺

Managing Your Mind

Ok, you've gotten clear about your outcomes and decided you want to do as much happiness-ing in life as you can. That's the first step. You now have to take congruent action — action that is going to continuously and appropriately support your outcomes.

The truth is though, there are going to be times when something or someone presses your buttons. It is naïve to expect that you are never going to '*get*' angry — to do angering. But every time you do angering, you'll be undermining your outcomes of happiness and joy in life. So what can you do about this?

Your Cybernetic Loop

To overcome this, you need to learn to manage your mind, emotions and behavior. The connections between these are known in NLP as the Cybernetic Loop. You'll remember this from earlier chapters. Your mind and body are connected in a control loop in such a way that what affects one affects the other — your thoughts, feelings and physiology are all connected.

Managing your mind therefore is about managing your thoughts and physiology. Together, these will help you manage your emoting. That's how you'll pattern-interrupt and halt the process of angering and retributing.

The first step in this process is ***anger awareness***.

Recognize the Signs

To begin with, you need to become skillful in recognizing the signs and symptoms of anger in yourself. What are your warning signs? For most people they will include increased pulse, faster breathing and irritable feelings — all indicators of Sympathetic Nervous System dominance. Often these feelings will be felt in and around your chest. Because of the interaction of the heart-brain you may strongly feel the anger around your heart region.

Figure out the Triggers

Also work out what the typical triggers are that fire you up. What are the things that *'piss you off'*? Track for and become aware of these. Analyze and neutralize them where possible using the success strategies provided later in this chapter. For those you aren't able to fully transcend, simply note what they are so you can recognize when they are occurring.

Accept your Reactions

Research shows that accepting your reactions helps the process of managing them. When you fight yourself or beat yourself up for getting angry, you escalate your cybernetic loop. You end up being angry about being angry. This meta-emoting amplifies the state and causes your heart and gut-brains to become more stressed and threatened.

By calmly accepting that you are angry — that you are doing a cybernetic looping process of angering — you neutralize the intensity of the experience and put yourself at choice.

Express your Feelings Appropriately

One of the findings from the psychology of anger management is that talking about the situation is correlated with a decrease in stress and depression. It is much better to discuss your feelings and explore them appropriately with someone supportive and reflect on the insights from the situation, than to ruminate internally about them. Indeed, anger discussion has been found to be linked with feelings of optimism about the situation. So talking it out can really help. Note that this is not the same as arguing it out. You need to learn to express legitimate anger in an effective way. We'll cover this in the section on assertiveness.

Focus on Outcomes

We covered this earlier. Focus on the values and outcomes you want to support in your life. Would you rather be calm and happy or stressed and angry? Talk to yourself — to your unconscious mind — in a loving and supportive way, telling yourself how you want to act and feel.

Take action

Finally take action to do the emoting you value. You can do this through appropriate breathing and adjusting your physiology and behavior to match your outcomes. You can also support your outcomes through challenging negative thoughts and exploring those that are more positive and supportive.

We'll cover both of these Success Strategies in the coming sections.

↻ Deeper Understandings — The language of angering

As discussed in Chapter 1, there are three basic modeling processes we use to create our maps or models of the world.

These are:

> ➢ Deletion

> ➢ Generalization

> ➢ Distortion

Each of these modeling processes has language elements that are indicators of the underlying process. In NLP, these language distinctions are described by what is called the NLP Meta-Model. By becoming aware of and tracking for these distinctions you can become more precise in your thinking and communicating with yourself and others. You can also gain more choice and control over how you are modeling and generating your world by choosing language that supports your outcomes.

Cause and Effect

Cause and Effect thinking is an example of linguistic distortion. This type of thinking is expressed in utterances that imply or presuppose belief that one thing causes another. When these beliefs don't match the way the world really works, they are semantically ill-formed and impoverish a person's model of the world. In this way, Cause and Effect beliefs limit your perceived choice or ability to act.

The most usual form that Cause and Effect distortions take are statements that a person's actions or environmental circumstances '*cause*' an emotional response in another person.

For example, the thought "*My boss makes me angry*" is a Cause and Effect belief that is inaccurate and not entirely rational. It doesn't match the way the world fundamentally works. No one can cause an emotion in another person. Your response to stimuli is effected within yourself. This is shown by the fact that a number of people can experience the exact same event and yet each of them will generate their own unique meaning and response. What one person gets angry about, another may find humorous.

This is a powerful and useful insight. Emotions are not something that happen to you from external agency. Emoting is a process your mind/body does, with unconscious competence, in response to your environment. You can influence and change how you are emoting and responding. No person or situation causes your emoting. However, if you operate from the semantically ill-formed belief that you do not have control, and that the world causes and creates your emotions, then you limit yourself and remove choice from your world. And that's an enemy to happiness.

To counter this, listen for language, thoughts and beliefs that have the form:

X causes Y

If you hear yourself saying or thinking things such as *"person X pisses me off"* or *"situation Y depresses me"* or *"Z causes me a lot of pain"* then you are distorting your world and limiting yourself with Cause and Effect modeling.

The way to expand your choice is to turn such causal relationships around so they are more sane and rational. Put the locus of control back into the expressions by re-languaging them as *"I cause Y when X."* For example, instead of saying *"My boss makes me mad"*, re-language this as *"I make myself mad about my boss."* Notice this now puts you at choice. You can now focus on outcomes and decide whether this is a response that is useful or whether perhaps there might not be a more generative way to respond. Remember, choice = control.

Blaming Others

The field of Rational Emotive Behavioral Therapy (REBT) has also determined a number of irrational beliefs that people use to anger themselves. Fundamentally, REBT has shown that the process of angering occurs when we blame others for not meeting unreasonable rules or expectations that we have generated in our model of the world. Beliefs such as *"people must never make mistakes or else they are totally useless"*, *"everyone must always treat me fairly"* and *"I must always be totally loved by everyone"* are irrational and unrealistic. Using such language to think about people and situations in this way can only lead to disappointment, anger and low self-esteeming.

Listen for such irrational self-talk and actively dispute it. Replace it with more useful beliefs that match the way the world works. The truth is, people are fallible and will occasionally make mistakes, treat you unfairly, or not meet your expectations.

Getting angry at this is pointless and un-sane. Of course you'd *prefer* that they not do this, but recognize this is just your preference. Don't take yourself and your expectations so seriously. Blame is an enemy to happiness, so listen for it in your languaging and challenge the irrational beliefs that underlay it.

Escalating Anger

Intelligent people do not use words that escalate anger. They understand the power of words and know that anger is an emotion that down-regulates intelligence and creativity.

> Thoughts and expressions such as *"How could they!!!??"* and *"How dare they!!!???"* will only create and escalate the unconscious process of angering.
>
> Really listen carefully to the languaging you are doing (both internally in your head and externally in your world) and refuse to use hateful or vengeful words or expressions that escalate anger.

Awareness Questions — Challenging Negative Thoughts

Ask Yourself:

- ➤ What am I really feeling and why? Do I want to feel this way or would I prefer to feel better than this?

- ➤ What thoughts am I thinking to cause my feelings? What angry, retributive or hateful thoughts am I ruminating over? How best can I challenge these un-useful thoughts?

- ➤ What over-generalizations am I making? Am I using unreasonable rules and attitudes to cause the angering?

- ➤ What are more useful ways of thinking? How can I reframe my thoughts to better serve me? What thoughts and ideas will help me to feel calm, positive and happy?

> *"Argue for your limitations and sure enough, they're yours."*
>
> Richard Bach

Asserting Yourself

There's a world of difference between assertion and aggression. Expressing yourself in a positive and assertive manner is the healthiest way to express angry feelings. Assertiveness is not pushy or demanding, rather it's about being respectful of yourself and others.

Assertion is also very different to passive-aggression. Passive-aggressive behavior involves suppressing your feelings rather than dealing with the situation, and then later finding indirect ways to get back at the person. Passive-aggression is a very negative way of dealing with anger and undermines relationships. It can also damage your emotional and physical health, so it's an enemy to happiness you absolutely must avoid.

The real key in dealing with unfair situations is expressing yourself constructively and respectfully. Just make sure before asserting yourself with others that there is reasonable and objective cause for your feelings — if not, deal with your own unreasonable or irrational beliefs, thoughts and feelings first.

If you're clear the issue is objective and fair, then it is very important you communicate with the person in a way that resolves or dissolves the conflict (or more accurately, that dissolves the way you are conflicting) and moves the relationship forward. We'll explore these skills in the coming sections.

Asserting yourself is really about relating well with yourself and others. It's involves communicating your thoughts, beliefs and feelings in a clear, open and unthreatening way. It's also about considering the beliefs and feelings of others.

The steps for asserting yourself are:

- Get clear about your thoughts, feelings, beliefs and outcomes for the situation

- Express your thoughts, feelings and outcomes in a direct, calm and tactful way

- Be objective and non-judgmental

- Provide constructive feedback and options for how to improve the situation

- Keep your posture and attitude open and relaxed

- Talk at a normal pace and volume and breath evenly

So rather than miring yourself in anger, deal constructively with any unfair situations by directly communicating and negotiating with the person. Begin by stating your issue clearly and specifically. Tell them how you are feeling and how their actions have affected you. Offer a solution and suggest what you'd like them to do. And be open to considering things they may suggest as constructive ways forward. Then give them the time and space to think about what you've said and for you both to take it all on-board.

Remember, be calm and respectful, it's your best chance of influencing others in a positive way.

☑ Success Strategy – Discharging Anger

Anger involves Sympathetic Nervous System arousal. It is a fight and flight response. As such, it mobilizes energy in your body. One very successful way to deal with angering, is to discharge this energy in more useful and generative ways. The following are some suggestions on healthy ways to utilize and release the physiological arousal of anger:

1. **Exercise**, especially aerobic exercise such as running, bike riding, swimming, kayaking etc. will burn off the excess energy and will at the same time remove stress hormones from your body and replace them with positive mood hormones such as endorphins, serotonin and dopamine. Make sure however that you start slow with exercise and only do as much as your fitness and health levels allow.

2. **Laughter**, having a good belly laugh or doing something you really find amusing or fun will help dissipate the negative arousal. Watch or listen to your favorite comedian or movie. Even faking laughter for a couple of minutes can really make a positive shift.

3. **Calming techniques** such as meditation and massage can really help discharge the nervous system arousal. Even having a walk in the park, calmly breathing slowly and evenly and repeating positive emotion words like *"calm abiding, peace, joy, love, relaxing"* will ensure that you interrupt and block any ruminating and can make a real difference to how quickly you come back to a peaceful and centered state.

4. **'StopStress' Breathing** is an *m*BIT technique that uses the fact that breathing strongly influences the Autonomic Nervous System (ANS). Whenever you breathe in the Sympathetic arm of the ANS is activated and as you breathe out the Parasympathetic arm is in turn activated. So when you are feeling angry, stop, take a breath for 2 seconds in, and 10 seconds out. Repeat 5 times. This will quickly calm you down and allow the Parasympathetic arm of the ANS to quell the Sympathetic dominant state of anger. Then begin to breathe for approximately 6 seconds in, 6 seconds out. This is called Balanced Breathing, and requires the in-breath and out-breath to be of the same duration, and quickly brings the ANS into a beautiful coherent balance i.e. a balance between Sympathetic and Parasympathetic. It is calming and healthful. Add into the breathing process that you imagine with every breath your heart, mind and body filling with a beautiful peaceful loving joy. Breathe this into your heart, up to your head and then down to your gut.

> *"The greatest predictor of failure is the inability to interact harmoniously with other human beings."*
>
> Dr. Leonard Ingram

High Quality Relating

Success and happiness in life are largely dependent on your relationships — your relating — with others. High Quality Relating is a fantastic friend to happiness. The better each and every one of your relationships are, the better your life will flow.

High Quality Relating is the opposite to '*piss me off, pay the price*'. High Quality Relating never involves anger, hostility, blaming, threatening, demanding, or sarcasm. These are the antithesis of great relating and can only do damage to how another person feels about themselves and about you. Remember the work of Professor John Gottman, discussed in Chapter 5?

In his research, John found there are four powerful destroyers of relationships:

- ✖ **Contempt**
- ✖ **Criticism**
- ✖ **Defensiveness**
- ✖ **Stonewalling**

If you think carefully, you'll see the links between these behaviors and the emotions of anger and revenge.

It's really important you do the opposite of these in all your relationships — all your relatings. Regardless of whether it's relating with work colleagues, friends, family, your beloved or simply an acquaintance, make sure you do more generative and positive behaviors.

Always focus on doing High Quality Relating. Practice forgiving and do appropriate asserting when necessary. Think about other people's values and how you can dovetail with them. Support people and you'll find they'll support you in return.

And remember…

> *"You can have anything you want in life, if you just help enough other people get what they want in life."*
>
> Zig Ziggler

Dissolving Conflicting

One of the key initiators of anger is conflict between people. Once conflict occurs in a relationship, anger is sure to follow.

In the workshop I teach on Conflict Resolution, I start by explaining and exploring how the words Conflict and Resolution are both nominalizations — disguised verbs. There's no such thing as *'conflict'*. Instead, there are just people relating in ways that leads to them conflicting with each other. It's an active process.

This is a very important realization. It places the locus of control where it belongs. It opens up choice and awareness.

I like to get participants of the workshop to think about what the opposite of *'conflicting'* is. Think about it now. What do you think the opposite of conflicting is?

The workshop participants typically come up with terms like harmony, working together, acceptance and rapport. I like to encapsulate all of these into the concept of *'High Quality Relating'* which we explored earlier. When you think about it, High Quality Relating is the antithesis of conflicting. When you are relating really well with someone, when you know their values and you dovetail with them, when you support them, communicate openly with them and really connect, you find that conflict just cannot occur. It's pretty obvious, isn't it.

So in the workshop, rather than teaching the old-fashioned method of conflict resolution that relies on attempting to fix conflict once it has occurred, I prefer to teach the skills of *'Dissolving*

Conflicting' — getting people to relate in high quality ways so that any conflicting is dissolved before it even occurs.

Now, I could write a whole book on Dissolving Conflicting and High Quality Relating, and maybe one day I will. Certainly the workshop takes a whole day in its cut down form, and really needs a couple of days to cement the skills into competencies. In this section we can only just touch on the key components of the strategies and skills. Nevertheless, it's a good start and will give you ideas and things to think about and practice in your relatings with others. Certainly it will help you remove any conflicting that might otherwise have led to angering, and that's a great thing.

Seeking Win-Win

Research from the Harvard Negotiation Project has found that conflict is minimized and greater success is achieved when people seek to negotiate win-win outcomes together. Operating from this perspective means looking for solutions and outcomes that help all parties get what they want. It's about dovetailing options and looking for mutual gains.

To do this, you need to understand your own values and the values of the person you are negotiating or relating with. Then you need to brainstorm ways in which everyone can have their needs and values met.

It's also important to recognize you are dealing with another human being. And all humans have frailties, emotions and their own unique views of the world. Most people endeavor to make the best choices from the options and possibilities available to them. So any time you find yourself in a situation where you are conflicting with another person, you need to search for and understand the positive intentions and needs behind the behaviors. Once you've figured these out, you can then find ways to help the person satisfy those needs, whilst still satisfying your own needs and values. This is the heart of win-win relating.

Understanding Positive Purpose

A really useful thinking tool from NLP is that *"All behavior has a positive intention."* When you operate from this perceptual filter, you begin to see people's behaviors in a whole new light. You start to understand their values and connect with their model of the world. You give yourself the best chance of dovetailing with them.

Let's explore an example. In one of the organizations I consult to there was a Senior Executive who would always interrupt in meetings and mismatch my presentations. It would have been easy to have seen his behavior as antagonistic and hostile and I could have responded in kind, attacking him back and escalating the way we were relating into an ongoing conflict.

Instead, I used the NLP thinking tool to ask myself, *"what is the positive intention behind this behavior?"* I intuited that his behavior may have been an attempt to elicit recognition from myself and others and may also have served the intention to help the group see all sides of the issue at hand.

At the next meeting I was presenting in, I started by mentioning to the group that it was important that we always examine all sides of every issue and that I would be asking people to take on this role at various times during the meeting. After my first point in the presentation, I then turned to this particular Senior Executive and asked him if he would use his experience and business wisdom to point out any issues that might have been missed so far in the presentation.

I could immediately see that he felt valued and validated. He made a couple of minor points and sat back looking very happy and satisfied. I repeated this process a couple more times in the meeting and strangely enough ☺ my friendly Senior Executive became more and more supportive. Instead of mismatching and being disruptive, his behavior changed and he became one of my key supporters within the organization. Through finding the positive intentions in his behavior and doing high quality relating, I dissolved any possible conflicting and turned the relationship around. There was no *'pissing me off'* and no *'paying the price'*. Now, that's the recipe for happiness.

🛠 Thinking Tools – Positive Purpose

All behavior and emotion has a positive intention.

🛠 Thinking Tools – Behavior

People are NOT their behaviors.

Separating People from their Behavior

Another useful thinking tool is that *"People are NOT their behaviors."* Just because someone makes a mistake, does not for example, make them a failure as a person.

Separating people from their behaviors removes the tendency to blame. It allows you to go easy on the person, while not condoning the behavior. It also stops you from character assassinating them.

Using this thinking tool helps avoid criticizing the person and assists you to calmly and assertively negotiate with them and relate together in ways that are win-win.

Criticism as Feedback

Yet another process that can generate conflict is by perceiving criticism in a negative way. This can lead to feelings of anger and a relationship loop that spirals into hostility and negativity.

Remember the NLP Success Strategy that treats all information as useful feedback. In this model there is no such thing as failure — so there's no such thing as criticism. Instead, using this model, you accept criticism as important and useful information. Don't take it personally. Thank the person for their feedback. You'll find they will appreciate your response. Then find the nugget of gold if there is one in the feedback and use it to change and adjust your behavior.

Also remember the NLP thinking tool that *'the meaning of your behavior/communication is the response that you get.'* The meaning that the person is making from your behavior is their meaning and it is valid in their current model of the world. As a communicator, focused on successfully achieving your relationship outcomes, you have just received very useful feedback about the meaning they are making. So use any *'criticism'* as the valuable feedback it is and flexibly change how you're behaving and communicating with the person until you get the outcomes and responses you want. It's your responsibility to achieve your outcomes, not theirs. In this way you'll dissolve any conflicting before it escalates or damages the relationship.

☑ Success Strategy — A Light Heart

This technique uses your heart-brain to dissolve angering and embody an attitude of light-heartedness.

1. One of the causes of anger is taking yourself and situations too seriously. When you take things to heart, you literally perceive them in a way that your heart-brain experiences as threatening and stressful. This leads to anger and hostility. So don't take things to *'heart'*. Don't *'awful-ize'* situations. Don't take life too seriously!

2. Instead, embody an attitude of *'light-heartedness'*. Focus loving feelings of peace and happiness in your heart. Take what happens to you with a healthy sense of humor and flexibility. Fill you heart with light. Relax, let go. Never take things so damn seriously. Instead, practice calmness and light-heartedness.

3. Whenever something happens that triggers feelings of annoyance, anger or transgression, simply stop and breathe peace and calm into your heart region using Balanced Breathing. You'll be surprised at how well this works to diffuse the situation and allows you to respond in a creative and positive way.

⚡ Pattern-Interrupt — Stopping the Process of Angering

The following process combines the ideas and skills described throughout this chapter. Use this to interrupt any angering or retributing. To make this pattern-interrupt effective, make sure you are well aware of your anger signals and indicators.

Interrupt any old unsupportive patterns in your life by:

- If you hear, feel or notice your anger signals, say calmly to yourself 'STOP!', take 3 or 4 deep calming balanced-breaths.

- Recognize and calmly accept that you are angering.

- Decide on how you want to respond — work out what your outcomes are and what values and feelings you'd prefer to be living.

- Take action to embodying your preferred values and outcomes.

- Use the Success Strategies from this chapter to dissipate the energy from the Sympathetic Nervous System arousal that was associated with the angering and to calm your heart-mind and gut brain and soothe them.

- Celebrate your new more positive responses, notice the positive differences and congratulate yourself as you enjoy your increasing patterns of happiness and success.

Strengths & Values In Action

Use the following table to determine which strengths, qualities and values to focus on and amplify in your life to support the processes and skills of happiness. Also notice if you have any elements of the absence, opposite or exaggeration of these strengths and remove them from your behaviors and your life.

Enemies to happiness	VIA Strength
Lack of State Control	Self-regulation
	Bravery
Anger & Hostility	Forgiveness & Mercy
	Kindness
Intolerance	Social Intelligence
	Open-mindedness
Blame & Retribution	Perspective/Wisdom

Notes from the Field — The Heart of Happiness

Dr. Deborah Rozman is a psychologist, author, educator and a key spokesperson for the HeartMath heart-brain system. She serves on the Institute of HeartMath's scientific advisory board and has worked for many years with Doc Childre the key developer of the HeartMath system. I spoke with her about heart-brain research and its links to happiness.

The HeartMath system is an award winning and powerful technology. It is scientifically based and designed to improve emotional, physical and cognitive health and well-being. The HeartMath products provide biofeedback tools to enable users to monitor and control the physiological processes that reflect their emotional state.

Connecting to Deep Happiness

According to Deborah, deep happiness is supported by aligning and connecting with your heart. The scientific underpinnings of this are that when your heart resonates at its natural frequency, your mind and deeper heart-mind become aligned and in synch. This leads to feelings of joy, fulfillment and happiness.

Your heart-brain responds to deeply heart-felt feelings and these positive, nurturing states increase your heart-rate coherence and bring about a balance between mind and heart. As Deborah points out, *"It's all about connecting with values and with your deeper heart. You can have momentary stimulation of happiness for example when you buy a new pair of shoes, but compare that with the deeper and more enduring feelings of happiness when you get a hug from someone you love."*

The more your heart and mind are in synch the more fulfilled you'll feel. *"This is not some 'mushy' idea of heart."* The research shows we have a true heart intelligence and there is a critical link between this and the main trunk-line of our nervous system. That's why our heart is so connected with our centre of being.

Overcoming the Enemies

So what blocks or stops happiness? Deborah believes that this occurs *"when the mind goes outside the wisdom of the heart."* The more we pursue the mind without connection to our heart wisdom, the more we end up feeling disconnected, dull and out of sorts.

As Deborah explains, *"Once basic survival issues are satisfied, it's about heart-mind connectivity. The mind can add a lot of things, but it can't add happiness. For happiness and balance you need to listen to the messages from your heart and align your life and mind with those."*

Your mind generates fear, dwells on grief, blame and judgment. Your thoughts feed these emotions. When you allow your heart to connect and direct your emotions, you'll find it easier to move on to forgiveness, peace and a more holistic connection with the world.

In terms of relationships and happiness, Deborah points out that your first relationship is with yourself; it's between your heart and mind. Get yourself in synch, otherwise you'll continue to see other people in limited, reactive and antagonistic ways. To overcome anger and negativity in your relating with others, *"Listen and speak authentically with the heart."* This is something that needs to be practiced, and the HeartMath systems and tools can help with this.

The Heart of Happiness

The key to happiness according to HeartMath wisdom is to put your deeper heart into all your communications and relationships.

Life today can be stressful, so make use of all of the available tools to overcome this and build the heart of happiness into your life.

☞ Remember This

✓ Anger, hatred and retribution are damaging emotions and behaviors. They have incredibly negative effects on your life. Recognize that angering is a process and that you have choice over how you are emoting.

✓ Angering is a signal. Learn to recognize when it is occurring, accept it and then use the signals to get clear about your purpose and outcomes. Commit to choosing more generative ways to respond to what you are experiencing.

✓ Never give away your control by letting people or situations anger you, and remember — violence is the last refuge of the incompetent.

✓ Revenge is an insidious enemy to happiness. Every time you perform a thought or action, it increases the probability you will perform that thought or action again. So beware of revenging as it will only lead to an escalation of this harmful behavior in your life.

✓ Practice forgiveness, kindness and heartfelt caring to increase your positive emotions and buffer against angering.

✓ Control your mind/body state to stop angering through:

> ➢ Awareness of the triggers, signs and signals

> ➢ Calmly accepting your reactions

> Expressing your feelings appropriately

> Focusing on your outcomes

> Taking action and dealing with the situation assertively and fairly

✓ Resolve conflicting before it occurs by doing High Quality Relating with everyone you meet. Find the positive intentions in their behaviors and then find ways to dovetail with the needs and values expressed in those positive intentions.

ⓘ Extra Info

Refer to www.enemiestohappiness.com for

- more information about the material covered in this chapter
- additional reading and references for this chapter

Avoiding the Enemies to HAPPINESS

Chapter 8

HALF way there...

You will learn to

- ✓ Align all parts of your mind and body
- ✓ Take congruent action
- ✓ Motivate yourself and overcome procrastination
- ✓ Courageously achieve your goals and outcomes

HALF way there...

While it's incredibly important to have inspiring dreams, goals and outcomes in life, it's equally important to actually achieve these. Only getting half way there... only partly achieving your goals and dreams sabotages happiness. Incongruence, inconsistency, procrastination and self-conflict create failure — a definite enemy to happiness and success.

In this chapter you'll learn how to align all parts of your mind and body to support yourself in achieving your goals and outcomes. You'll learn strategies for motivating yourself, overcoming obstacles and encouraging yourself. Congruence and alignment are key skills for happiness-ing. So keep moving and achieving by reading onwards to success.

Enemies to your Happiness

✘ Incongruence, inconsistency and self-conflict

✘ Procrastination, not taking action or following through

✘ Self-sabotage — fear of success and fear of failure

✘ Self-dishonesty

Aligning your Multi-mind

According to the noted Stanford University neuro-scientist and psychologist Prof. Robert Ornstein, we don't have a single unitary mind, rather we are a multi-mind made up of numerous simple and relatively autonomous mini-minds. The cognitive scientist Marvin Minsky calls it a *'society of mind'*.

We appear to experience a single mind and stream of consciousness, but the scientific evidence suggests that this sense of unitary self and consciousness is really a fiction. In reality, our mind is the result of a synthesis of many unconscious processes operating and negotiating together.

Let's examine this idea in a bit more detail. For a start we know we have at minimum three separate brains — the head brain, the enteric or gut brain and the cardiac or heart brain. The head brain itself is also composed of two relatively autonomous functional half-brains — the right and left hemispheres. Within each of these brains, groups of neurons and structures operate, build and perform competencies and unconscious skills. And importantly, these mini-minds communicate with one another to operate the totality that appears as the *'self'*.

This is all very fine when all the parts of your multi-mind, your *'society of mind'* are aligned and congruent. It's problematic however when there's disagreement or dissension in the camp; when parts of your mind are incongruent or at odds with one another. Such incongruence or mismatch undermines your resolve and leads to incongruent behavior and outcomes. You literally sabotage your own success.

We all have experiences of this. Think of times when you've felt torn on a decision. Where one part of you has agreed but another part has not. Notice also that the two '*sides*' of this disagreement are often represented on the two sides of your body. You'll see and hear people say "*on the one hand I feel/want/believe X… but on the other hand I feel/want/believe Y*"; and you'll literally see them hold their hands out as they say this.

In NLP terms, this is a literal descriptor of the unconscious process of their two hemispheres being in disagreement with one another. Remember that the left side of the body is connected to and controlled by the right hemisphere of the brain, and the right side of the body is controlled by the left hemisphere. When the two hemispheres are in disagreement with one another, this incongruence is represented and embodied across the physical body and often experienced as mismatched feelings at the midline of the body.

Think about something you are undecided on now, or something that was important but you were divided about in the past. You'll probably experience exactly what I've just described. Notice also that the left and right brains also communicate to the heart brain and gut brain and lead to feelings of discomfort or disagreement in your gut region or heart region — in your gut brain and heart brain.

Remember the Cybernetic Loop model from NLP that says that the mind and body are connected in a control loop, and what affects one part affects all other parts. When there is disagreement or incongruence within the system of your multi-mind, it leads to incongruence in your feelings and your behavior and physiology.

A great example of this is when someone gives you a gift you really don't like. It's almost impossible to congruently express gratitude and thanks without some non-verbal indicator of your dislike for the gift. In fact, psychologists have developed tools to read the fleeting and small micro-muscle movements that occur whenever you attempt to lie. The part of your multi-mind that knows it hates the gift will fleetingly take control of the muscles in your face and show a micro-expression of disgust before your conscious mind directs the muscles to make a smile and voice your appreciation of the gift. These fleeting micro-expressions are picked up by the other person's unconscious mind and form part of the intuitions that we all use to know when someone is being genuine or not.

Another great example of the effects of incongruence occurs in sport. Golfers are well aware of the *'yips'* — unconscious and involuntary patterns of movement that derail successful shots. Even the most skilful sportsperson knows that if they allow any part of their mind to think a negative thought or focus on failure then their performance will suffer.

> *"A house divided against itself cannot stand."*
>
> Abraham Lincoln

There are two important things to note from this insight about your multi-mind and the effects of incongruence within it. First, if you want success, you need to make sure all parts of yourself are aligned and supportive of that success. Incongruence and inconsistency are enemies to happiness. You need to learn to detect incongruency within your society of mind and be able to negotiate with all parts of your mind to bring them into alignment and agreement.

Secondly, incongruence within a person's multi-mind is usually embodied and expressed (typically outside of their conscious awareness) in their physical stance, their micro-muscle movements and facial expressions and in their non-verbal communication. You can learn to notice and track these signals and detect when someone is not fully supportive of the outcomes you are working towards with them. Equally, any incongruence you are feeling will be non-verbally expressed to other people's unconscious minds and will undermine your chances of successful outcomes with them. In part, this is how self-fulfilling prophecies work within human relationships. We literally express and communicate all the messages from our multi-mind, and get responses from others that recapitulate our expectations.

So I hope you are fully and totally realizing right now, with all your heart and mind, all the parts of your society of self, that congruence is a key and vitally important skill. You need to become a master at *'congruence-ing'* — at tracking for and generating congruence and alignment within your mind/body. And with that in mind, let's learn about detecting congruence and incongruence signals.

> *"Your life changes the moment you make a new, congruent, and committed decision!"*
>
> Anthony Robbins

Congruence and Incongruence Signals

Congruence is the experience of being in rapport with all parts of your mind, body and behavior. It occurs when there is an internal and external consistency. Incongruence is of course the opposite of this.

When you are congruent or when you are incongruent, there are feelings and signals that occur in your body and brain. By paying careful attention you can learn what these signals are. They may be specific feelings in parts of your body or certain tonalities or sounds in your internal dialog. The signals can also occur in your internal and external visual field. For example, some people generate fuzzy or cloudy internal images when they are incongruent, and experience crystal clarity in their visual representations when they are congruent.

In one fascinating experiment, researchers at the University of Bath in the UK, induced signals of incongruence between muscle movement intention and actual movement by placing a mirror between the limbs of subjects while they moved their limbs. This created incongruence between actual movement of the limb as directed by one part of the brain and the visual feedback experienced in another part of the brain via the mirror image. The incongruence between motor intention and movement lead to 66% of subjects experiencing feelings of numbness, pins and needles, moderate aching and in 15% of subjects, actual pain. This research shows how strong an effect incongruence signals and feelings can generate.

Learning your Signals

The key is to learn what the signals are for you — to learn how your unconscious mind signals the process and experience of congruence and incongruence.

To do this, think of 3 or so times in the past when you were totally aligned and congruent and a similar number of situations or experiences in which you were massively incongruent or in conflict. You may find it easiest to write these onto a piece of paper.

Then as you recall each event, really associate back into the memory of the experience, and note the thoughts, pictures, feelings and sounds. Look for patterns that are similar within each of the congruent and incongruent experiences.

For most people, incongruence is signaled by a feeling — often sinking, squeezing or sometimes sharp — somewhere in the region of their stomach or heart. Congruence is often signaled by a rising, expanding or even a warm feeling in the chest.

Whatever the signals are for you, just notice and memorize them. They are messages from your system that either all is well, or there is an issue, a disagreement within your multi-mind, and you need to attend to it. These are very powerful and useful messages that can serve you in achieving success and happiness.

🛠 Thinking Tools — Cybernetic Loop

Everything that happens inside a person, has a physiological effect observable on the outside. The mind and body are connected in a Cybernetic Loop.

Generating Congruence

There are many ways to generate congruence. At their heart though, they all rely on aligning your multi-mind to a common purpose or set of values. Purpose and values are key to all aspects of success and happiness, and you'll see that throughout this book we keep coming back to them.

A very powerful and enduring way of generating congruence is to use the NLP technique of Reframing. This technique was used in Chapter 4, and is also described fully in the following Success Strategy. It's based on negotiating with the various parts of yourself that are in disagreement and getting them and the rest of your multi-mind to align around an agreed purpose. When you focus on a truly compelling purpose or value, it's easy to align all parts of yourself.

Another potent technique for aligning two parts that are disagreeing, is to perform what in NLP is called a *'visual squash — collapsing anchors'*. In this technique you anchor or associate each part on to your hands and then collapse them together by clasping your hands together. It's very, very simple, fast and quite powerful. We'll cover it later in detail later in this chapter. I've coached many people with it and seen amazing shifts as parts were aligned and long-standing incongruency dissolved in seconds.

Whichever technique you use, be sure to use the skills and knowledge you gained from the previous section on tracking your congruence signals. Once you are adept at listening, feeling and watching for congruence and its converse, along with negotiating and aligning your multi-mind, you'll find that life gets easier, and that you gracefully continue to spiral upwards from success to success. Happiness-ing is a skill that in large measure relies on ongoing congruence and alignment between all parts of your manifold multi-mind. Your happiness very much depends on support from your heart brain, your gut brain and the many parts of your head brain. So make sure you track for and remove incongruence in your thoughts, behaviors and decisions. Make congruence an important and guiding value for your life.

🛠 Thinking Tools — Congruence

Congruence is vital for Happiness & Success!

🔎 Awareness Questions — Finding Incongruence

Ask Yourself:

➤ Are there any areas or contexts in my life in which I am incongruent, confused or at odds within myself?

➤ Do I have any values that don't match with each other or are in conflict?

➤ Do I have any beliefs that might limit my success in achieving my dreams, goals and outcomes?

☑ Success Strategy — Negotiating Congruence

In NLP there is a technique called the Six-Step Reframe that is used to communicate with the unconscious parts responsible for any particular process or outcome in your life. In this technique you literally talk to parts of your multi-mind and ask what their positive intention is. You speak to the parts of your mind and ask what positive thing they are trying to achieve for you. You then negotiate between all the parts so that you find ways to achieve the positive intentions.

There is a presupposition in NLP that every behavior has a positive intention. By exploring and finding the underlying positive intention of each part, you can then negotiate within yourself to find a better and more generative way of achieving and satisfying the positive purpose or need that exists in your life.

Six-Step Reframe

The steps of the Six-Step Reframe technique are:

1. **Identify the parts, behaviors or signals you want to align**

2. **Communicate with the parts responsible for the behaviors or signals**

   Literally talk to each part. Respectfully ask *"Will the part responsible for X communicate with me consciously now?"* Then carefully notice the signals, messages or responses you get. It may be words, sounds, images or feelings.

3. **Determine the positive intention of each part**

   Thank the parts for communicating with you and ask each of them *"Please tell me what your positive intention is. What are you trying to do for me?"* Notice the responses you get. What intuitions or messages does each unconscious part respond with?

4. **Ask the parts to work with the whole of your unconscious mind, including your creative parts, to generate new and more generative ways of accomplishing your outcomes**

Ask each part to communicate internally with the other parts of your mind to find new behaviors and ways of achieving the positive purpose.

5. **Ask each part if it will agree to use the new behaviors and choices rather than the old behavior to achieve its outcome**

   If you don't get a yes signal from the part, then return to step 4 until all parts of you have worked together to find values, behaviors and choices that work and that the part in question will support.

6. **Do an ecology check of all parts of your mind**

   Ask *"Does any other part object to my new choices?"* If you get a response that indicates there is an issue of ecology or potential negative consequences then return to step 3 and ask what positive intentions this new part is attempting to communicate about and work with it and the original part to generate behaviors and choices that work for the whole of you.

As indicated in Chapter 4, this technique can work quite powerfully. You'll be surprised at just how clearly parts can communicate. You need to trust your unconscious mind and work with it respectfully. It's trying to do the best it can with the knowledge and skills you have at this point in your life. You may need to support yourself with new skills and patterns, and reading and studying this book is a great step in that direction.

Do this technique in a quiet place. Relax, calm your mind and then gently talk to the parts of your mind that have a message for you. Be very positive and explicit in your communicating. With trust, you'll be surprised at how amazing this communication process can be. It's about getting in touch with your intuitions. It's about hearing the messages from your gut brain, heart brain, non-dominant hemisphere and other distributed intelligences around your brain and body. It's about aligning all parts to support common values and purpose. By looking deeply within and explicitly communicating with the parts of your multi-mind, you can gain important insights and messages from your unconscious mind. You can also directionalize the whole of your multi-mind to work together for success and happiness.

☑ Success Strategy — Aligning Parts

This technique uses the NLP technique of *'visual squash — collapsing anchors'* to align two parts of your multi-mind that are in disagreement, conflict or are not congruent. Use it anytime you want to feel and act more congruently and aligned.

1. Hold out your hands in front of you, with your palms facing upwards.

2. On your left hand, make an image or representation of one of the parts that was in conflict, or of what its outcome is. Really focus on the image. The image may be a still picture, a movie, it might even be the image of a word; just as long as the image is meaningful to you. If you don't find it easy to visualize clearly an image in your hand, then simply perform the exercise by acting *'as if'* you are seeing a clear representation. You'll find the strategy works just as well whether you see the

image clearly and solidly or not.

3. On your right hand, make an image or representation of the other part that was in conflict, or of what its outcome is. Really focus on this image.

4. While continuing to look from hand to hand — from image to image — slowly bring your hands together until you can clasp them together at the midline. See the two images coalesce together. Then bring your clasped hands together to your heart. Really feel the two parts coming together and calmly warming your heart. The parts and their outcomes are both important and deserve your love and respect.

5. You may notice that as your hands finally touched, you felt an interesting sensation at the midline of your body. Many people feel this in the gut or heart regions. It's a signal that your parts are integrating, negotiating and aligning together.

6. Now test for congruence by thinking about the issue you were previously in conflict about. You should find strong signals of congruence and no dissonance feelings. Repeat the exercise if you are not completely congruent. Once you've achieved full congruence, you'll find that the parts work together and stay aligned towards your goals and happiness.

Excellence versus Perfection

One of the ways that people stop themselves from completing or following through on their dreams and outcomes is via a quest for perfection. If they can't have or achieve perfection they give up or stall. Believing you have to do something perfectly is a recipe for stress and disappointment.

More importantly... perfection doesn't exist in the world. Let me say that again: *"Perfection doesn't exist in the world!"* Perfection is an ideal, a concept, an abstraction.

Nothing is ever perfect. Focusing on perfection can create a lot of anger, frustration and negativity. A need for perfection can be a recipe for unhappiness. Perfection is merely an idea, it is not real. Instead, a much more useful focus is on *Excellence*.

Excellence implies fitness for purpose. It's about something being excellent for its intended outcome. Even if it's not perfect, it can still be excellent for what you want to do or have with it. A book with a small blemish on its cover, or one of its pages dirtied, is not perfect, but it's still excellent for conveying the knowledge or story inside it. It's still eminently readable.

> *"Perfection is the enemy of excellence."*

So focus on excellence-ing, on achieving outcomes, on purpose and values. Go for *'satisficing'* rather than maximizing. With satisficing, you aim to achieve the best outcome in the situation, one that meets your purpose and needs, rather than on attempting to achieve the absolute best result, the perfect result. Research in

Positive Psychology has shown that individuals who focus on maximizing lead far less happy lives than those who satisfice appropriately.

Limiting beliefs and attitudes about perfection are an enemy to your happiness. Many of these are unconsciously installed by our culture and the micro-culture of your family. They are often so ingrained and unquestioned that at first you may not be aware of them. So look carefully at your beliefs and attitudes, and if you find yourself looking for perfection or agonizing over completing something because it won't be perfect, then recognize you are limiting yourself by grasping after an impossible ideal and instead follow through with doing the best you can in your current situation and skill-set.

Remember, happiness comes from focusing on achieving excellence in what is an imperfect, but wonderful world.

Happiness Sabotage

Some people have an incredible skill at creating happiness in their life and then just when things are going wonderfully they crash and burn. Something happens that causes them unhappiness or misery. It's like their unconscious mind is operating from a belief that they don't really deserve to be happy and so with unconscious competence and outside of conscious awareness they undermine and sabotage their own success.

Sometimes this can occur from a deep sense of worthlessness, sometimes from fear of failure and sometimes it is even motivated from a fear of success. Whatever the reason, it is the underlying core beliefs about deserving success and happiness that are the drivers of this enemy of happiness.

If you ever find yourself sabotaging your own happiness, then read Chapter 2 and the section there on overcoming the beliefs and processes that lead to Happiness Sabotage. Find out what is motivating this incongruence in your life. Then follow that by using the New Belief Generator Success Strategy described in Chapter 2 to install empowering beliefs and help you generate all the ongoing happiness and success you desire and truly deserve.

> *"Your incredible brain can take you from rags to riches, from loneliness to popularity, and from depression to happiness and joy — if you use it properly."*
>
> Brian Tracy

○ Deeper Understandings — Wants versus Shoulds

The way we think and express ourselves is crucial to how we make meaning and how we unconsciously motivate ourselves. Language is one of our key tools for thinking and making sense of our world. It's also how we communicate between parts of our multi-mind and with other people around us.

As has been pointed out throughout this book, un-sane use of language leads to un-sane thinking and this in turn leads to un-sane actions and outcomes in life.

When you create absolutist rules and generalizations about what you '*should*' do and what you '*have to*' do, you limit your freedom and apply pressure that can lead to parts of your multi-mind sabotaging your success. No one likes to be pressured or forced into action. In NLP, generalizations such as *'must'*, *'should'* and *'have to'* are called *'modal operators of necessity'*. They indicate rules about the mode of operation you are following or requesting. Thinking that you *"absolutely must do X"* often leads to stress and procrastination.

A much more generative and useful way to communicate to yourself and others is to use *'modal operators of desire'*. Words such as *'want to'*, *'like to'* and *'desire to'* are much more compelling and are linked with notions of value and attraction.

So when you are thinking and talking about your outcomes and goals, notice the words you are using. Practice and form habits of replacing the modal operators of necessity with modal operators of desire. For example, rather than saying something like, *"I should go wash the car now"*, instead choose to express the statement as something like, *"I want to wash the car now so that it looks fantastic."* You'll notice it has a different feel to it when expressed that way and is much more likely to lead to the intended outcome.

Powerfully using language that supports your outcomes can really make a difference to the happiness and success you are generating in your life. Remember, words are powerful. Do languaging that aligns, encourages and supports all the parts of your multi-mind.

Overcoming Procrastination

One of the ways people stop themselves from achieving success and happiness is through procrastination. They know what they want; they simply don't take action or follow through on what they've started. They distract themselves or de-motivate themselves. Then wonder why they feel so bad and why nothing is going right in their lives.

Procrastination is the thief of success! You achieve nothing by doing nothing. It's a blinding flash of the obvious, isn't it?

So how do you overcome and stop procrastinating? Well, start by recognizing that it's a skill, an unconscious competency. And like all skills, you can control it. You can also increase and utilize the opposing skill of operacy — the skill of achieving outcomes and goals, of taking massive congruent action to achieve success.

Let's look at how to do this.

Chunking the Task

One of the key skills of operacy involves breaking tasks and outcomes up into small bite-size chunks and then tackling each in turn. This is also known as time-boxing. The idea is to divide the outcome into small sub-goals that can be easily achieved in relatively small time windows. For example, scheduling 30 minutes each day to work on your outcome. In this way you build momentum, keep yourself motivated towards completion and see steady progress. It also removes the obstacle of overwhelm that some people experience when they contemplate starting a big goal or task.

You know the old aphorism: *"how do you eat an elephant… one bit at a time"*. Well, chunking the task is exactly like this. Divide your outcomes and available time windows into manageable, *'bite-size'* chunks, and then schedule them and take action. Focus on how little time and effort each next chunk or step involves and celebrate and reward the completion of each. Before you know it, your outcomes will have been easily and happily achieved.

Two further distinctions worth noting are to use a written plan and to schedule your time-windows. These may sound simple and obvious, but you'd be surprised how often people don't put their plans in writing and schedule them in writing on their calendars. Another small and powerful distinction is to never write '*To Do*' at the top of a list — instead a much more useful unconscious motivator is to write '**To Have Achieved**' at the top of the list. Try it, use it, you'll find it makes a subtle and potent difference.

Removing Distractions

Distractions and interruptions are always there if you look for them. Funny that... isn't it! If you are looking for ways to stop yourself from achieving your goals, then your powerful Reticular Activation System — the part of your brain responsible for attentional orientation, filtering and selection — will always manage to find them for you.

Using the skill of operacy you recognize these processes and prepare your environment to remove and minimize distractions and interruptions. Most interruptions occur in identifiable patterns. So notice when they occur and take action ahead of time to prevent them.

Similarly, most distractions are readily identifiable. So remove them ahead of time. Make it easy for yourself to stay focused, on-task and in flow. Remember, operacy is about taking massively congruent action. It's about focusing your whole cybernetic loop, your whole mind/body, your attitude, thoughts, feelings and behavior on your intended outcome. Support yourself by setting up an environment that encourages this.

Let me share with you an example. My father ran an automotive workshop for many years and I would often spend time assisting him in the repair of an engine or gearbox. The first thing he would do before starting on a new job was to clean the bench and workspace completely, removing any rubbish or clutter from a previous job. He would then lay newspaper down to place the parts onto as they were removed and cleaned.

The clever thing he would do though, was to place the newspaper upside down, so that it couldn't be easily read. He'd noticed that if it was right way up, he would occasionally find himself being distracted by an interesting article. By consciously making sure ahead of time that the paper could not be easily read, and by removing clutter from the environment, he minimized distractions and interruptions to the flow of the job. He got more done and enjoyed the process of achieving his outcomes more fully.

Overcoming Obstacles

Operacy also involves being able to recognize, remove and overcome obstacles ahead of time. The skill of procrastinating on the other hand involves ignoring obstacles until they halt progress and then using them as an excuse and rationalization for delay and lack of action.

Obstacles are inevitable. Many outcomes involve obstacles and challenges. The skill is in determining what obstacles might occur and resourcing and planning around them so they are minimized or removed. It's all about forethought, planning and design. You know the expression, *"Prior Planning Prevents Poor Performance"*? Well, that's the skill of operacy. Planning and designing ahead of time so you are already prepared to overcome the challenges you may face.

All of this might sound incredibly obvious, and it is. Yet, it's the obvious that often gets overlooked in the hectic experience of life. To overcome procrastinating and replace it with operacy, you need to become a master of following these simple and effective processes.

So before starting any goal or outcome, ask yourself, *"What are the possible obstacles to achieving each step?"* Then write the answers on your plan and figure out what resources, skills or assistance will help you overcome them. Make gathering these and preparing for challenges part of the chunks of the outcome.

And a very important attitude shift: make sure you view obstacles as challenges and not as problems. Your attitude makes all the difference to how you unconsciously motivate yourself and your multi-mind. Absolutely refuse to see or language obstacles as problems. From now on, only refer to them as challenges and tackle them with passion, courage and tenacity.

Reinforcing and Rewarding Yourself

Another important way to ensure you complete what you start is to reward yourself along the way. This is important for two key reasons. The first is to help encourage your steps towards your outcome. The second however is even more important. It's about the ongoing patterns you create in your life.

The patterning systems of the neural networks of your brains learn new patterns through both repetition and through reward and reinforcement. This is how you build unconscious competencies.

If you achieve a goal or sub-goal, and reward yourself for doing this, then you build an unconscious competency — a part — that will take responsibility for and ensure that you continue to achieve and complete goals, sub-goals and outcomes in your life. This process will then generalize across contexts in your life, and you'll find yourself becoming more goal/outcome oriented and achieving success effortlessly and without having to put conscious attention or effort into motivating yourself.

However, if you continuously fail to complete goals, or fail to reinforce the completion of goals, then you will build a skill — an unconscious part — that will ensure that failure continues and generalizes across contexts in life. Such a skill will undermine your success and create ongoing unhappiness and misery.

It is really important to understand how your mind works. It's so obvious once you realize that you are dealing with a self-reinforcing patterning system. Whatever patterns you put into your life, are the patterns you'll get out of your life. Garbage in, Garbage out! Conversely, Excellence in, Excellence out.

So if you want a life of happiness, joy and success, you need to put in patterns that reinforce positive results into your life. You do this by encouraging and rewarding yourself every time you do something that supports your outcomes, dreams and goals.

Research on Learned Industriousness also backs this up. Prof. Robert Eisenberger from the University of Delaware and his colleagues found that when individuals are rewarded for completing tasks, they are more likely to persist on future tasks. Most importantly, it was also found that persistence is encouraged when a reward conveys positive feedback about competence and increases the intrinsic motivation for doing the task.

So make it a positive habit to reward yourself every time you achieve a step towards your goals and outcomes. Plan ahead with these. Make a list of small rewards and encouragements. It might be buying yourself a small gift, such as a book or movie tickets. It might be pampering yourself with a massage. It might even be something as simple as patting yourself on the back and telling yourself out loud how wonderful you are for completing that goal.

I know this may sound strange, but talking out loud has a stronger effect on the unconscious mind than talking inside your head. Small distinctions such as this can make a BIG difference over time when dealing with complex patterning systems such as the human mind/body.

> *"A pessimist sees the difficulty in every opportunity; an optimist sees the opportunity in every difficulty."*
>
> Winston Churchill

Optimistic Attitudes

As described in previous chapters, research has shown that people with optimistic attitudes are more resilient, have greater resistance to depression and discouragement, and are better at achieving goals and outcomes.

So a simple way to support and encourage yourself is to refuse to give in to pessimism and instead foster and embody attitudes of hope and optimism. Focus on what might go right rather than what might go wrong. Continuously hold hope in your heart. Your heart brain and gut brain will thank you for it. ☺

Overcome fears and discouragement by concentrating on the meaning and purpose of your goals. Really motivate yourself by surrounding yourself with posters, images and signs about your dreams, desires and outcomes. And choose optimism every day. Hope is the food of happiness and success. So reward each day with a healthy diet of hope, joy and optimism.

> *"Focus on where you want to go, not on what you fear."*
>
> Anthony Robbins

🛠 Thinking Tools — Optimism & Success

Hope is the food of Happiness & Success.

Motivating Yourself

Motivating yourself is easy… Just figure out your values, then honor and uphold them. Create bright, compelling futures. Focus on and celebrate what you really want in life. And use move-towards and move-away values and strategies to ensure you are continually energized towards your goals and dreams.

With move-towards values, you focus on what you want, on the positive benefits of achieving your outcome. This is about pleasant feelings and values of achievement and success.

Move-away values are the opposite. Here you focus on the consequences of not achieving outcomes, on what will happen if you don't achieve your goals. You focus on the pain and disgust of not taking action and not getting what you want.

By combining these two processes you create a sling-shot effect that empowers achieving success and happiness. You utilize both positive and negative reinforcement to get and keep yourself moving.

Let's look at an example. If your outcome is to achieve a certain amount of slenderness. Let's say for example that your goal is to achieve a healthy slenderness of 150lbs. (Note that the outcome is stated with what we want *"achieve slenderness"*, rather than with what we don't want i.e. *"to lose weight"*.) Then you might focus on and celebrate the positive move-towards values of feeling great, looking good, fitting into those new clothes you'll reward yourself with, being healthier etc.

You'd also motivate yourself using move-away values by reminding yourself whenever you considered over-eating, of how fat disgusts you, of how much you hate not fitting into clothes, of how bad it feels when you are bloated and how much you dislike looking in the mirror and seeing that fat.

The key with this sling-shot strategy is to use both sets of values and to use them in the right sequence. Start with a focus on your positive towards values, then think about the away from values and how much you don't want to experience them any more, then finally refocus on your positive motivating and compelling outcomes. Make sure there's more positive focus than negative, at least 3 times more positive than negative and start and finish on the positive.

You'll find you are more attracted to contemplating the positive values. But you'll also find you will move away from pain and disgust quicker than you'll move towards pleasure. It's an evolved survival mechanism and one that you can use powerfully to help motivate yourself to go the whole way to achieving and completing your outcomes.

Motivation and Action

Another great insight into motivating yourself comes from Zig Ziglar, one of the top motivational speakers of all time. According to Zig, *"motivation follows action"*, and the research backs him up.

Most people think that action follows motivation… they erroneously believe they'll be more likely to take action once they feel motivated. But that's not the way it works. It's counterintuitive, but the patterning system of the mind/body works the other way around.

You generate motivation by taking action. Just start it. Just do it!

Begin taking action on a goal or outcome you've been procrastinating on, or a goal or outcome you've been waiting for motivation on. You'll find that as soon as you take action, even the smallest of steps, your feelings of motivation will immediately increase. You'll feel more positive and encouraged. Your energy will increase. It's an amazingly simple and very powerful insight. Use it!

🛠 Thinking Tools — Motivating Yourself

Motivation follows Action!

⚡ Pattern-Interrupt — En-Couraging Success

The following process combines the ideas and skills described throughout this chapter. Use this to interrupt any procrastination, sabotage or blocks to achieving success.

Interrupt incongruence in your mind/body by:

- ⚡ Adjusting your cybernetic mind-body loop to a more positive and relaxed attitude. Lift your head up, balance your body on both feet equally, breath fully in your abdomen and chest, smile, open your eyes and embody flexibility and courage.

- ⚡ Think about someone or something you love. Hold and amplify those feelings in your heart and chest region. Breathe these loving feelings into your heart. Really build and

> amplify this.
>
> ✶ Slowly move and expand your loving heart feelings up into your head and down into your gut. Really feel those powerful and supportive feelings moving and spreading, up and down along your body. Feel the positive feelings strongly in your stomach, in your gut brain.
>
> ✶ *'Gutsy-ness'* and courage come in large part from messages and responses from your enteric (gut) brain. So encourage and empower it by radiating and amplifying positive supportive feelings in this region of your body.
>
> ✶ Celebrate your new positive feelings of courage and commitment, congratulate yourself and enjoy your increasing happiness and success.

> *"The secret of success is constancy to purpose."*
>
> Benjamin Disraeli

Strengths & Values In Action

Use the following table to determine which strengths, qualities and values to focus on and amplify in your life to support the processes and skills of happiness. Also notice if you have any elements of the absence, opposite or exaggeration of these strengths and remove them from your behaviors and your life.

Enemies to happiness	VIA Strength
Incongruence	Self-regulation
Not Taking Action	Persistence
Procrastination	Integrity
Fear	Bravery
	Vitality

Notes from the Field — Going the Distance

Tammy van Wisse is an absolutely amazing person. She's a world-record holding long distance swimmer with an impressive list of firsts. She holds World Records for the fastest person to swim the length of Loch Ness in Scotland, the fastest person to swim the English Channel, the fastest person to swim across Cook Strait in New Zealand and the fastest person to swim Bass Strait in Australia. She has also won numerous swimming marathons such as the grueling Manhattan Island 48km Marathon Swim. In total, she has swum the equivalent of 1.5 times around the planet!

Tammy is also an amazingly happy, positive and bubbly person who knows an incredible amount about endurance, perseverance and that only going part way doesn't achieve success or results. I spoke with Tammy and asked her for her secrets of success and her ideas on the enemies to happiness.

"Happiness comes down to attitude — it's one of the few things we get a conscious choice over." Tammy's advice is to take a positive view on life and focus on the positives. When swimming she continuously visualizes success and looks for opportunities and positive challenges in what she is doing. *"Make a conscious choice to be someone who takes a positive outlook."* As Tammy points out, beaming out positivity in your life attracts those with a similar outlook. Gather people who support your goals and values, and your success will lead to more success in a positive spiral.

Tammy also believes it's important to have big goals and outcomes and to commit fully to these. For Tammy, personal growth equals happiness. She recommends goals that stretch you and that link to your passion. *"Get out of your 'box of safety', your comfort zone and don't be afraid of failure"* is her advice. *"Focus instead on the process and the journey rather than the end result."* Also, support yourself with role models and mentors that really inspire you — people who have achieved something you'd like to do.

"Make a decision to commit to your goals." As Tammy well knows, only getting to the half-way point will not win the race or make the record. Tammy's strategy is to make the mid-point a trigger for excitement and success. That way she can focus on and enjoy the success of the process rather than putting all her attention only on the final destination. *"When I get to my halfway point, I get really happy and excited. It's a trigger point. It gives me a*

boost in spirits." Tammy's well proven advice is to see the halfway point as a real celebration of nearing your goal, one that motivates you to continue to completion.

Tammy also suggests you need to have a strong sense of purpose for all your goals. *"You've got to have a 'why', got to have a strong motivation and stay constant on this."* When she was preparing for her swim across Bass Strait — a grueling swim that had never been successfully completed by anyone before her — she got lots of negative advice and blocking. On those 5am midwinter morning trainings, she motivated herself by continuously focusing on and reinforcing her *"strong driving reason"* for getting up and pushing herself through the cold, tiredness and pain. As Tammy points out, *"it's a mind battle fighting against and quashing the dark side, but you can achieve it by having a big enough 'why' and re-motivating yourself to get back on track and focusing on what you've already achieved."*

According to Tammy, the key enemies to happiness and success and what will stop you going the distance are:

- *Surrounding yourself with people that hold you down or are negative*

- *Not helping yourself first*

- *Getting stuck in a rut through fear of change or not wanting to change*

- *Not focusing on your passions and dreams*

- *Not doing enough planning, training and preparation to achieve your goals*

- *Setting goals that are too big, too difficult or too soon for your current levels of skill and experience*

- *Not reflecting on your learnings to build and improve*

As Tammy points out, overcoming the enemies to success in life, like success in long-distance swimming is *"all about attitude, positive conscious choice and focus."* You can easily go the distance if you, *"adapt, overcome and continuously improve."*

☞ Remember This

✓ We don't have a single unified consciousness, but instead are made up of a myriad of small autonomous multi-minds. Happiness and success depends on congruence and alignment in this society of mind. You need all parts of your mind and body working together harmoniously and in unison.

✓ Search for and recognize the signals of congruence and incongruence in your mind/body. Then use reframing or collapse anchors to negotiate and align your multi-mind to common outcomes, values and purpose.

✓ Focus on excellence rather than perfection and on wants, desires and values rather than *'shoulds'*. Satisfice rather than maximize.

- ✓ Overcome procrastinating by using and practicing the skills of operacy:
  - ➢ Chunk the tasks and schedule time-windows
  - ➢ Remove distractions before they occur
  - ➢ Overcome obstacles through planning and resourcing
  - ➢ Motivate and reward yourself through positive reinforcement
- ✓ Apply Learned Optimism in your life and focus on building hope to support yourself to complete your outcomes, dreams and goals.
- ✓ Motivate yourself by focusing on both move-towards and move-away values to create a slingshot effect. Don't wait to feel motivated, take action and motivation will follow. Remember *"Motivation follows Action!"*
- ✓ Amplify and embody positive attitudes of focus, congruence and success.

ⓘ Extra Info

Refer to www.enemiestohappiness.com for

- more information about the material covered in this chapter
- additional reading and references for this chapter

Avoiding the Enemies to HAPPINESS

Chapter 9

More GREED is better?

☺ *You will learn to*

- ✓ Appreciate and savor your life
- ✓ Control your desires to overcome greed
- ✓ Do *'bliss-pointing'* to maintain enjoyment
- ✓ Focus on wealth rather than money

More GREED is better?

Greed, excessive materialism and hedonism are addictive behaviors that destroy inner peace and happiness. We are challenged daily by a world that encourages and supports these addictions. They're insidious and deceptive. And once you're on the treadmill of escalating desires, it's not easy to get off.

By understanding the natural processes that lead to these destructive emotions and behaviors, you can learn to control your desires and re-balance your life. Happiness is created, not by satisfying greed, but by truly savoring and appreciating what you already have and do in life. True wealth involves more than money and true joy requires more than the mere satisfying of desires.

In this chapter you'll learn knowledge and skills to overcome evolved patterns of greed, envy and selfishness. You'll learn to truly appreciate a life filled with contentment, happiness and joy.

Enemies to your Happiness

✘ Greed and excessive materialism

✘ Negative emotions of envy and selfishness

✘ Lack of gratitude and appreciation

✘ The hedonic treadmill of wanting more and more

More GREED is better?

> *"Trying to get everything, you often get nothing."*
>
> Ivatan

Addiction to Greed

It's becoming exceedingly obvious we live in a world filled with selfishness and greed. The evidence surrounds us. Take a look at the state of the world! The media is filled with stories and images that are testament to the greed that has stealthily overtaken society.

We are living well beyond our means. The planet cannot support so many humans living such rapacious lives. We are destroying our world and our future. Our economy is in massive disarray. Our ecosphere is in massive decline. We are raping our world in the name of greed, desire and avarice.

This has all come about due to the craziness and un-sanity of following an economic model of infinite growth in a finite system. Yes, an infinite growth model... For hundreds of years our society, politics and economics have been managed using a year on year growth imperative. Our businesses and financial systems have been measured and directed by expectations of year on year growth — that's growth on previous growth.

This is an infinite growth model. It relies on exponential growth, of continuous and never ending expansion on top of previous growth. And as we are now experiencing, it is unsustainable. We live in a finite world. We cannot keep digging and siphoning up limited resources and expect that to continue forever. It's un-sane!

And I'm sure I don't have to convince you of that...

However, we may have more of a challenge getting you to see your own addictions to personal patterns of greed, desire and selfishness that are feeding this un-sane system and that are enemies to happiness and peace of mind — both your own and those of others.

Why is that?

Because many of these patterns, the very patterns that have created our current world issues, are naturally evolved and inbuilt propensities. They are '*normal*'. And in controlled amounts they're even useful and appropriate. They have largely driven the successes we all enjoy and are highly valued in society. But they're also insidious, addictive and lead naturally ever onwards to more and more and more of the same.

So while en-masse and globally they are now evidenced as crazy and destructive, in your own life they're often still accepted, overlooked or even applauded. Tracking and changing these insidious greed and selfishness patterns can be challenging.

The first step of course is awareness. The next step is to interrupt the patterns. Then finally and continually you need to practice emotions and behaviors that oppose these negative greed patterns and inoculate yourself against them.

Greed is a Verb

Let's get one thing sorted at the start. Greed is a *verb*. It's a process. We often talk about greed as if it's a noun, an object, a thing. However, people don't '*have*' greed. They '*do*' greed — more accurately, they do *greeding*. It's an active process, a skill, and an unconscious competency.

The behavior of greeding occurs naturally, uses primitive biological survival circuits of the brain and body and is in large part instinctually driven. That's why it's so insidious. As we'll see later in this chapter, the research shows that greeding is linked to hunger and sexuality. So it can be very powerful.

But the key point is that it's a process that can be controlled and moderated. It's a skill that has counter skills that can be used to constrain and control it. And awareness of its component behaviors and instinctual processes is important.

> "We've been raised to compete, to want more! More! More! It's a way of life. It's about greed."
>
> Sandy Duncan

The Materialist Imperative

We have a long evolutionary history of hunter-gathering and an instinctual predisposition towards ownership. We love owning and gathering things. It's the materialist imperative. We desire things: houses, cars, boats, clothes, toys and all the entrapments and enchantments of bling. It's also the ownership trap! Because everything you own, owns a small piece of you, and the more you own, the more it owns you. Remember this!

The psychology of ownership is fascinating and understanding it is crucial to overcoming patterns of greed.

Ownership changes perceptions. Research by Social Psychologists has shown that once a person owns an item they place higher perceived value on it than on an identical item they do not own.

Stop and think about this. The mere fact of owning something increases how much you value it!

Ownership is also linked to Loss Aversion. The research shows that people prefer avoiding losses to acquiring gains. Indeed, some studies suggest that losses are twice as powerful psychologically, as gains. So once you own something, it really does start to own you emotionally and psychologically. You become attached to it and form a relationship with it. It takes up your time, thought, energy and life.

Marketers are well aware of these traits and use them to manipulate you. Partial ownership confers similar effects on perceptions, so they encourage free 30 day trials and money back guarantees, knowing that the majority of people will grow attached to the item and not return it. Similarly, in on-line auctions, people start feeling they own the item even before the auction has completed and so drive the price higher than they would pay if they'd bought it from a shop.

Sure, owning stuff is useful. Where would we be if we owned nothing? Probably still swinging in the jungle and living from hand to mouth. The problem occurs when we own too many things; when we get stuck in the greed of the ownership trap — of wanting more and more and more.

A very wise man taught me many years ago to live life guided by the thinking tool that, *"the more you own, the more it owns you."* If you keep that in mind, and watch your patterns of ownership and acquisition, you'll be able to find a balance between utility of ownership and the grind of greed.

Before buying every item, ask yourself: *"Do I really need to own this?"* You might be better served in not owning it. Or you might be able to rent, lease or borrow the item for the small amount of use that in reality you will make of it.

Let me share an example from my own life. I always wanted to own a sportscar. But when I sat down and ran a spreadsheet on it, when I asked myself whether I really needed to own it, I figured that for the couple of weeks a year that I'd actually drive such a toy, I'd be better off renting one. So for many, many years that's exactly what I did. I'd rent a BMW open-topped sportscar and take it on a wonderful adventure holiday for a week or two each year. It was more cost effective both monetarily and life-wise to hire than own.

Then a few years ago, the rental companies stopped renting the sorts of sportscars that I liked to drive and could afford. I was forced into buying my own in order to have the joy of using one for the couple of weeks a year that I actually could find time to drive it.

Now I own the costs of registration, insurance, repairs, depreciation, insurance and eventual replacement. I also have to store it, wash and clean it, take it for servicing and have the worry of theft and damage.

Sure I love my car. But I'll tell you, it was much better when I rented one each year, because the rental car didn't own a piece of my life!

I share that example to show how owning things, owns a bit of you. So, every opportunity you can, refuse to be sucked into the ownership trap. It's a subtle greeding pattern and while owning stuff appears to increase your happiness — in the larger context of life and if not controlled, it can be a pernicious enemy to happiness.

🛠 Thinking Tools — Ownership

The more you own, the more it owns you!

> "Joy has nothing to do with material things, or with man's outward circumstance... A man living in the lap of luxury can be wretched, and a man in the depths of poverty can overflow with joy."
>
> William Barclay

The Status Game

Status is a primary and universal human motive and a very powerful contributor to social success. Research has shown for example, that women are more attracted to men they perceive as having high status. Status is also linked to financial success. It's powerful and ubiquitous.

The need for status is a game that largely drives society and can lead to a never ending greed spiral of status anxiety and misery. The more status a person has, the more they want. Uncontrolled, the Status Game is an enemy to human happiness.

While status awareness is a biologically driven function, supported and reinforced by societal moirés and learnings, at its heart it is mediated by the process of who and what reference groups you compare yourself with. While it can be challenging to suppress status awareness entirely, it is much easier to control it by carefully selecting your focus for comparison.

Comparing yourself to those who are richer, more attractive by today's current societal standards, or to those who are more privileged, will inevitably lead to status anxiety. On the other hand, comparing yourself to those who you are more fortunate than, will lead to positive feelings of higher status.

As psychology professor Peter Salovey suggests, figure out what's really important to you and mentally withdraw from status competitions that aren't close to your heart. You can also draw upon memories and references in other domains in which you are successful to buffer against envy and status anxiety in a challenging domain.

The key is to realize that you can and need to control how you play the Status game and make sure that it is you who is controlling your perception of status and not someone else. The desire for status can be a greed pattern that drives materialism and undermines your self-esteem and happiness. Recognize and control your focus of comparison and refuse to play show-off games of greed. Your happiness and peace of mind depend on it.

Sexual Selection

Another important unconscious process you need be aware of and control is based on the evolutionary function of sexual selection. Sexual selection is a special case of natural selection and makes many organisms go to extreme lengths to obtain sex. For example, male peacocks have evolved elaborate tails to attract and mate with female peahens.

The problem is that sexual selection is often powerful enough to produce features that are harmful to the individual's survival. In the case of peacocks, extravagant and colorful tail feathers are just as likely to attract predators as they are to attract interested members of the opposite sex.

In the case of humans, some researchers believe a number of human behaviors not clearly tied to survival benefits, such as humor, music, visual art, verbal creativity, and some forms of altruism, are courtship adaptations that have been favored through sexual selection. They are the equivalent of the peacock's gaudy tail, used to attract mates.

What's important to note about this, is the idea that certain human behaviors are instinctually driven by the need to attract sexual attention. As such, they are powerful motivators and unless tracked for and controlled, can lead to *'the more, the more'* patterns of greeding.

The need for a faster, sexier car, a larger house, a better physique, a more expensive suit, are all examples of *'peacock feathers'* — of sexual selection emblems. The individual who displays these is unconsciously trying to send a message to potential mates saying that not only do they have sufficient reproductive fitness that they can provide good mating success, they have enough additional biological fitness that they can also provide all of the added societal bling.

This may be all well and good if it's what you've consciously chosen to invest your time, money, energy and life in. But if you get unconsciously caught up in such patterns of pandering to sexual selection, you may get lost in the never ending materialism of desiring and obtaining more and more — constantly seeking for larger and brighter sets of peacock feathers!

This is an un-sane pattern that is more valid to the forest than to a modern human life. Do you really want partners who only respond to you because you are displaying the trappings of materialism? Will this really bring you the happiness you desire in your life? Think carefully about the peacock feathers in your own life and decide whether their dubious benefits outweigh the costs.

The Biology of Greed

The primitive emotion-driven biological circuits of your brain become intensely aroused when you anticipate greed behaviors. Research at Stanford University has shown that anticipation and desire for money during behaviors such as financial investing and gambling cause the same areas of the brain to activate as those responsible for sexual desire. In one study, the brains of young adult men were scanned with magnetic resonance imaging while they viewed sexually arousing pictures and also when they made risky financial decisions. The study found the same areas of the brain light up during financial gambles as during sexual desire.

This is something to be aware of: Greed utilizes many of the same biological circuits as hunger and sexual desire. Greed feels good. It's quite an insidious trap.

The other important thing to note about the biology of greed is that satiating desire does NOT feel as good as the greed itself. One study found that the hot state of anticipation cools down as soon as you gain the financial reward, yielding lukewarm satisfaction. As Jason Zweig, author of the book *'Your Money and Your Brain'* describes it, "*Making money feels good, all right; it just doesn't feel as good as expecting to make money. In a cruel irony that has enormous implications for financial behavior, your investing brain comes equipped with a biological mechanism that is more aroused when you anticipate a profit than when you actually get one.*"

> "He who is greedy is always in want."
>
> Horace

Contentment versus Greeding

According to the Dalai Lama, "*The true antidote of greed is contentment*" and a reliable method to achieve inner contentment is, "*not to have what we want but rather to **want and appreciate what we have***" (The Art of Happiness by Dalai Lama and H. Cutler).

These deep and ancient insights from Buddhist philosophy have been recently supported by research in Positive Psychology. The studies show that savoring and appreciating what you currently have can significantly increase levels of joy and happiness.

Savoring involves relishing and paying special attention to the pleasurable and meaningful things and events in your life. It's about truly appreciating and celebrating your experiences, including those occurring in the present, those that are now fond memories and those you are looking forward to with positive anticipation.

The studies also show that savoring positive experiences is correlated with a greater sense of well being, increased happiness and better physical health — All great benefits and wonderful antidotes to greeding!

By shifting your attention to a focus on contentment, you'll have broken the vicious spiral of wanting more and more. You'll have allowed your multi-mind to experience and enjoy the life you have right now. You'll overcome the enemy to happiness of greed and never-ending desiring.

Remember also that the mind/body is a patterning system, so the patterns you put into your mind and life create the patterns and results you get back from life. I liken the practice and focus on savoring and contentment to the Native American story about the wise grandfather talking to his grandson. He tells the young boy that we all have two wolves inside of us struggling with each other. The first is the wolf of peace, love and kindness. The other wolf is fear, greed and hatred. *"Which wolf will win, grandfather?"* asks the young boy. *"Whichever one you feed,"* is the thoughtful reply.

So make sure you feed the patterns you want in your life.

> *"The doors we open and close each day decide the lives we live."*
>
> Flora Whittemore

Supernormal Stimulus

If a bird is given the choice between nesting on a large plastic egg or on its own egg that it recently laid, it will choose the larger egg, even though it is cold, smells of plastic and has the wrong texture. This tendency in nature, for any stimulus that is an exaggerated version, to elicit a stronger response than normal is called the Supernormal Stimulus effect.

It was first observed by the ethologist Konrad Lorenz in brooding birds. Since then it has been observed in a wide variety of creatures. For example, there is an Australian beetle species whose males are sexually attracted to large and orange females — the larger and more orange the better. This creates a problem as the males attempt to mate with beer bottles that are just the right color — the males are more attracted to the bottles than to actual females.

In humans, it is argued that phenomena such as sexual fetishes and our delight for junk food can be largely explained as examples of supernormal stimulus effects. Candy bars are a great example of supernormal stimulus, they contain more concentrated sugar, salt, and fat than anything that exists in our ancestral environment and we love them. Some people are so strongly attracted to candy and chocolate that they'll continue to eat them to the point of damaging their own health.

Other examples of human responses to supernormal stimuli are evidenced in how we like the colors of flowers so we breed bigger and brighter ones; we like sweet scents, so we manufacture strong perfumes; we like sexual stimuli, so create clothes and cosmetics to exaggerate them. We also prefer tall people, large breasts in women and super-models who have exaggerated levels of human beauty such as large eyes and facial symmetry.

The key and important thing to note about the effect of supernormal stimuli is the instinctual preference we have for those things that are larger, shinier and more exaggerated than normal.

The effects of supernormal stimulus can link to and drive patterns of greeding. They can lead to behaviors of over-indulgence due to the strong unconscious responses we have to super-stimuli. So it's vitally important to track for these effects in your life and then use conscious decision making to moderate your behavior. Make life choices through intelligence rather than through evolved instinctual patterns and desires. More greed is not better!

> *"There are limits to self-indulgence, none to restraint."*
>
> Mahatma Gandhi

Bliss-Pointing

As researchers in psychophysics know, almost all human processes and behaviors have a *'bliss-point'*. Indeed, sensory satisfaction is largely driven by the bliss-point phenomenon. What is a bliss-point? It's the optimum sensation or experience that results when the level of a constituent is *'just right'* — neither too low nor too high. Our physiology evolved to search for and maximize these bliss-points.

For example, with sweet foods our palate is optimized for a certain level of sweetness. Too little sugar and the dessert tastes bland, too much sugar and it tastes sickly.

Similarly, there are optimum levels for brightness and other forms of sensory stimulation. The import of this for understanding and overcoming greed involves finding and maintaining the bliss-points in your life.

You see, the challenge is that the human nervous system is built around the use of hormones and receptors to control and communicate within the system. Our body continually adjusts the amount of these chemicals and the number of receptors based on our ongoing experience.

Let's look at an example. There is an optimal bliss-point level for the amount of endogenous opiate (endorphin) receptors in our tissues. These are used in the control and signaling of pain and pleasure. However, when a person floods their body and brain with an opiate like the drug heroin, over time the body down regulates the amount of endogenous opiate that is produced and the number of receptors that respond to it.

In other words, the system attempts to maintain the evolved bliss-point for internal opiates. Then when the person tries to give up the drug, they find themselves in terrible withdrawals, in massive pain and heightened response to normal stimuli. Even the slightest touch becomes painful, because their body can no longer produce sufficient endorphins to control the pain signals.

During the addiction phase, it takes more and more of the drug to produce the high, as the body continues to down-regulate the response to maintain the bliss-point — the point of optimal opiate response. During the withdrawal phase, it takes many weeks or months for the body to regrow the receptors and the ability to produce and respond to internal opiates, as it once again attempts to maintain the bliss-point.

The *"take home"* message about bliss-pointing, is that to maintain optimal enjoyment from any experience in life, you need to carefully manage not to flood your system. If you have too much of anything, you will overflow the inbuilt bliss-point and your body will down-regulate its response. You need to give everything a rest. Moderation in all things is the key.

You will only be able to maintain the bliss-point of happiness in your life if you carefully manage your behaviors and experiences so that you never continuously over-do or continuously over-indulge. Your wonderful brain/mind/body is like a garden, the plants need just the right amount of water and nutrients; too much or too little and the plants wilt and suffer. The neurons in your multiple brains are the same.

Track for the bliss-points in your life and carefully manage and maintain them. Remember: use moderation in all areas of your life. Your ongoing happiness depends upon it.

🛠 Thinking Tools – Moderating your Life

Moderation in ALL things.

Appreciating your Life

According to the father of Cognitive Psychology, Dr Albert Ellis, psychologically healthy people are usually glad to be alive and accept themselves simply because they are alive and have some capacity to enjoy themselves and appreciate their lives. *"They refuse to measure their intrinsic worth by their extrinsic accomplishments, materialistic possessions and by what others think of them."*

This ability to appreciate your life circumstances and situations is an adaptive coping strategy. It helps you overcome obstacles and buffers you against greed, stress and difficult life circumstances.

Sometimes patterns of greeding are a futile attempt to cope with stress or problems in life — *"when the going gets tough, the tough go shopping"* syndrome. But as we've seen, the satiation of desire never feels as good as the desire itself, leading to a vicious cycle of wanting more and more. Alternatively, by accepting and appreciating yourself and your life and focusing on gratitude and appreciation you can overcome the enemy to happiness of *'more greed is better?'*

The Blessings of Gratitude

Dr. Robert Emmons, a psychology professor at the University of California-Davis has spent the last decade studying gratitude. His research has shown that people who regularly practice grateful thinking are more than 25 percent happier, suffer lower levels of stress, are healthier and even sleep better.

The practice of gratitude has also been found to be incompatible with negative emotions, and can inhibit feelings of envy, bitterness, anger, and greed. You simply can't do greeding and other negative emoting while focusing on gratitude and appreciation. The expression of gratitude also stimulates moral behavior, such as kindness and helping, and increases social bonding.

So to increase gratitude in your life, use the easy and very beneficial Positive Psychology exercises covered in earlier chapters. For instance, make a practice of counting your blessings via a Gratitude Journal. In this process you write 3 or more things each day that you feel blessed with in life and really savor and appreciate them.

Or use a Gratitude Rock or Item as a trigger to remind yourself to remember things you feel grateful for. You can also send Gratitude Letters or messages to those who have helped you and you appreciate.

In a sense it's about creating and evoking a spirit of joy and generosity in your life and your interactions with others. There's always something or someone you can feel grateful for or towards.

Generously celebrate your blessings, savor them and focus on the positives in your life. Even in the midst of the worst of life's challenges, you can always choose to place your focus on past blessings and future possibilities.

Awareness Questions — Savoring Gratitude

Ask Yourself:

- What are the blessings in my life? Who and what can I show appreciation for?

- What positive aspects of my life and my self can I fully savor and appreciate?

- How can I focus more on the delights and abundance of the simple joys in my life?

> *"The secret of contentment is knowing how to enjoy what you have."*
>
> Lin Yutang

⚡ Pattern-Interrupt — Satiating the Hunger of Greed

Since greed utilizes many of the same biological circuits as sexuality and hunger, you can satiate these primitive mechanisms by sending messages to your heart brain and gut brain to quell them. Remember also that positive emotions undo and inoculate against negative emotions and that gratitude and appreciation overcome greed.

The following technique uses heart-based Balanced Breathing and creative feeling to pattern-interrupt the process of greeding.

Interrupt patterns of greed by:

- Recall an act of kindness you did for someone. Feel pleasure in having performed it. As you remember this experience fully, focus on breathing your feelings of love, caring and appreciation into your heart.

- As you are feeling deep and strong feelings of positivity, love, kindness and generosity in and around your heart, begin to expand and move these kind and loving feelings up into your head and down into your stomach and gut region. You can even send them lower into your groin region.

- ✗ Continue to breathe in feelings of love and kindness and spread and expand them throughout your body, with specific awareness to deep in your gut.

- ✗ Talk to your heart and gut brains and tell them they are satiated. Reassure them they are well and that your life is filled with a wealth of happiness. Tell them you are satiated and replete. Really feel the fullness of your life at a gut level.

You'll find this technique is very powerful and can stop selfishness and greed in its tracks. Greeding comes from parts of your primitive multi-mind attempting to gain more and more because they have not received the message that you have achieved your outcomes and enough is now enough. By sending appropriate messages to your unconscious mind via your heart brain and enteric brain, you bring your system back into balance and stop the vicious cycle of patterns of greeding.

⟲ Deeper Understandings — The language of ownership

In the field of General Semantics, there is a linguistic technique called '*E-prime*' that involves using English in a way that excludes the use of the verb '*to be*' and its various forms.

The idea underlying this suggests that the '*is*' of identity and the '*is*' of attribution can lead to un-sane thinking and consequent behavior. For example, if you say "*I am stupid*" you are linking the process of stupidity to your identity, rather than expressing the behavior as one of many skills or traits that you do. This can lead to self-fulfilling prophecies that maintain an unconscious competency of doing stupidity at all levels of your life.

Since language influences perception, the use of E-prime encourages the choice of verbs and meanings carefully. E-prime can also lead to a less dogmatic style of expression and reduce the possibility of misunderstanding and conflict.

O-prime

The ancient philosophy of Buddhism maintains that the nature of the universe is impermanence and that consequently much suffering stems from attachment and grasping. The need for ownership and attachment can lead to unhappiness.

Everything you *'own'* owns a piece of you, and that ownership and grasping can cost you dearly. Nothing lasts forever and everything is always in a state of flux and change. So grasping and ownership, as insidious enemies to happiness, can lead to suffering.

Based on these deep insights from this ancient wisdom, and following on from the neuro-semantic concept of E-prime, I have created the technique of *'O-prime'*.

O-prime involves the use of English in a way that excludes the use of the verbs, adjectives and predicates of ownership — especially in the case of ownership of intangible experiences. O-prime is a semantic tool that helps you notice and filter for processes of attaching and ownership that can impoverish your model of the world, your experience, thinking and ultimately your behaviors.

For example, if you say *"I have an understanding of General*

Semantics" then you are indicating ownership. You are saying you *'have'* understanding.

This suggests a grasping and need for understanding and nominalizes the process of understanding into an object that you own. However, understanding is a process that can change with time, experience and knowledge.

If you feel you *'have'* an understanding of General Semantics and then someone shows you your current understanding is not complete, how do you feel? There's every possibility you may feel threatened since *'your'* ownership of *'your'* understanding is about to be lost.

Contrast this with the O-prime version that replaces ownership with process — that shifts "*I have understanding*" to "*I do understanding*".

With O-prime, you could more accurately say, "*I feel I do understanding of General Semantics very well.*" Or perhaps you may express it as, "*General Semantics is something I understand well.*" These O-primed ways of thinking and communicating remove the semantic presuppositions of ownership and grasping.

Removing all forms of ownership expression from your language is not really practical and not what is suggested. The key message of this deeper understanding is to note that the language of ownership can at times be pernicious and lead to unsane thinking and behavior.

Instead, use O-priming appropriately to allow yourself to gain more choice and control over how you are modeling your world. Where useful, track for and replace the language of ownership in how you communicate and express your experiences so that the language you use supports your outcomes.

> Stop grasping after permanence and allow yourself to flexibly flow with the ongoing processes of change.

Pos Ψ Hedonic Treadmill

There is a tendency in our lives to adapt to the prevailing conditions and for things, no matter how distorted or extreme to become *'normal'* before long. Research has found that people who have either experienced incredibly positive events such as winning the lottery, and people who have experienced extremely negative events such as becoming blind or quadriplegic, have an initial positive or negative response respectively, then within less than a year largely revert to their normal levels of happiness. The joy and sadness of good and bad events tends to fade with time.

In the field of Positive Psychology, this effect is called the *'Hedonic Treadmill'* and it's particularly germane to the subject of greed. Research on the hedonic treadmill has shown that as a person makes more money, their expectations and desires typically rise, resulting in no permanent gain in happiness.

Part of the process of greeding is the belief that the satiation of a desire will lead to ongoing positive feelings and experiences. But, as the research on the hedonic treadmill suggests, the initial positive response to satiating your desires will be fleeting. Before long, your feelings and levels of happiness will return to the norm, leaving you back on the treadmill. You'll then need to increase your wants and desires and continue questing for more.

Over time you'll end up stuck on the tiresome hedonic treadmill of greed and all this will ultimately achieve is leave you feeling no better than before and with a constant unsatisfied need for more and more. Now that is a definite enemy to happiness!

The hedonic treadmill effect is particularly applicable to happiness based on pleasure. Remember, research in Positive Psychology has shown there are three components to a happy life — pleasure, engagement and meaning. The antidote to the hedonic treadmill is to shift your focus from pleasure to a greater focus on engagement and meaning. By living a life filled with purpose and meaning and focusing on helping others you'll experience a life that is deeply satisfying and doesn't rely on an ongoing greed for pleasure and surface enjoyment.

Also, stop basing happiness on external objects and possessions. Instead, look to your own inner resources and competencies to generate joy and happiness in your life and the lives of others. Watch out for patterns of greed and hedonic treadmill effects in your life, and avoid them as the true enemies to happiness they really are.

☑ Success Strategy — Loving-Kindness Meditation

Research by Positive Psychologist Dr. Barbara Fredrickson has shown that the practice of the Buddhist technique of Loving-Kindness Meditation can mitigate the effects of the hedonic treadmill. When practiced for as little as an hour per week, Loving-Kindness Meditation can enhance positive emotions, increase cardiac vagal tone (a measure of heart and autonomic health) and buffer against negative emotions such as greed, fear and envy.

Loving-Kindness Meditation is a meditational practice in which you send out thoughts and feelings of love, kindness and well-being to all sentient beings. It involves 4 phases, with each phase lasting approximately 5 minutes each. The meditation can be done as a visualization in which you imagine and feel a sphere of love and light around yourself and then radiate it out from yourself. It can also be done as a verbal exercise in which you repeat phrases or mantras while remembering and recalling positive memories of love and kindness.

1. The practice begins by focusing on developing a loving acceptance of yourself. This is the first phase. Fill yourself with thoughts, feelings and images of love, caring and acceptance. Repeat words like *"I love and care for myself. I deserve happiness, health and love."* Visualize yourself filled with a radiant ball of love centered round your heart and radiating throughout your body and your life. Do this for 5 minutes.

2. The second phase involves meditating on loving-kindness for someone you already care about and love. This could be a close friend, a parent, a lover, a mentor, teacher or benefactor. Concentrate on sending them feelings and messages of loving-kindness. Visualize the light of your loving-kindness and compassion spreading from your heart out to them, surrounding and filling them and their life.

3. In the next phase, you shift your visualization and meditation to someone you are neutral to, perhaps a stranger or an acquaintance. Do this for 5 minutes also, before moving on to phase 4.

4. The final phase is more challenging. In this phase you focus on sending loving-kindness to people that you dislike or who have been difficult or hostile towards you. Feel and imagine enveloping them in compassion, forgiveness and kindness. You can also spread your thoughts of loving-kindness out to all beings in the world, encompassing all sentient creatures, all people.

You will find that this meditation exercise feels fantastic and has a lasting effect that stays with you for many, many hours. Indeed, Dr. Fredrickson's research shows that the more you practice the meditation the longer the effect lasts and spreads across the contexts of your life, generating emotional and psychological resources that support ongoing happiness and success. And remember to enhance your meditation using the *m*BIT technique of Balanced Breathing as it really brings greater levels of calmness and amplifies the effects.

Wealthing

This chapter on overcoming greed would not be complete without exploring the issue of money, prosperity and true wealth generation.

Sure, as the research shows, money doesn't buy happiness. Once you have enough money for the basic necessities of a good life, more money tends to bring little additional and meaningful happiness and can even bring its own hassles and additional risks and responsibilities. Nevertheless, wealth provides freedom, choice and the ability to purchase life experiences and adventures such as overseas travel, inspirational adventure activities and the time and resources for advanced education.

The key with wealthing your life is to bypass the greed for mere money and instead build skills and strategies into your life for creating true wealth. Of course, I could write a whole book on Wealth Creating and many people have written excellent books on the subject. I suggest you read some. And I must stress that what follows in this section is general life advice and in no way constitutes financial advice. For specific financial advice, pertinent to your life, personal situation and requirements, you should always seek professional advice from a registered Financial Advisor. With that disclaimer out of the way, let's explore some tips, distinctions and thinking tools that support wealth creating.

Producing versus Consuming

Many years ago I worked with a fellow consultant who was constantly broke. Though he earned hundreds of dollars an hour, he had no money in the bank and no investments or assets to his name. His problem was he consumed more than he produced! He would waste his money on expensive meals, pointless and costly toys and high priced rental accommodation. Everything was hired, leased or rented. We called him *'gadget boy'* because he always had to have the latest gadgets or technology on the market and as soon as it was a few months old he would give it away to someone else.

He owned no real wealth of any sort and his outgoings were equal to or larger than his income. He often lived on a buffer of credit card debt while he waited for his next payment to arrive. I would occasionally have to loan him money just so he could eat a meal with me or fill his car with fuel. What a crazy life!

While he literally had a 6 figure income every year, he was one of the poorest people I know.

Thankfully, my father taught me from an early age the vital

importance of producing more than I consume. He gave me the powerful thinking tool of the insight that *'It's not your incomings — it's your outgoings'* that are crucial for generating wealth and living a great life. You see, you can earn a relatively modest income and be wealthier than my friend described above.

All you have to do is ensure that your expenses are much less than your income, and save the wealth that you thereby generate. Use that wealth to create investments and assets that in turn generate more income. Make your wealth work for you. Before long you'll find you are rich in freedom and choice with a healthy buffer of wealth to support you no matter what happens in life — you'll be financially free. It's quite simple, maximize your incomings, minimize your outgoings and save the difference. Invest wisely and your wealth will steadily grow.

Thinking Tools — Produce more than you Consume

It's not your incomings — it's your outgoings!

Using Money

I was at a local produce market where I spied a flower stall filled with beautiful bouquets. *"I know,"* I thought, *"I'll buy my beloved some beautiful flowers, she'll love them."*

Now you see, since I teach and run workshops on negotiating skills I always like to practice my skills and techniques whenever I can. So I walked over to the vendor and started negotiating.

"How much discount will you give me now, for those two bunches of

flowers, and make such a great customer like me, really happy?" I asked with a smile. With a cheeky glint in his eye, the vendor smoothly responded, *"Ah, my friend, I can see you like a bargain. However, my prices are as low as I can go. So there's no discount available. However, if you buy the flowers now, I can give you a bonus that is worth much more than a few dollars. How does that sound?"*

We bartered back and forth for a few more rounds, as I attempted to determine how firm he was on not dropping his price and to find out what this *'bonus'* was.

"I'll give you some very powerful advice as the bonus" he said. *"Advice that has such value it will make you much more money than you could ever get from the few dollars you could bargain on these flowers." "And I'll tell you what, if you don't feel the advice is worth it, then I'll give you the flowers for free. But I know you'll see how powerful the idea I'll share with you is."*

He had me very intrigued now. He'd done his negotiating job well. So I capitulated, and agreed to buy the flowers at the original price and waited anxiously for him to wrap the flowers and share with me his sage advice.

"Ok," he said, handing me the flowers and taking my money. *"When you first came over to my stall, I heard you say 'I think I'll spend a few dollars on these beautiful flowers for my beloved,' is that not true?"*

"Yes," I replied, *"I do believe you are right."*

"Well," he asked, *"Once you have spent your money, what has happened to it?"*

I pondered… what does he mean? What happens to money once you've spent it? I looked quizzically at him.

"It's simple," he smiled, *"It's gone! When you spend your money, it's gone. You don't have it any more."*

"However," he continued, *"if you 'Use' your money, rather than*

spending it, what happens?"

I looked at him, thinking... *"I guess when you use money, you have created value with it and you still have the value,"* I replied.

"Yes!" he laughed, *"you've got it! When you find yourself about to purchase something, ask yourself: will buying this use my hard earned money wisely or will it merely be spending it? Will this be the best use of my money? Do I really need to spend this money?"*

"If you follow this powerful advice, you'll find yourself generating true wealth. Your purchases will add value to your life and you won't waste money spending it on frivolous purchases."

His face lit up with the biggest of smiles, as he asked, *"Now tell me, isn't that powerful advice, and isn't it worth more than a couple of dollars saved on these beautiful flowers!"*

He was right! It was fantastic advice: *"Use money, don't spend it!"* What a powerful thinking tool. I thanked him profusely. He had added another useful distinction to my understanding of how to generate wealth in my life.

I truly suggest you commit this thinking tool to memory and use it and practice it every time you consider making a purchase. The tool orients you to questions of purpose, outcomes and value. Do you really need to make the purchase, will it be the best use of your money, and will it add true wealth to your life? If not, then don't make the purchase, save your money.

Link this tool with the previous distinction of watching and managing your outgoings, and you'll find yourself growing and creating much wealth in your life.

🛠 Thinking Tools — Using Your Money

Use money, don't spend it!

Generosity

True wealth goes beyond money and assets. Wealth is an attitude and a way of living. It's about peace of mind, flexibility and generosity of spirit.

You can have millions in the bank, but if you won't share it or use it wisely to live a great life, then you'll suffer a more miserable life than the poorest pauper.

There is little point being rich and miserable, or being a selfish, lonely and miserly billionaire. Being rich as a life purpose is not something to aspire to. More greed is NOT better. A richness of spirit and a life of meaningful purpose will outweigh money every time for achieving happiness.

So ask yourself what true wealth means for you? Then invest your time, thought and energy in creating it.

Research shows that helping others, being generous and caring increases happiness and life satisfaction. You are wealthy when your life is filled with community, family and love. You are also truly wealthy when you have choice, freedom, health and peace of mind.

Yes, money is useful and important, but not at the exclusion of other values. Money is a means to an end and not an ultimate purpose in itself.

On the other hand, generosity is a friend of wealth and happiness. So share your good fortune and it will return in good measure. Donate to charities. Help those less fortunate than yourself. Generosity is a great antidote to the enemy of greed.

Focus on building real and meaningful wealth in your life and you'll truly create a life filled with contentment, happiness and joy.

> *"It is neither wealth nor splendor, but tranquility and occupation, which give happiness."*
>
> Thomas Jefferson

Strengths & Values In Action

Use the following table to determine which strengths, qualities and values to focus on and amplify in your life to support the processes and skills of happiness. Also notice if you have any elements of the absence, opposite or exaggeration of these strengths and remove them from your behaviors and your life.

Enemies to happiness	VIA Strength
Greed & Materialism	Self-regulation
Envy & Selfishness	Kindness
Not Appreciating & Savoring	Social Intelligence
Hedonic Treadmill	Perspective/Wisdom

📋 Notes from the Field — A Tropical Paradise

Lazing in the shade of a coconut palm, golden white sands at my feet, the crystal blue ocean sparkling across the horizon, I asked Mere what the Enemies to Happiness are in her experience:

- *The desire for material objects — constantly wanting the things you don't have*

- *Treating people like objects — not connecting and forming deep relationships with others*

- *Rushing and stressing — not taking time to enjoy the moment, experiencing the 'now'*

Mere lives on a small island off the coast of Fiji, in a tropical paradise. She works in a resort, cleaning and servicing Bures and giving wonderfully relaxing massages. The island provides all the necessities of life, and though her work pays minimal wages, she is the embodiment of joy, happiness and positivity. Mere also gets to see and interact with thousands of travelers from all over the world. She gets to see all levels of happiness.

So what does Mere find works for happiness?

- *Have a goal — work and save for the future*

- *Do something that is meaningful for your life and the lives of others*

- *Build friendships — connect and form deep relationships with family and others*

- *Share — give small gifts of kindness to others*

- *Relax — take time out to relax, release and revitalize yourself*

- *Laugh — have fun, make life a joyous adventure*

☞ Remember This

✓ Greed is an insidious and powerful instinctual drive. You need to be aware of the inbuilt processes and tendencies that lead to the process of greeding and combat them with counter skills and awareness.

✓ Ownership is seductive and changes your perceptions so that you become attached to the things you own. Everything you own, then owns a piece of you. Beware of the ownership trap that leads to rampant materialism and an addiction to owning more and more.

✓ The desire for status is a primary and universal human motive, and if not controlled can lead to never ending greed spirals of status anxiety and misery. Eschew playing the status game or showing off, it is an enemy to happiness. Comparing yourself to those who are richer, more attractive or more privileged will inevitably lead to status anxiety. Instead, recognize and control your focus of comparisons, so that you feel blessed compared to those who are less fortunate than yourself.

- ✓ Beware of the instinctual drive to accrue and display sexual selection emblems. These *'peacock feathers'* are costly and may not add real value to your life, relationships or happiness.

- ✓ An antidote to greed is provided by the positive feelings engendered by savoring, appreciation and gratitude. Really focus on making the most of what you currently have in life and the enjoyment of positive experiences, rather than focusing on what you don't currently have.

- ✓ Track for and control your response to the Supernormal Stimulus effect — the tendency for any stimulus that is an exaggerated version to elicit a stronger response than normal.

- ✓ Almost all human processes and behaviors have a *'bliss-point'* — an optimum sensation or level. Make sure you don't flood your bliss-points and cause adaptation and down regulation of these. Maintain optimal bliss-pointing by doing everything in moderation.

- ✓ Watch out for the hedonic treadmill effect and in particular to how it relates to happiness based on pleasure. Instead, put a greater focus on engagement and meaning into your life. By living a life filled with purpose and meaning and focusing on helping others you'll experience a life that is deeply satisfying and doesn't rely on an ongoing greed for pleasure and surface enjoyment.

- ✓ Use the Buddhist technique of Loving-Kindness Meditation to enhance positive emotions and to mitigate the effects of the hedonic treadmill and buffer against negative emotions such as greed, jealousy and envy.

✓ Bypass the greed for mere money and instead build skills and strategies into your life for creating true wealth. Produce more than you consume. Use money rather than spending it. Wealth is an attitude and a way of living. It's about peace of mind, flexibility and generosity of spirit. Generosity is a great antidote to the enemy of greed.

ⓘ Extra Info

Refer to www.enemiestohappiness.com for

- more information about the material covered in this chapter
- additional reading and references for this chapter

Avoiding the Enemies to HAPPINESS

Chapter 10

Life is FANTASTIC!

You will learn to

- ✓ Create dream lists, inspiring goals and compelling futures

- ✓ Generate well-formed outcomes

- ✓ Follow the NLP Success Strategy to achieve your dreams

- ✓ Clarify your values and use them to guide your life

Life is FANTASTIC!

Life without goals and dreams is mere existence. For life to be fantastic, you have to live fantastically. You do this by dreaming big dreams, generating inspiring goals and outcomes and creating compelling futures. You also need to ensure all your outcomes are well-formed to give yourself the best opportunity for success.

The Failure Formula — focusing on the various strategies for failing, is an enemy to happiness. You need to be aware of this formula and its opposite, the NLP Success Strategy, and learn to track for and pattern-interrupt failure in your life.

Finally, life is fantastic when you live by your values — when you are clear about what's important to you and you ensure all your behaviors, decisions and outcomes are aligned with your true purpose in life.

Enemies to your Happiness

✘ Lack of dreams and desires

✘ Poorly formed outcomes

✘ Focusing on failure and following the Failure Formula

✘ Not knowing your values

Living your Dreams

The opposite of happiness is not misery, it's apathy and boredom. The opposite of happiness is living a life of mind-numbing mediocrity, just counting down your days and numbers until you die. You know, first you are 20, then you're 30, 40, 50 and each day you peel another sheet off the calendar…

Next thing you know you are at the end of your life and you look back and regret all the goals and dreams you never experienced or achieved. That's a life that is the opposite of happiness!

Remember the three components of happiness from Positive Psychology? Happiness is composed of pleasure, engagement and meaning — and of these three, true life satisfaction and abiding deep happiness are underpinned by living a life of meaning.

Life is fantastic when you live life fantastically. Life is like a sausage machine. If you put beef into one end of a sausage machine, you'd expect to get beef sausages out the other end. If you put chicken into the sausage machine, you'd be sure that chicken sausages would pop out the other end. The last thing you'd expect would be to put lamb in one end and get vegetarian sausages out the other.

Well, life is like that sausage machine. If you want happiness to come out the machine, what do you have to put into it?

Yes, that right! You have to put the ingredients for happiness and meaning into the sausage machine of life. For life to '*be*' fantastic, you have put fantastic behaviors, thoughts and outcomes into it. Life '*is*' fantastic when you '*do*' yourself and your life fantastically.

So how do you do a fantastic, meaningful life? Well, that's what this chapter is all about! ☺

> *"The more you can dream, the more you can do."*
>
> Michael Korda

> *"There is nothing like a dream to create the future."*
>
> Victor Hugo

Dreaming BIG Dreams

Without dreams, what is life? Your dreams and desires create your life. They lead you to your goals and outcomes and ultimately inspire you to create the life you live. At least they do when you put life enhancing actions to your dreams and outcomes.

Dreams come from your heart's desire. They're motivated by your values and strengths. What is important to you? What do you value? What are your strengths? The first step in dreaming big and inspiring dreams is to work out and get clear on your values.

As you know we have a fully functioning brain in our heart — a *'heart brain'*. As described earlier in this book, Neuroscience has recently discovered that we actually have a functioning system of neural tissue consisting of up to 120,000 neurons in our heart. This heart brain connects to our head brain and other body systems and integrates information and sends messages out across our mind and body.

There is wisdom in your heart — in your heart brain. Your heart is the seat of your desires and many of your emotions. Learn to tune into its signals and messages. Trust your heart. Ask it:

♥ what will truly make me happy and fulfilled?

and then listen and look for the answers it provides. It will tell, share and show you dreams and yearnings. Often the heart brain communicates in your sleep-time dreams and via visions, hunches and symbols. Continue to ask your heart to guide you and show you what's deeply important and what you truly desire. And as it does, write these dreams up on a *'Dreamlist'*.

Create a Dreamlist

Create a Dreamlist — a list of all the things you dream about and want; a list of what's important and inspires you. Capture your heart's desires here in writing. This is important!

Also, make a collage of photos and pictures from magazines of these things. Make it beautiful and colorful. Put it up on the wall next to your Dreamlist as a poster of dreams.

Desires vs Shoulds

Notice also whether the things you're dreaming about are based on *'shoulds'* versus *'desires'*. Society, family and culture fill your head with generalizations and stereotypes about what's right and what you *'should'* want and do in your life. Some of these *'shoulds'* are useful, but many are restrictive and will dampen and minimize your life — they are life denying and enemies to your happiness.

Question all your rules, beliefs and *'shoulds'*. Make sure your Dreamlist is truly filled with what you want for your life, with what motivates and inspires you. Remember it's the life *you* lead — it's your life, so dream BIG and amazing dreams and then lead yourself in achieving them.

Fantasy Dreams vs Realistic Dreams

There is an important distinction to note between fantasy dreams and realistic dreams. Fantasy dreams are ones that are unlikely or impossible to make happen in real life. For example, the ability to grow fairy wings and be able to fly through the air, like a bird, soaring, and gliding high above the earth. This is obviously a fantasy and could never occur in reality.

However, fantasy dreams are very, very useful for informing realistic dreams. If you examine the fantasy and ask what's the important driver or value inherent in the fantasy, you can often find key criteria and ideas to bring to the real world.

In the case of the fairy wings dream, you might morph it into a more realistic version by seeking practical and potentially possible versions of the dream. A practical equivalent would be to do paragliding, base jumping, hang-gliding or even to own or hire one of the newly released jet-packs. There are certainly a number of people on the planet right now, who have invented technologies that allow them to soar and fly like a bird. Though of course, not with fairy wings. ☺

The other way you could utilize the fantasy dream of fairy wings is to explore the underlying values driving it and then dream of more practical ways to achieve these.

For example, the fantasy of flying may be driven by a desire for freedom. Understanding this, you could dream of practical ways to achieve more freedom in your life. You might decide an overseas trip is in order and therefore place an adventure holiday in a foreign country up on your Dreamlist.

The key distinction here is that you should not limit or constrain your dreaming. Wild fantasies can often lead to practical outcomes. Allow your imagination free reign. Play and explore. Have fun!

Then hone and adjust your dreams into practical and doable equivalents and put them on your Dreamlist.

Dream-storming

A very powerful way to generate new dreams and ideas and to brainstorm on your heart's desires, is to play with *'what-if'* scenarios. I call this *'Dream-storming'*. By using wild and extreme scenarios you open up your mind and release boundaries and limitations on your thinking.

Ask yourself, what would you do, what would you achieve, what would you want and what would you focus on if:

- You were going to live forever (or say for 200 years)
- You only had one year to live
- You had an infinite amount of money
- You had no money whatsoever and owned or desired nothing
- You could never be harmed, you could never fail, you were invincible
- You allowed yourself to fail and knew it was OK not to succeed
- You controlled the world or the universe

Also, for each of these scenarios explore what you would definitely NOT do, NOT achieve and NOT focus on. Play with and work through the scenarios and write up or mindmap each of them. Then see what comes out that's common across them and what's different, what stands out and what seems like something you might want to do in your current reality.

This is a fun exercise, you can do it in a group, over dinner or when driving in a car with friends. It makes for fascinating conversations. The thoughts you generate can then inform your realistic dreams and may trigger ideas for what you can implement more practically into your '*LifeDesigning*'.

LifeDesigning

Many years ago I realized the importance of living a life of success by design rather than accident. It was a BFO (Blinding Flash of the Obvious) to me at the time and ultimately it motivated me to create a process I called '*LifeDesigning*' that I have been living and teaching ever since.

In this process, (which is the subject of an upcoming book), you treat your life as a '*LifeProject*' and you design and document what you want in your life across all levels.

You then build mechanisms and activities into your life to ensure you achieve the success and happiness you desire in the various contexts of your life. You also develop simple metrics and measures that help track your success and allow you to change and adjust your design. It's a fascinating and fun process and has made an incredible difference to my life and to the lives of those I've taught it to.

In this chapter, I'm introducing you to some of the key concepts and techniques from the LifeDesigning process. A fantastic life starts with knowing what you want from life. You need to dream BIG and inspiring dreams. Figure out what motivates you. Come up with a list of things you want for and from your life. Explore and determine what creates meaning in life for you. Then once you've generated your Dreamlist, you need to prioritize your dreams and start to put them into action as Outcomes and Goals.

> "If you can imagine it you can achieve it. If you can dream it, you can become it."
>
> William Arthur Ward

Dreams versus Outcomes

Here's an important distinction: *dreams are not outcomes*.

Yes, that's right, there's a huge difference between dreams and outcomes. Dreams are those things you desire and would love to have or do in your life. But making dreams into reality takes time, effort, money, knowledge and resources. Not all dreams can come true.

For a start, some outcomes are incompatible with others. I'd love to spend my life travelling the world, not living in any one place, just wandering like a gypsy from experience to experience.

I'd also love to live quietly and peacefully on a mountain retreat. Living and meditating in a cave, living an austere and transcendent existence.

But then, I also dream of living in a city like Tokyo or London, filled with people and life and adventure and stimulus. I can't live all these three dreams at once. They don't match. And of course, your dreams don't have to match. They don't have to be sensible. That's what outcomes are for.

Prioritize your Dreams

You need to begin by prioritizing your Dreamlist. Given the time limited lifetime we have and given the cost/risk/benefits involved in achieving your various dreams, which dreams would you most like to live first? What is the one dream you'd choose if you could only choose one? What would the next one be? What sequence do you want to achieve your dreams in? Prioritize your list.

Now, let's talk about outcomes. Outcomes are those things that you are actively working towards achieving in your life. They're the goals, plans and results that you're making happen in your life. Outcomes set directions that you action. And according to NLP, for success in life you need to set well-formed outcomes.

Well-formed Outcomes

A well-formed outcome is one that:

- Is positive, worded positively and says what you want rather than what you don't want
- Is specific and behaviorally measurable — you can see, hear and feel what it would be like to have achieved the outcome
- Is self-initiating and self-maintaining — only relies on yourself, not on others
- Is supported by positive beliefs
- Is ecological — has no negative consequences to you or the people you relate with or the systems in which you live
- Is sufficiently resourced — you have all the resources, money, time and skills you need to achieve the outcome
- Doesn't have anything that can prevent it — it's physically possible and you can overcome any obstacles
- Is linked to and motivated by a clear purpose and set of well-formed values.

Move your Dreams to Outcomes

You see, the way to work with dreams and outcomes is to keep dreaming big dreams, making a prioritized list of them and then when you are ready, moving your dreams one at a time into becoming clear and well-formed outcomes.

Once you have set an outcome, use the NLP Success Strategy to make the outcome happen. Remember, the Success Strategy is:

The NLP Success Strategy

1. **Clearly know your Outcome** — know exactly what you want and ensure your outcome is well-formed, that it's positive, achievable, believable and ecological.

2. **Take positive Action** — congruently and wholeheartedly take action to achieve your outcome.

3. **Learn from Feedback** — use your sensory acuity to determine if your actions are moving you closer or further away from your outcome. There's no such thing as failure, just great feedback, since if what you are doing is not moving you closer to your outcome then you need to perform the next step —

4. **Flexibility** — change and adjust your behavior (step 2) until you move closer to your outcome.

To know which dreams to make into outcomes do a cost/risk/benefit analysis of each dream at the top of your list. Grab a piece of paper and put 3 columns on it, then list each of the Costs, Risks and Benefits that the dream entails. Note that costs include more than money — there are costs in time, effort and the loss of other things that achieving the dream will cost. Note also the distinction between 'risk' and 'risky'. Some things are risky — that is, they involve risk that cannot be mitigated or controlled. Other experiences have associated risks, but these can be controlled.

For example, rock climbing using a rope and protection has an element of risk that is controlled by how much protection you use and how well you place it. Free climbing with no rope, no partner and no protection is risky. You just don't know what is going to happen and have no mitigation against accidents and harm. If a rock dislodges and causes you to fall or be knocked unconscious then you suffer the fatal results. If you use a rope and protection to control the risk, an accident will merely leave you dangling from the rope and able to be lowered so you can climb another day. It's important to ensure that your dreams are not risky before you move them to outcomes.

Once you've analyzed the cost/risk/benefits of your dreams you can decide which ones are worthwhile turning into outcomes. Then think them through clearly to ensure they are well-formed and redesign them or fine-tune them until they are. Now you're ready to take action. And that's where being gutsy enough to live your dreams and goals comes in.

🛠 Thinking Tools — Dreams to Reality

Dreams >> Outcomes >> Actions >> Success!

Awareness Questions — Empowering your Life

Ask Yourself:

- What are my dreams? If I could have ANYTHING in life, what would it be? What do I want from and with life?

- What amazing things would I like to have achieved in my life?

- What is the purpose of my life? What for me creates meaning in life? What would make my life even more deeply meaningful?

Being *'Gutsy'*

Just like we have a brain in our heart, we also have a brain in our gut — it's called the *'enteric brain'*, and consists of a functioning neural system that thinks and communicates with the other brains in our body and head.

Being *'gutsy'* involves aligning your gut with your heart and head. The gut-brain is attuned to fear and danger and is used to evaluate and prepare for risk. It's also the seat of courage, strength and determination.

To help yourself do *'gutsy-ness'* — to have the courage to make your dreams into outcomes and then live them — you can use your heart brain to talk to your enteric brain and get all of your brains aligned. You do this by thinking of times and situations in which you've been positive, strong and courageous and the values that drove this. Fill your heart with positive, strong, loving feelings and values. Amplify and centre those feelings. Breathe them into your heart and chest. Then when you are really feeling these positive heart feelings, move them down into your gut. Fill your gut with the messages of passion, values and the importance of taking courageous action now! You'll experience an amazing flow of strength and motivation in the pit of your stomach, across your torso. Some people feel it as warmth or tingling or an uplifting sense of positive courage.

This is how you build courage in yourself — how you encourage yourself. It's how you flood your life with the passion and strength to live your dreams. Hold your dreams on high. Make them into compelling and inspiring outcomes. Align your head, heart and gut. And move yourself forward into a life of loving and fulfillment.

For more information and detailed exercises on embodying courage and aligning your head, heart and gut brains, please visit www.mbraining.com and read my book, *'mBraining'*.

> *"The only thing that will stop you from fulfilling your dreams is you!"*
>
> Tom Bradley

☑ Success Strategy — Creating a Compelling Future

This technique is a visualization process that uses the NLP concepts of timelines and submodalities to create a compelling future to inspire yourself to success and happiness.

I'm sure you've heard the saying *"he or she is looking forward to a bright future"*. This expression represents our unconscious neuro-linguistic understanding of the natural process by which we create compelling futures.

In essence, a compelling future is a representation of a future state or experience that is so strongly realized and powerful that it has ongoing compelling effects on your unconscious mind. It creates and generates inspiration in your life and excites and draws you forward to the completion of your goals.

The technique comes from behavioral modeling of high achievers in fields such as sports and business. Typically, these people visualize themselves having already achieved success, making the winning goal, or receiving their reward. By having already vividly experienced it in their mind, they create compelling feelings that shape their ongoing behavior and inspire them to take action. The clearer and brighter the picture of success, the stronger the feelings and the more irresistible the compelling future is.

Create a Compelling Future:

1. Think of a goal or outcome that you'd like to have achieved in the future. Think about the details of this outcome. What will it entail? What are the steps and sub-goals involved? How will you know once you've achieved it? Create a picture in your mind of having achieved your goal or outcome now.

2. Next, imagine a line drawn out on the ground in front of you, running from left to right, or front to back. This is your timeline, running from past to future (with the past on whichever side makes sense for you). Step to one side and see or imagine an image of yourself on the timeline at the point of *'now'*. Then watch yourself move through time, doing the steps

required to achieve your outcome. Create a movie of achieving your outcome. See yourself in the movie.

3. When you are ready, step onto the timeline at the point of now and step inside your own image, into your own shoes and see the experience through your own eyes, as if it is happening to you now. Live out the experience of having achieved your outcome. Run the movie in your head, and feel the experience of achieving success in your body (in your heart and gut) as you move and step along your timeline to the point of success. See what you'll see and hear what you'll hear as you achieve your outcome now. And as you do, really feel the positive feelings of how good it is to have achieved your outcome. Enjoy and savor the sweet taste of success. Revel deeply in your achievement. Let your heart thrill with joy.

4. Now adjust the submodalities of the experience. Brighten it up. Make everything larger and closer. Add sparkle to the periphery of the image. Make it scintillating. Notice how as you do this it intensifies your positive feelings of success and achievement. Amplify these feelings. Expand them through your body. Intensify them deliciously.

5. And when you are ready, step off your timeline, and look again at the image of yourself having achieved that wonderful success now. Feels fantastic doesn't it! Re-orient yourself back to here and now, with a strong and deep sense of how compelling your future success is now. You can and will have completed that outcome soon now, won't you have!

6. Get cracking! Take action! You've now started the process to having achieved your dreams. So continue your momentum and use your bright, sparkly image to inspire and motivate yourself to the success you know you want, desire and deserve.

Use this technique with each of the key goals and outcomes in your life. The more you do this exercise, the faster and more streamlined it will become. Eventually you'll find that you've built an unconscious competency in creating compelling futures and you'll naturally use it whenever you think about anything you want to have achieved. It's powerful and it works.

> *"Failure is not a single, cataclysmic event. You don't fail overnight. Instead, failure is a few errors in judgment, repeated every day."*
>
> Jim Rohn

Failing the Failure Formula

It takes more work to fail than to succeed. Failing is a skill. There is a structure to failure and it is encapsulated by the following formula which turns the *NLP Success Strategy* on its head:

The Failure Formula

1. **Ignorance** — Don't know what you want or what's important to you.
2. **Don't do anything about it** — don't take congruent action.
3. **Ignore all feedback** — don't learn from experience.
4. **Don't change** — be very inflexible, keep doing what doesn't work.

It's obvious really… repeated failure comes from being very skilled in one or more of the steps above. You can easily sabotage success by not knowing what you want, or following poorly-formed outcomes; by not taking action or taking incongruent and ineffectual action; by ignoring feedback or advice; and by being stuck or inflexible and not changing as required.

The old aphorism of *'a stitch in time, saves nine'* expresses quite well the fact that failing creates more work and requires more energy from life. If you are clear on your outcomes and proactively do the *'stitch in time'* to fix things before they fail, you've only invested a small amount of energy to succeed. However, if you neglect to get clear about what you want and need in life or fail to take action in time, then you'll end up having to do *'nine'* times the work to remedy the failure. You will constantly be expending far more energy, time and resources just to get by.

And here's a cool idea… If you are skilled at failing, then why not fail at failing? Turn failure around and do its converse — success.

Yes, failure takes work and is a skilled incompetence. Anytime you find yourself not getting what you want in life, examine your behavior to see if you're unconsciously following any of the steps of the Failure Formula. Look for examples of the Failure Formula in your life. Then assiduously and passionately pattern-interrupt them and do the converse.

Place your focus and motivation onto the steps of the Success Strategy. Get clear about your goals, values, strengths, outcomes and dreams. Prioritize and focus your well-formed outcomes. Take congruent action and follow through. Learn from the feedback life provides as you take action and then change flexibly to keep adjusting your behaviors till you've achieved your desired results.

If it's possible in the world, then it's possible for you. It's never a question of *'if only I could do it'*, it's simply a question of learning *'how'* to achieve your desired success. Learning comes when you are open to feedback and open to advice. Look for role models — people who have already achieved the results you desire. Then learn from them and model their actions.

⚒ Thinking Tools — Modeling Success

Possible in the World, Possible for me, not a question of 'if', just a question of How.

> *"Life gives you the minimum you are prepared to accept... so set high minimum standards!"*
>
> Grant Soosalu

High Minimum Standards

Here's something I'd like to share with you. It's an insight that has made an enormous difference to my life over the years. And whilst it may appear to be another BFO (Blinding Flash of the Obvious) I do think it's worth bringing to conscious awareness and using as a life enhancing thinking tool.

Dreams vs Minimum Standards

As I hope I've convinced you, dreams, goals and outcomes have power. If you want a great life, you absolutely have to aim for the stars and dream BIG dreams. These things are important!

However, there's a crucial backup process that I've discovered in life, and it's encapsulated in the aphorism I coined and shared in the previous quote. In the everyday cut and thrust of our busy lives, in the paying of the bills, working full time jobs, running a house and family, getting the car, the dog and the mortgage serviced... life tends to give you the minimum you are prepared to accept. If you are willing to work for $10 per hour, guess what... you'll end up earning around $10 per hour. If you are prepared to let people push you around, guess what... you'll end up being stood over and pushed around. It's inevitable.

On the other hand, if you are truly prepared to only accept $1000 per hour, to never be pushed around, to really set high minimum standards, then life falls into line and delivers on that. At least, that is my experience and it's backed up by the experience of those I've shared this rule and philosophy with.

Every time I've decided that regardless of the outcome, I'm only prepared to accept a certain specific level of income, or particular behavior or results, I've amazingly gotten what I've expected and demanded. It almost seems like magic. It isn't of course; there is science and logic to why this works.

Most importantly, the take home message is...

"Set high minimum standards in every area of your life!"

Why does this work?

I think the reason that this works is due to a number of factors. A key one is the self-fulfilling prophecy effect. Your beliefs and attitudes are expressed non-verbally in your behaviors and communications and picked up by other people who then act in ways that fulfill your unconscious expectations. There is a ton of research from the fields of cognitive and social psychology to back this up.

In one classic experiment, known as *'the late bloomers study'*, researchers Dr. Robert Rosenthal and Dr. Lenore Jacobson, gave children in an elementary class an intelligence test and told teachers that a small group of these children were unusually clever *'late bloomers'*, though in reality they were average. The researchers then returned at the end of the school year and tested the same class again, and not surprisingly, the children singled out as intelligent *'late bloomers'* had improved their intelligence scores far more than the other children, showing that they had responded positively to the teachers unconscious beliefs and expectations.

> *"Psychological research shows that beliefs and expectations are the strongest predictor of the future."*

In a more recent example, a group of researchers from Iowa State University examined whether mothers' and fathers' beliefs about their children's alcohol use had cumulative self-fulfilling effects on their children's future drinking behavior. Analyses of longitudinal data showed consistent synergistic and cumulative effects of parent's negative beliefs. And these beliefs predicted the greatest degree of confirmatory behavior from children when both mothers and fathers overestimated their children's alcohol use. The results show that beliefs and expectations really are powerful and send out unconscious messages that have real effects on people's behaviors over time.

Another factor for why the rule works is that much of life involves negotiation, and people and society tend to be good at working out your bottom line and offering that to you. If you are time pressured or feeling a bit insecure or distracted by all the other things going on in your busy life, then you'll tend to accept the initial offer, or at least, not hold out to get your ideal result. Thus over time you end up accepting and receiving the minimum you are prepared to accept, rather than your ideal outcomes and dreams.

Linking Dreams with High Minimum Standards

To live a fantastic life, you need to design your life by creating clear and well-formed outcomes, that link to big dreams and inspiring purposes. In this way, you motivate yourself by having meaningful outcomes and goals and filling your life with intentions and behaviors that link to your highest values.

At the same time, set high minimum standards in every key area of life and hold firm to those. Set in concrete, in your mind, the minimum standards you are prepared to accept in yourself and others. Then stick to them.

Your goals, dreams and outcomes set the direction for your life.

Life is FANTASTIC!

They inspire you. Your minimum standards act like a platform and springboard. They are the base from which you support yourself to live a wonderful life and achieve your dreams and outcomes.

Note that setting high minimum standards is not a recommendation to indulge in perfectionism or focus on unreasonable expectations and unobtainable standards. Research in Cognitive Psychology has shown that setting unrealistic goals can contribute to depression. So set achievable and obtainable outcomes and high realistic standards.

Do it NOW!

Ok, grab a pen and paper and right now think about and get specifically clear about your minimum standards for:

- How much money you will work for?
- What sort of loving behavior you want from yourself and your beloved?
- How fit you'll be, how much exercise you'll do?
- What sort of language you'll use both externally and in your internal dialogue?
- How you'll spend/invest your time?
- How much stress you'll put up with?
- How much pampering you want in your life?
- How much learning you'll do?

- What you'll eat and what body mass index you're happy with?

- How healthy you are?

- How successful you'll be, by your own definition of success?

- How you'll treat your friends and how they'll treat you?

The more specifically you define what you'll accept and what you definitely won't accept, the more you'll find your life magically improving. You won't even have to negotiate about these things. People will read the messages in your life language and your unconscious responses. Life starts to get better and better as it delivers to your expectations and high minimum standards. And stick to those standards. Don't accept anything less!

"Life gives you the minimum you are prepared to accept... so set high minimum standards!"

Yes absolutely, definitely, dream BIG dreams and set lofty goals and outcomes; and truly, take the time to clearly and firmly set high minimum standards in your life, you'll find they'll help avoid many enemies to happiness and support a fantastic life of ongoing happiness and success.

Balance and Ecology

Some dreams are not worth having! You need to beware what you dream and ask for. There is a balance and ecology required for well-formed dreaming. Focusing solely on money for example, is an enemy to happiness.

In a number of studies performed by psychologists Dr. Tim Kasser and Dr. Richard Ryan at the University of Rochester, it was found that individuals who aspired to financial and monetary success over other life goals such as interpersonal support, affiliation, community feeling or self acceptance, were significantly more likely to experience negative psychological outcomes such as anxiety and depression and poor psychological adjustment.

Additionally, such individuals were more likely to evidence a need for over-control than those who focused less centrally on financial success. The results show that focusing on monetary wealth over other life goals is counterproductive and leads to emotional and psychological problems.

Those are not the sort of outcomes you want in life!

Intrinsic vs Extrinsic Goals

Further studies have shown that a focus on intrinsic goals such as personal growth, emotional intimacy and community involvement are inherently psychologically rewarding and lead to increased emotional and psychological well-being.

In contrast, extrinsic goals such as financial success, image, and fame are less satisfying of innate human psychological needs and tend to impact negatively on well-being and happiness, especially over the long term.

The message is to find a balance between extrinsic and intrinsic goals and dreams. Fame without personal growth, or money without sharing can lead to misery. Make your dreams, goals and outcomes meaningful and connect them with your deeper and more heartfelt life purpose. Your happiness depends on it.

> "Seek out that particular mental attribute which makes you feel most deeply and vitally alive... and when you have found that attitude, follow it."
>
> William James

◯ Deeper Understandings — Directing your RAS

As described earlier in Chapter 2, there is a part of your nervous system, called the Reticular Activating System (RAS) that sits near the core of your brainstem. The RAS acts like a filter or way station for almost all the information that feeds into your brain from the outlying sensory nerves.

The RAS is responsible for ensuring that your brain isn't swamped by useless and unimportant data and signals. It only let's through to the higher centers of your brain the information that is deemed as important and salient.

For example, the RAS is involved in what is known in psychology as the *'Cocktail Party Effect'*. This is the effect you'll have experienced when at a club, restaurant, party or bar; a noisy environment where it's difficult to hear conversations. In order to pick out just the voice of one of your companions, your RAS manages to filter out that auditory signal from the blooming confusion of noise and voices around you. Whilst doing an excellent job of that, and without any conscious awareness on your part, your RAS also monitors other conversations for anything of importance or salience.

This is why, if someone three tables over, mentions your

name, or starts speaking about something that is of significance to you, their voice or conversation will somehow jump out and come to your awareness. This is the cocktail party effect. Your RAS manages to filter what appears to be noise from your conscious mind, but nevertheless manages to bring to your conscious awareness anything important. An amazing and necessary feat.

The key to the RAS and its operation is salience and values. Your values, goals and dreams direct and guide your RAS. If there's something you strongly desire or value highly, then your RAS will notice examples of it and highlight it in your environment. These will then be incorporated into and magnified in your ongoing map of the world.

The more specifically you delineate and define your values, goals and dreams, the more your RAS will assist you in achieving them. It works like magic and is the basis for so called esoteric goal achievement techniques like *'the secret'*. The real secret however is to focus and direct your powerful RAS by using the skills and techniques highlighted in this chapter.

"Happiness is that state of consciousness which proceeds from the achievement of one's values."

Ayn Rand

Valuing your Life

Values are those things you are prepared to invest time, money, energy and resources to gain and achieve. They're what you want in life. Values drive and motivate your goals and outcomes. The clearer you are about your values, the more powerfully your multi-mind will work to deliver them. When you are confused or unclear about your values, you undermine your chances of success.

Values and Meaningfulness

The neural network of the brain is a values driven patterning system. As an evolved survival mechanism, it tracks for and maps what is important, salient and of value. Whenever new experience occurs, the strength of the synaptic connections that are firing during the experience get strengthened in proportion to the biological and semantic salience or meaningfulness of the experience.

The brilliant Neuro-Biologist, Gerald Edelman, in his research on the mind and brain has shown in his theory of Neuronal Group Selection, that values are at the heart of how we construct our maps of the world. Meaningfulness drives and determines what gets stored in the neural network of the brain. Your values sort and prioritize which memories, experiences and cognitive structures eventually come to live in your map of the world. Values and meaningfulness interconnect to determine how you make sense of the world, how you make decisions and ultimately how you come to live your life.

Values also are at the heart of what information comes through your nervous systems to impinge on your frontal lobe processes and higher brain functions. As described in the *'Deeper Understandings'* section, your Reticular Activating System (RAS), a core component of your central nervous system, acts as a filter or way-station to information coming from almost all sensory processes. And the key to the RAS is salience or values. The RAS only allows information through that it deems to be meaningful.

So values filter and prioritize the information your nervous system attends to and therefore learns from and builds new maps and meaning from. Values filter and directionalize learning.

Types of Values

There are numerous ways to categorize values and each has its benefits and uses.

Values can be:

1. **Move Towards** or **Move Away** values

2. **Content** or **Process** values

3. **Means** or **Ends** values

4. **Espoused** or **Operating** values

Let's explore each of these briefly and look at how you can use them to ensure you are living a fantastic life.

Move Towards vs Move Away values

Towards values are the things you want and desire. Away values in contrast are the things you abhor and definitely do NOT want in your life. Sometimes it's as important to clearly know what you don't want in life, as it is to know what you do.

Most people naively think that if you have a strong move towards value for something then you'll naturally have a strong move away value for its converse. However, this is not necessarily so.

For example, you may highly value honesty, yet be ambivalent about certain types of white lies. Or you might strongly value adventure but be unfussed about mundane activities. Sure you'd prefer and desire adventure, but when subjected to normal or boring experiences you don't have a strong move away from response to them.

On the other hand, it is entirely possible to have strong move away from values to the converse of your move towards values. In our example above, you might strongly value adventure and intensely move away from the mundane. The key is that move towards values do not always necessarily define and determine your move away values.

That's why it's important to explore, understand, define and consciously articulate both what you want in life and what you don't want in life. The clearer you are about these things, the more your unconscious mind will track for and create the reality you desire.

If you aren't clear about what your move away values are, without realizing it, you may insidiously end up living with things that don't serve you and are enemies to your happiness.

Content vs Process Values

Content values are the '*what*' of life. They're the things you want in life. Process values are the '*how*'. They are the qualities by which you live and achieve your content values.

Content values are things like houses, relationships, careers, cars, holidays and educational degrees. Wealth is a content value. Honesty, passion, resilience and flexibility on the other hand are process values. They are the qualities you operate from as you achieve the things you want in life.

Most people focus on articulating the content values they want and desire. They fail to get clear about '*how*' they will live each day and fail to articulate and design the quality of how they will action their goals and outcomes.

I think it's incredibly important to understand and clarify both the content and process values for your life.

In particular, process values are important because they are more immediate and ongoing. Many content values take a long time to procure or achieve. It can take years to pay off and own a house, or to complete an academic degree, or amass a certain amount of wealth. Along the way, you can get lost in the journey and end up with a miserable life.

Your process values and qualities can be lived every single day. If you value strength and resilience for example, you can practice these in small ways daily, even as you are slowly working your way towards your larger more long term content values.

Means vs Ends Values

Some things are ends in themselves. You want them simply for what they are and what they bring. Love is an example. You want loving relationships and people you care for and about in your life, simply because they make life worthwhile.

Other values are means values. They are a means towards the ends you desire. Wealth is an example of a means value. Money provides the means to support other values and outcomes. You don't have money as an end in itself because it is meaningless outside of what it can buy, bring and enable.

It's incredibly important to be aware of this difference between means and ends values and to make sure that you don't confuse one with the other. There are numerous examples in life of famous wealthy people who have made wrecks of their lives by confusing money as an ends value. They've ended up lonely, depressed and unwell because they focused on accumulating wealth above all else, as an end in itself.

Make sure you understand what each of your values is and that your means values support your ends values. Your happiness and true success depend on it.

Espoused vs Operating Values

Espoused values are the things we say are important to us. Operating values show up in what's unconsciously/behaviorally important and attractive to us. Our operating values are evidenced by our actions and by what we do as compared to what we say.

When there is congruence and alignment between your espoused values and your operating values then life flows smoothly. Mismatch between your articulated values and operating values is an enemy to happiness and leads to undermining of your goals, dreams and outcomes.

Well-formed Values

For values to serve you, they need to be *'well-formed'*. That is, they need to align, match and work with each other in a way that supports success.

I've spent a number of years researching values and modeling the well-formedness rules for values. To go into this in detail requires a book in its own right. However, I'll cover the basics here to get you started.

Well-formedness Rules for Values:

➢ All your values must be congruent with one another and aligned with your Life Purpose

➢ Values must be sorted in a well-structured hierarchy

- There needs to be a balance between means and ends values

- There should be no means values above the ends values they support in the hierarchy

- There should be no means values right at the top of the hierarchy

- There should be a balance between towards and away-from values

- There needs to be congruence between espoused values and operating values (values-in-action)

- All values must be ecological in all contexts of your life and have no negative consequences or impacts (e.g. not illegal, not damaging to health or property, not damaging to relationships, not damaging to key life outcomes)

- All values must be sustainable

Submodalities and Values

When you think about something you value, when you picture it in your mind's eye, the content of the picture carries and codes the meaning. What is *'in'* the picture forms and determines the meaning. The submodalities of the image (brightness, size, position, color etc.) on the other hand, code the meaningfulness. In other words, how meaningful a value is, is structured through the submodalities of your representations and images.

Let's make this clear with an example. Picture something you strongly value, something you feel very strongly about and that's very important to you. Something you value highly. Now notice how bright and close the picture is to you. Push the picture way, way off into the distance and dim it right down. Notice that subjectively it no longer seems so important, so salient, so meaningful. Now zoom it back in to where it was originally and brighten it up. Your subjective experience of the value is intrinsically linked to the submodalities you code the image with.

Notice also that the things that are important to you, that you value highly, tend to have pictures that are physically located high in the visual field. They are *'highly valued'*. And notice also that this extends into other patterns of how we value our world.

Where are the most valued and expensive *'top shelf'* drinks stored? — On the highest shelf. Where do we physically place the most important people in an organization? — The office of the CEO is usually on the top floor, and similarly on an Organization chart, the most highly valued (in importance and in remuneration terms) people are placed on the top of the chart. Have you ever seen a short Super Model? Research indicates that tall people are more highly valued, they get better jobs, more opportunities and their median income is higher. Society is replete with examples of the vertical sorting of values.

So the submodality of vertical dimension codes for move towards and move away from values. Up is move towards, down is move away. The higher or lower, the more the towards or away salience.

Distance and brightness combine together, as a means of increasing or decreasing the flux density of photons impinging on the retina, to code for intensity of value or salience. By brightening an image or moving it closer, you increase the intensity of the meaningfulness. You make it much more meaning-full.

Central and Peripheral physical location also code for

meaningfulness. We value those things that are central to us much more than those that are peripheral. Note however that change in the peripheral view has high salience from the perspective of danger and fear. Left and right also code for meaningfulness.

These are just some of the many ways we use submodalities to code how meaningful experiences are to us. There are numerous others related to time coding, color coding, patterns of change etc. and I'll write more about them in a future book and on my blog *'Life Enhancing'* (http://enhancingmylife.blogspot.com).

The more you understand how values and the process of valuing works, the more you'll know how to drive your own mind and life.

Values Mastery

The message of this chapter is that to overcome the enemies to happiness and to support a life of meaning and purpose, you need to become a master of tracking, designing and flexibly operating from very clear, well-defined and well-formed values.

You need to become a master of how you are value-ing your life.

Remember, values aren't something you have, they're processes that you do. How are you valuing your life? Are your values well-formed and clearly focused? Prioritized in hierarchies that support your life purpose? If not, you now have the knowledge, skills and techniques to design and live a fantastic life. It's up to you to use these and put them into action now.

☑ Success Strategy — Values Hierarchy

It is vital that you are both clear about what matters to you in the various contexts of your life and that these values are sorted in a clear hierarchy of importance. This will allow your unconscious mind to align your decisions and behaviors with your desires.

1. Mindmap or create an unstructured list of the key values that are most important to you in life. Do this exercise separately for your process values and content values.

2. Ask yourself: *"If I could only have one of these values in life, just one, and no others, what would that one be?"* For example, if you have values of *'love'*, *'money'* and *'health'* on your list, and you decide that if there's only one value you can have it must be love, then ask yourself as a clarity check: *"If I could only have love, not health or money, would it be what I want? If I could have love, but I didn't have health, would that be ok?"* Explore these issues and questions deeply. On reflection, you may decide that it's hard to be loving and feel and enjoy love if you are in bad health, if you are suffering great pain or locked in a coma. You may decide that health is more important to you, since you need health to do and enjoy the other values in your list.

3. Once you have decided what the number one value is. Move to working out number two. Ask yourself: *"If I could only have two values, what would they be? Only two?"* Explore this.

4. Continue to work through your list until you have your values sorted in a hierarchy of importance. List them in sequence on a piece of card or paper, with the most important value (the

highest value) at the top of the page.

5. Memorize your list and its sequence. Keep it pinned somewhere high in your visual field, for example on a wall in the kitchen or bathroom or bedroom. Somewhere where you will see it regularly and value it both highly and deeply.

6. Monitor your life to ensure that your operating values — the values in action in your life — match this espoused list of values. Do this by comparing what you're spending time, energy, money and resources on. If your life doesn't match the values you have consciously decided upon, then change and adjust your actions, behaviors and decisions to match your values hierarchy.

⚡ Pattern-Interrupt — Looking Back on Life

The following process combines the ideas and skills described throughout this chapter. Use this to get clear about what you want in your life and to motivate yourself to generate inspiring dreams.

Inspire yourself to create and live great dreams and outcomes by:

⚡ Imagine for a moment that you are on your dying bed, in the last moments of your life, at the end of a long, wonderful and satisfying life...

- Looking back over your life, what would you have wanted to have experienced and achieved?

- What do you want people to remember you for?

- What do you want your life to have meant?

- What adventures do you want to have completed?

- What places do you want to have visited or explored?

- What do you want to have learned?

- What will you have done for other people?

- Who will remember you and why?

- What will your legacy be to the future?

- If you knew you couldn't fail, what would you do in your life?

- Now, returning to your life right now, grab a pen and paper and write up your *'bucket-list'* — your list of things you want to have done, experienced, created and achieved before you die.

- Continue to think about and explore your list and be on the lookout for fascinating things to add to your list.

- Make sure you put action to these ideas and insights by adding them to your Dreamlist and as appropriate make them into outcomes that you make happen in the fantastic life

Life is FANTASTIC!

> you are creating for yourself now.

> *"Do not spoil what you have by desiring what you have not; but remember that what you now have was once among the things only hoped for."*
>
> Epicurus

Being and Doing

It's vitally important to find a balance between stretching and inspiring yourself to live and do more, whilst enjoying and truly appreciating what you've currently achieved.

Too often people focus solely on achieving and rushing from one goal to the next —- and in doing so, they don't remember to sit back, savor and enjoy the journey. Isn't it the case that we sometimes put too much value on quantity at the cost of quality? And too much focus on doing versus simply *'being'* — on achieving rather than making quality time to enjoy the simple pleasures of being alive on this wonderful planet?

Transcendental Change vs Generative Change

The challenge is that modern society has grabbed rigidly onto the Generative Model of Change. This is the model that says that no matter how good life is, we can always make it better. It's about more passion, fun and achievement NOW!!! This is a model that fields like NLP have been promulgating and installing for over 30 years and it has crept insidiously into many areas of management, training, education and marketing.

It's very seductive and it certainly does support success. However... if you follow it slavishly, you'll end up on the treadmill of a *'more the more pattern'*... the more you follow the model, the more success you'll enjoy and achieve, the more reinforced you'll be to continue making bigger and bigger dreams, goals and outcomes and the more you'll focus on achieving more. And along the way, if you aren't careful... you'll get lost in the constant drive for more and trapped by the enemies to happiness of *'more greed is better'* and *'too much, too soon'*.

In Positive Psychology, as indicated earlier in this book, this process is described as the *'hedonic treadmill'* and is an enemy to human happiness. So whilst the achievement of goals and outcomes makes you feel good fleetingly, the constant pressure and drive for success, stresses you unconsciously and wears you down, ultimately eroding your true happiness.

The Generative Model can be contrasted with what I call the *'Transcendental Model of Change'*. In this model, we focus on meaning and purpose; on exploring why you think and feel you're on this planet for, with this particular life, and what you're here to experience and learn.

It's about transcending the constant need for *'$uccess'* and *'Achievement'*. Indeed, it's more about the *'how'* and the *'quality of being'* by which you are doing whatever achieving and success-ing that you are doing in your life.

Focus on Qualities

With transcendental change — with a focus on being versus doing — it's OK to have times where you don't actually need to do any changing and material achieving. If the *'how'* of your life is aligned with your purpose and with the deeper meaning of life, then you can happily stay exactly where and how you are.

Of course in the massively changing world we live in, it's impossible to stay *'exactly'* the same. However, at the level of process, of *'how'*, of qualities and process values, you can *'change to stay the same'*. In other words, you can stop constantly striving for more and more, and make quality time in your life to just be connected, centered, happy and flowing. In other words there's a bliss-point for being and doing, for achieving and then taking time to rest and savor your success.

As of today, right now, begin to notice more and more the opportunities for making *'Quality Time'* an important process value in your life. Create the time and space to think about and focus on what sort of Qualities you want in your life each and every day and then put them gently and surely into practice.

Take time out from the hectic race for more and more, get off the hedonic treadmill, and just enjoy *'being'*. Learn and make time to meditate. Make time to pamper yourself. Get out for a walk in the forest. Connect with nature. Enjoy quality time and conversing with people you love and care about. Connect with yourself.

At the end of your life, looking back, it won't be how many material items you accrued, or how big your house was, or how many cars you owned that makes your life worthwhile. It will be the quality of your relationships, the quality of your experiences and the quality of the person you are that really counts.

Invest in Yourself

This life is yours! It's the life *you* lead! So lead it well. Your life can be fantastic if you stay strong, stay focused and put action to your dreams.

Invest in your life and your future. Build up your knowledge and skills. Determine your strengths and then build on them. Focus your life. Gain as many and as varied experiences as you can.

Educate yourself. The more you invest in yourself and in creating a meaningful life, the more you'll be able to live great dreams. Life is a wondrous adventure and there is nothing like living an amazing dream to create an amazing future now.

Strengths & Values In Action

Use the following table to determine which strengths, qualities and values to focus on and amplify in your life to support the processes and skills of happiness. Also notice if you have any elements of the absence, opposite or exaggeration of these strengths and remove them from your behaviors and your life.

Enemies to happiness	VIA Strength
Lack of Dreams & Desires	Purpose/Spirituality
Poorly formed Outcomes	Hope & Awe
Following the Failure Formula	Curiosity
Unclear Values	Creativity

Notes from the Field — Embracing Your Dreams

Author and Pulitzer Prize nominee Thomas *'Sully'* Sullivan has been a coach, a "*Rube Goldberg*" innovator, a teacher, a city commissioner, and an All-American athlete. Currently he lives in Minnesota, writing full-time and lecturing across the country.

I came across Sully a couple of years ago and liked his writing so much I subscribed to his on-line newsletter. Every month Sully shares his thoughts and adventures and his missives are so full of lyrical wisdom and inspiring, uplifting anecdotes that I feel he is a great exemplar of someone who lives a fantastic life.

As an example of Sully's attitude to life, I'd like to share a couple of excerpts from recent *'Sullygram'* newsletters:

> *"I run the risk of falling short by living for ideals, but when my dreams are frustrated the solution for me is to keep on reaching for them, whereas giving up on ideals would be fatal to my soul."*

> *"Whatever your personal hurts and limitations, you can always find a way to live to the max. That's because life actually takes place between the ears. Your dreams never rejected you, but you may have rejected your dreams. Surround yourself with the stuff of your fantasies, and you will rise to the level of ideals they represent. They will become real as you become real."*

Inspired by Sully's writing, I contacted him and asked if he'd share his ideas on happiness, on avoiding the enemies to happiness and on the importance of filling your life with dreams, purpose and outcomes.

What do you think are the secrets to happiness? What do you believe are the key states, processes and strategies for achieving happiness and joy in life?

For many, as they go through the stages of life, there seem to be transitory states of happiness based on perceptions and strategies that position them well in the rank order of their society. It might be as simple as having a well-kept lawn in relation to the neighbors or as complex as power dynamics in a career or being desirable to the opposite sex. Having a good image of ourselves — whatever that means at a given point in one's life — seems to be paramount.

Personally, I have chased and continue to chase my own vain idols, but almost uniformly throughout my life, whenever I've been unhappy, the ultimate solution for me was to get outside myself. I'm not an aggressive do-gooder by any means, but I'm a lot more satisfied when I remember that it isn't about me and when I become lost in analyzing (not judging) and inspiring others.

What do you believe are the key enemies to happiness i.e. what do you think are the strategies, values, beliefs or behaviors that destroy or limit happiness and joy in life?

Mindless competitiveness is certainly high on the list. Insecurity about one's worth in the eyes of others is almost the same thing. But perhaps a more insidious enemy of happiness is the addiction to acquiring markers in the pecking order of society. Those symbols of *"happiness"* might be material goods or leverage over others.

Eventually each symbol of achievement gives way to an addiction for the pattern itself, and we require the sense of momentum we get with the next possession or control. This kind of self-appeasement becomes redundant and hollow eventually, especially if it meets little adversity.

We are problem-solving animals trained through eons of evolution. Getting what we want too easily weakens our growth and capacity to adapt. If you want a species to become vulnerable, let it succeed without obstacle. Ditto the individual.

With regard to dreams, goals and purpose are there any specific beliefs, patterns, strategies or techniques that you feel support happiness or destroy happiness? Are there any strategies that you use in your own life to enhance your happiness and meaning in life?

Dreams can become goals, and fulfilling them answers a purpose. You could juxtapose the order of those words and shift the semantics, but for me the sequence remains. Whether or not I am subconsciously trying to answer a purpose, my dreams are the first conscious/willed step for me. They give me a foretaste of the perfection/idealism which is the tap root of my existence. That is the motivator for me.

I've always been seen as having impossible dreams, and yet that is precisely what produces the greatest successes, the magic in life, and the romance. The dreams may harden into concrete goals, and always in retrospect over time, it turns out that I have understated what was possible. There are no impossible dreams; only those which are still in the process of fulfillment.

Dare to Dream

According to Sully, and I totally concur with his insight, *"most people do not dare to dream"*. They are caught up in fear, guilt and *"the images of other people's imaginations"*.

Sully's advice is to put aside fears, wounds and the hauntings of others' expectations. Venture into creative areas. Risk something. *"Get outside yourself and see what's there."*

It's all about inspiring yourself, stretching yourself and embracing your dreams.

You can read more of Sully's wisdom and check out his books at his website: www.thomassullivanauthor.com

---

☞ Remember This

- ✓ To create and live a fantastic life, make a prioritized Dreamlist and move your dreams into inspiring well-formed outcomes and compelling futures.

- ✓ Encourage yourself to take action and fulfill your dreams by aligning your head, heart and gut brains.

- ✓ Beware of the steps and behaviors of the Failure Formula and pattern-interrupt these by replacing them with their opposing skills from the NLP Success Strategy.

- ✓ Life tends to give you the minimum you're prepared to accept, so set high minimum standards in every area of your life and use these as a base foundation to support living a wonderful life and achieving your dreams and outcomes.

✓ Focus on intrinsic goals such as personal growth, emotional intimacy and community involvement rather than extrinsic goals such as money, fame or image. Make your dreams and outcomes meaningful and connect them with your deeper and more heartfelt life purpose and values.

✓ Clearly articulate your values. Values drive and motivate your goals and outcomes. The clearer you are about your values, the more powerfully your multi-mind will work to deliver them.

✓ Create a Values Hierarchy of prioritized values for both your Process Values and Content Values and examine these lists to determine and adjust them so they are well-formed. Ensure that you understand and focus on:

   ➢ Move Towards and Move Away values

   ➢ Means and Ends values

   ➢ Operating versus Espoused values

✓ Find a balance between stretching and inspiring yourself whilst enjoying and truly appreciating what you've currently achieved. Focus on Qualities and savoring your success.

ⓘ Extra Info

Refer to www.enemiestohappiness.com for

- more information about the material covered in this chapter
- additional reading and references for this chapter

Avoiding the Enemies to HAPPINESS

Chapter 11

HAPPINESS is a verb

You will learn to

- ✓ Experience happiness as a process and journey
- ✓ Use success strategies to do exquisite happiness-ing
- ✓ Help others and add value to their lives
- ✓ Gain well-being by building on your strengths and focusing on purpose and meaning

HAPPINESS is a verb

As you've discovered in this book, happiness isn't something you *'have'* — it's not an object — it's the result of specific skills and behaviors that you *'do'* in your life. In essence, the process of happiness-ing is an ongoing journey and not an end point or destination in itself.

Happiness comes from behaviors that focus on purpose and meaning. Actions that help others and allow you to utilize your core strengths increase the deep feelings of satisfaction, well-being and joy you experience.

You don't *'get happiness'* by focusing on happiness. You experience happiness-ing by systematically and continually removing the enemies to happiness in your life, and replacing them with strategies for happiness success. That's the recipe for a great life, and a great life leads to exquisite happiness-ing.

Enemies to your Happiness

- ✘ Treating happiness as an object
- ✘ Demanding and expecting happiness ALL the time
- ✘ Focusing only on yourself and not helping others
- ✘ Not inspiring yourself through purpose and strengths

Denominalizing Happiness

As indicated throughout this book, happiness is an active process and not a passive object. You don't *'have'* happiness. It's a disguised verb, a doing word, and NOT a noun, NOT an object.

It's an enemy to happiness-ing to think of happiness as if it's something you can grab hold of and own. Or to think of happiness as if it's something you can keep constant and *'have'* all of the time.

The reality is that you experience happiness when you use the skills of happiness-ing in your life. As I'm sure you've come to realize from the many deep insights throughout this book, happiness is the result of specific actions and behavioral competencies. Happiness is a process. Happiness is a *verb* — a *'doing'* word.

I like to think of happiness as similar to a speedometer in a car. When you are travelling, the speedo shows you how successfully you are traversing the miles. The outcome of the journey is not to do a particular speed, the outcome is to arrive at your destination. The speedo indicates how swiftly and safely you are achieving your outcome.

Happiness is like the speedo. The outcome in life is not to constantly *'have'* happiness. Instead, happiness is an indicator of how well you are journeying through life.

When you are living a wondrous life — when you are living a life of meaning and purpose and utilizing your core strengths — you'll experience high levels of happiness, joy and life satisfaction. If you lose momentum and get bogged down or swamped by the enemies to happiness, you'll experience the opposite of happiness and succumb to negative emotions and feelings.

The key message of this final chapter is that it is unproductive to constantly focus on and demand happiness. Instead, focus on and embody behaviors of happiness-ing. Build your life around meaning, purpose, values and strengths. Follow the wisdom of your heart and gut brains. Help others. That's the true secret to happiness-ing!

> *"Happiness is like a butterfly: the more you chase it, the more it will elude you, but if you turn your attention to other things, it will come and sit softly on your shoulder."*
>
> Henry David Thoreau

Bliss-pointing Happiness

As we learned in Chapter 9, almost all human processes and behaviors have a *'bliss-point'*. This is the optimum sensation or experience that results when the level is *'just right'* — neither too low nor too high. Our physiology evolved to utilize and maximize these bliss-points, but unless you are aware of this you can end up overdoing what you desire and going beyond the bliss-point, swamping your system, and losing the enjoyment of the very thing you're after.

As indicated previously, the *"take home"* message about bliss-pointing is that to maintain optimal enjoyment from any experience in life, you need to carefully manage not to flood your system. If you have too much, you'll overflow the inbuilt bliss-point and your body will down-regulate its response. Moderation in all things is the key.

This principle applies to the process of happiness-ing too. If you try to experience intense feelings of joy and happiness all the time, you'll end up on the *'hedonic treadmill'* (also described in Chapter 9).

You'll end up needing more and more stimulus to achieve the same level of bliss. Feelings of happiness, joy and bliss are largely mediated and produced by levels of neuro-hormones such as serotonin, dopamine and the endorphins. And as explained in Chapter 9, there is a *'sweet-spot'* or bliss-point for how much of these your body can produce and utilize. If you overdo their use, your body will decrease its response to them, making it harder to re-experience bliss and joy.

You can only maintain the bliss-point of happiness if you carefully manage your behaviors and experiences so that you never continuously over-do or over-indulge in happiness and bliss. Your wonderful brain/mind/body is like a garden, the plants need just the right amount of water and nutrients; too much or too little and the plants wilt and suffer.

So don't focus on trying to experience intense feelings of happiness and joy in every single moment of every single day. It's just not physically, psychologically, emotionally or physiologically possible. This is why focusing on purpose and meaning leads to a much more enduring sense of deep happiness. It's more sustainable and ecological in your life. It may not flood you with a continuous high of emotional bliss, but it will make you feel that life is great and worth living.

> *"Enjoyment is not a goal, it is a feeling that accompanies important ongoing activity."*
>
> Paul Goodman

Believing your Happiness

As a wise man once taught me, *'happiness is a state of mind'*. What he meant by this is that if you believe you are happy, if you choose to act happy, if you do the processes of happiness-ing, then you'll *'be'* happy. It's a choice. You are the master of your own happiness-ing, the master of your emotional destiny. You don't have to change your external circumstances, you just need to adjust your internal beliefs and expectations. You truly can choose to create a happy state of mind at any time. It's up to you.

As you know, throughout this book we've been exploring and highlighting the enemies to happiness and showing you how to replace them with strategies for happiness-ing that you can use to create your own happy state of mind and body. Knowing and believing that this is possible is a key step in doing this.

Remember that happiness-ing involves a set of skills and strategies. And as you practice what you've learned from this book, you'll become more adept at mastering the process of creating a happy state of mind, anytime, anywhere.

🛠 Thinking Tools — Happiness-ing

Happiness is a verb! Happiness is a state of mind.

🔍 Awareness Questions — Doing happiness-ing

Ask Yourself:

- ➢ Who and what in my life makes me feel happier?
- ➢ What can I do to feel happier now?
- ➢ What is a happier way to think about this?
- ➢ How much more can I appreciate who I am right now?
- ➢ How much more can I appreciate and enjoy what I have right now?

Pos ψ Enjoying Each Day

It's the little things that matter. Not the huge one-shot deals. People erroneously think that happiness comes from winning lotto, from major '*success*' events, from achieving fame and fortune. But the reality is very different. Positive Psychology research by Prof. Dan Gilbert has found that we are notoriously bad at estimating what will make us happy or about guessing how happy we'll be after a particular event or experience. His research shows that happiness gained from large events like winning the lottery evaporates fairly quickly. Instead, he suggests greater levels of enduring happiness come from the small and regular delights of daily life. You are better served in happiness-ing your life if you fill your day with small

Avoiding the Enemies to HAPPINESS

simple joys.

For example, hugs make people happier. Dr. Sonja Lyubomirsky found that subjects who were instructed to give or receive a minimum of five hugs per day and record the details became much happier than subjects who merely recorded their reading activity.

Smiling also makes you happy. As indicated in Chapter 4, research has shown that smiling leads to measurable changes in nervous system and immune function. One experiment found that simply getting people to simulate a smile by holding a pen in their mouth for 15 minutes a day lead to measurable increases in the hormones of happiness in the blood stream along with corresponding self-reported feelings of happiness.

Psychologist Dr. Ed Diener has found in his research that the frequency of positive experience is a much better predictor of happiness than the intensity of the experience. Someone who has a dozen mildly nice things happen per day is usually happier than someone who has a single incredible and intense thing happen.

So find the simple pleasures in life that bring you joy, and fill each day with a selection of them. If taking a walk makes you feel good, then plan a walk several times a week, or start the day with one. Make sure you schedule in time to connect with those you love. Give them daily hugs. Take pleasure in the simple joys of life, do lots of them each day, and you'll find they'll lift your spirit and mood.

There is an admonition in NLP that says, "*if you keep doing what you've always done, you'll keep getting what you've always gotten.*" This is an important insight. While it's the little things in life that make a positive difference to your happiness, it's also true in the converse. Small negative things, done repeatedly can destroy your happiness.

If you don't stop doing old patterns of negativity, you'll not be able to stop experiencing deep levels of misery and unhappiness. People don't become obese by eating one huge meal. It's lots and lots of poor eating decisions over long periods of time that lead to pathological overweight. Similarly, smoking one cigarette won't kill you. But smoking a cigarette every hour or two, over many years, will destroy your health. Smoking kills one in two people who habitually smoke.

So pattern-interrupt those enemies to happiness and replace them with patterns of behavior that generate joy and happiness. Fill each day with joyful activities, and keep doing those. You'll then keep doing and getting the happiness and well-being you so desire and deserve.

> *"Success and happiness are not destinations, they are exciting, never-ending journeys."*
>
> Zig Zigler

☑ Success Strategy — Tunnel of Happiness-ing

Here's a simple yet powerful Success Strategy you can use every day to increase the feelings of happiness in your life. I developed this technique using insights from NLP and Neuroscience and called it *'the tunnel of happiness-ing'*, and you'll see why in a moment. I always use it on the way to work whenever I go to visit one of my Clients so that I setup my mind-body state for optimal happiness-ing.

The way I do this is by creating a *'tunnel of happiness'* that I walk through as I traverse the City on the way to the Clients. This *'tunneling'* is done by looking for, noticing and amplifying every bright light, glint, and reflection that I can see high around me.

I use my peripheral vision to see these and I fantasize/visualize these bright, happy, glinting lights as part of a delightful tunnel encircling high around me. As I walk through my tunnel, I build strong and uplifting feelings of happiness inside my torso, chest, face and head — in my heart, gut and head brains. I do this using breathing and a mix of creative visualization and creative feeling. In this way I truly appreciate and notice the beauty of the buildings, the sky, the windows and reflections, the lights and all the shiny wonderful surfaces that make up our world.

If you are tracking the NLP concepts and strategies behind my *'Tunnel of Happiness-ing'* technique then you'll notice the use of visual submodalities that pay homage to the pragmatic wisdom of the designers of great churches and cathedrals. In such places, for the last two thousand years, stained glass, high windows and candles have been used to imbue and stimulate a sense of awe and the numinous. Sparkle and glinting high in the peripheral visual field is associated with the experience of fascination, delight and awe.

So everyday as you walk to and from work, or go about your business and life…

Build your own tunnel of happiness-ing:

1. As you walk around, look for and notice any and every bright light, glint, and reflection that you can see high around you.

2. Use your peripheral vision to experience this halo of brightness around you. Amplify the sense of glint, sparkle and shininess

that surrounds you.

3. As you use your peripheral vision to see all of the sources of sparkle and light, fantasize/visualize these bright, happy, glinting lights as a delightful tunnel encircling high around you.

4. Take the image you have created in your mind, that is overlaid over the *'real'* world, and intensify and magnify it 10 times! Really brighten it up.

5. As you walk through your tunnel, begin to build strong and uplifting feelings of happiness inside your heart and gut brains — your torso and chest — and up into your face and head. Smile! Really fill your body, face, heart and mind with feelings of joy and happiness. As you do this use Balanced Breathing (6 seconds in, 6 seconds out) and a mix of creative visualization and creative feeling to generate a beautiful vibrant sense of joy and aliveness in your body, and link this strongly to a sense of you moving through your tunnel of happiness-ing that stretches out into your future, out across the whole of your coming day!

6. Now relax, smile deeply both inside and out, and truly appreciate and notice the beauty of the buildings, the sky, the windows and reflections, the lights and all the shiny wonderful surfaces that make up your life, and carry your tunnel of happiness-ing with you wherever you go.

◯ Deeper Understandings — The three brains of happiness

As discussed in Chapter 0, we have three complex and functional neural networks or *'brains'* in our body — a head brain, a heart brain and a gut brain. Our brains are also influenced by the Autonomic Nervous System (ANS) and can operate in one of three modes:

- **Stressed** — Sympathetic dominant

- **Depressed** — Parasympathetic dominant

- **Balanced/Coherent** — A flow state balanced between Sympathetic and Parasympathetic

(There's also a fourth mode where you bounce between Sympathetic and Parasympathetic dominance, where both systems are maxed out.)

Most importantly, the modes the brains are operating in determine how they function.

The three brains also enact their own individual functions and core competencies, and of these research has found that there is a single core competency for each brain that represents the most adaptive, generative state for that brain. In the field of *m*BIT (multiple Brain Integration Techniques) these optimal states are known as the *'Highest Expressions'*.

For the heart the Highest Expression is Compassion, for the head it's Creativity and for the gut brain it is Courage. When all three brains are operating in Highest Expression and in balanced/coherent flow state, there's an emergent wisdom that

> unfolds within your mind-body system, you tap into the deep intelligence and intuition of all three brains and experience an incredible uplifting sense of joy and happiness.
>
> Compassion brings joy to the heart. It helps you connect deeply with others. It makes your heart sing. Creativity unlocks your mind. It opens you to new possibilities. It brings forth new ways of being and fresh experiences into your life and world. And gutsy courage allows you to move forward, to push through apathy and fear. It motivates you and makes you take massive action.
>
> When you learn to align your three brains, to bring them into Autonomic Balance and to operate through their Highest Expressions, magic begins to unfold in your life. Your intuition deepens and intensifies. You feel more in touch with yourself. And you begin to create a wiser and happier life.
>
> For more information and to learn simple and powerful techniques for integrating your head, heart and gut brains, please visit www.mbraining.com.

Pos ψ Gratitude and Appreciation

As you learned in Chapter 9, gratitude leads to happiness. Prof. Robert Emmons at the University of California-Davis found that people who regularly practiced gratitude were more than 25 percent happier, suffered lower levels of stress, were healthier and slept better.

So practice being grateful for the blessings in your life on a daily basis. Focus on the positives in your life and truly savor them. Share your gratitude. Tell the people you care about how much you appreciate them and the things they do for you. Become a daily messenger and purveyor of gratitude, thanks and appreciation.

Each morning think of at least three things or people in your life you're grateful for. Make this your morning ritual. And each night before sleep, do the same. Really appreciate the positives from your day. By sandwiching your daily experiences with an attitude of gratitude you'll direct your unconscious and conscious minds, your Reticular Activating System, and your head, heart and gut brains into tracking for, noticing and producing more positive experiences. You'll create a success spiral of happiness-ing.

I'll say it again, since it's worth repeating… In order to get happiness in your life, you need to do the actions of happiness-ing. And focusing on and experiencing gratitude is a key component for this. Yes it takes work to do, but the benefits are manifold. You get out of life what you put into it. Happiness is a choice, a state of mind, and it requires you to do the strategies of happiness-ing. Appreciate that and put it into action in your life. As you do, you'll thank yourself for the gift of happiness-ing that you have given to yourself every single day!

> *"Happiness is a choice that requires effort at times."*
>
> Aeschylus

☑ Success Strategy – Counting your Blessings

Are you savoring and appreciating your life, your world and as many moments of each day as possible? As the research in Positive Psychology has shown, focusing on gratitude increases your levels of life satisfaction and happiness. So make the effort every day to *'count your blessings'*. The following simple Success Strategy involves using a *'Gratitude Journal'* that you write in every night in order to truly savor and appreciate your life.

And the best thing is... with practice, the skills and strategies of savoring and appreciating form deep unconscious competencies that start to operate without the need for constant reminders. The more you do it, the easier it becomes and the more your unconscious mind finds and brings to your conscious awareness the wonderful, serendipitous, beautiful and joyful experiences that occur all around you.

1. Purchase a journal or notebook that will become your *'Gratitude Journal'* and place it with a pen beside your bed.

2. Each night, before sleeping, write 3 or more things that you feel blessed about in your life and really savor and appreciate them.

3. Ask yourself, *'What are the blessings in my life? Who and what can I show appreciation for? What positive aspects can I fully savor and appreciate from my day?'*

4. Review your journal each morning to fill your heart with gratitude and appreciation as a positive way to start your day.

In a sense this exercise is about creating and evoking a spirit of joy and generosity in your life and your interactions with others. There's always something or someone you can feel grateful for or towards. So generously celebrate your blessings, savor them and focus on the positives in your life. Even in the midst of the worst of life's challenges, you can always choose to place your focus on past blessings and future possibilities.

It's the Life <u>you</u> Lead

This is your life, not someone else's. You are in control of your destiny and it is not a practice run. So make an effort and make it count!

People sometimes ask me *"So how is life treating you?"* and I always respond *"Life treats me the way I treat it, and I'm treating my life very, very well!"*

Think about it… you've heard the expression *"it's the life you lead."* Well, the emphasis here is on the *'you'*. It's <u>your</u> life. It's the life <u>you</u> lead, so lead it well, and lead it towards happiness-ing.

Of course, leading implies purposive action, change and movement. And given that it's your life and you are leading it, then you need to stop relying on others to provide you with motivation and direction. Relying on others to guide your life can be an enemy to happiness. It's fine if they happen to be skilful and have your best interests at heart. But there comes a time where you need to take control of your own destiny. Happiness-ing is best served by *"self-satisfaction services"* — by you working out what you want for your own life and then guiding and leading yourself on a daily basis into achieving your own success.

Thinking Tools — It's YOUR Life

It's the life <u>you</u> lead, so lead it well!

Mindfulness

Research shows that people who are high in mindfulness, who practice being mindfully attentive to the here and now and keenly aware of their surroundings, are models of flourishing and positive mental health. Mindfulness involves bringing your complete attention to the present moment, non-judgmentally, so that each thought, feeling, or sensation that arises is acknowledged and accepted as it is. Mindfulness allows you to stay present and leads to an increased appreciation of each individual moment.

Mindfulness techniques, inherited from the Buddhist tradition, are increasingly being employed in modern psychology as an adjunct treatment for a variety of mental and physical conditions such as anxiety, depression, compulsive behavior, chronic pain and stress. Research has shown that in as little as two months the practice of mindfulness can produce positive changes in both brain function and immune response.

In the field of *m*BIT, mindfulness involves '*Mind-full-ness*' — that is, being mind-full of the messages, feelings and sensations from all of your brains. All three brains (head, heart and gut) working together make up the emergent process of the '*mind*', so being totally '*mindful*' means bringing awareness to the states, messages and integration or lack of integration of all three brains on a moment by moment basis.

The opposite of this is mindlessness, and this means ignoring information, messages and signals from your three brains. As we've shown in Chapter 3, *'Ignorance is NOT bliss'*, so ignoring valuable information from your heart and gut brains is an enemy to happiness! In our modern society, most people are relatively mindless about their heart and gut intelligences. We have tended to focus on and elevate the importance of head based experiences, thoughts and sensations. But this has caused our lives and world to get out of balance. Mindfulness means bringing back balanced, integrated awareness and attention to all three brains.

As pointed out throughout this book, much of our intelligence and cognition is *'embodied'*; a large and important proportion of our processing of our world is done through the intelligence in our heart and guts. So by practicing multiple brain mindfulness you are able to experience fully and viscerally the temporary, fleeting and ever changing nature of your sensations, feelings and thoughts that occur within and between your neural networks. The evidence from both Buddhist teachings and modern research is that when you practice mindfulness, more creative solutions emerge spontaneously and this leads to greater wisdom. By bringing a multiple brain approach to this you amplify the creativity and generative wisdom produced by mindfulness techniques.

So every day, practice being mindful and attentive to the signals and messages from your body. Feel your heart. Attend to the signals from your gut. Become aware of your thoughts. Be mindful and not judgmental. Allow the sensations and signals that are happening throughout your body to permeate through to your conscious awareness. Mindfully live each day. You'll find that life gets easier when you do and that your life naturally becomes wiser and happier.

Bouncing Back — Overcoming the Bumps in the Road

To stick with the travel metaphor we started this chapter with... sometimes when you are traveling down the road of life, you inevitably hit a bump. Life isn't always smooth. And you need to be able to cope with the negative experiences that life will surely and occasionally provide. This is where knowing about the '*Losada Ratio*' can really help.

In 2005, Positive Psychologist Barbara Fredrickson and her colleague Marcial Losada uncovered a fascinating finding. Dubbed the Losada ratio or Losada zone, it suggests that there is a critical positivity to negativity ratio for human resilience and flourishing. The research was based on a mix of mathematical modeling, psychological theory and quantitative data. While more recently the mathematical modeling has been shown to be somewhat problematic, nearly ten years of ongoing research across many domains has shown that the basic findings are solid. There is a critical ratio or zone of positivity for psychological flourishing.

What Fredrickson and Losada found is that individuals (and groups) flourish when they exhibit a positivity to negativity ratio of greater than around 3:1 (and less than 11:1 — you can have too much positivity and this is known as the '*Pollyanna effect*').

For example, in a more recent study completed in 2011, Fredrickson and colleagues examined the behavioral differences between individuals who were flourishing in their lives, those who were non-flourishers, and people who were depressed. The results showed that flourishers experienced the same number of negative emotions as the non-flourishers and depressed individuals, but that they had a higher positivity ratio. Those who flourished did so due to being nourished by a greater focus on small, yet consequential positive emotional experiences.

And within reasonable bounds, the research suggests that more is better. Prof. John Gottman for example found in his research that flourishing, resilient marriages have a positivity ratio of around 5:1, whereas marriages that are headed for failure exhibit a ratio of approximately 1:1. Other research across a wide range of life circumstances and ages shows that people with a higher positivity ratio have superior mental health and adjustment. Higher positivity ratios also predict greater creativity in employees.

So the evidence is in, but how can you use this to increase the happiness in your life and cope with adversity? Well, to build resilience and to cope with the inevitable *'negative'* experiences in life, you need to create a 3:1 minimum ratio of positivity to negativity in your ongoing experience. Whenever you are hit with something negative, you need to balance it with at least 3 positive experiences. When you talk about and think about a negative situation, you must ensure you counteract this with a minimum of 3 positives. This is important. You can easily spiral down into stuck states if you focus too much on negativity. However, by balancing negatives with a Losada ratio of at least 3:1 positives, you'll enable yourself to best overcome the bumps in your road.

Yes, negative things in life can get you down, but there's no excuse for staying down. Using your new knowledge of the Losada ratio, combat the enemy of negativity by over-riding it with three times as many positives, and you'll shift yourself into greater levels of resilience and flourishing. In this way, negative experiences can become the stimulus for greater focus on positivity and happiness-ing.

🛠 Thinking Tools — Losada Ratio

You need a minimum of 3 positives to every negative in order to maintain resilience.

> *"A calm mind is key to happiness."*
>
> Dalai Lama

> *"If we were able to maintain a calm and peaceful mind all day long, we would never experience any problems or mental suffering."*
>
> Geshe Kelsang Gyatso

☑ Success Strategy — Calm-abiding

To cope with the vicissitudes of life — the times when life serves you with overwhelming challenges and hassles — it helps to be able to do what the Buddhists call *'calm-abiding'*. This is a state of mind/body calmness that helps you balance your Autonomic Nervous System and bring peace to your heart and gut brains. Using this process you can experience a form of calm inner-peace even in the storms of life and then bounce straight back.

Your ability to calmly abide the challenges of life can make the difference between living a life of heart-felt peace versus a tumultuous life of suffering and misery when things don't go your way. As the Buddhists point out so perspicaciously, the nature of the Universe is impermanence. Nothing lasts forever. So it's a certainty that you'll experience times when something you love and value breaks, dies or disappears. You can upset yourself to no avail over this, or you can learn to calmly abide with peace in your heart, mind and gut.

To do '*calm-abiding*' use the following process:

1. Whenever you're feeling stressed or in need of some uplifting or calming, simply take a few minutes to sit and start *m*BIT Balanced Breathing. Breathe in and out calmly and evenly, taking approx. 6 seconds on the in-breath and 6 seconds on the out-breath. As you know, make sure your in and out breaths are of the same duration.

2. As you breathe in, imagine that each breath is uplifting your heart with light-hearted calming joy. Really feel that uplifting feeling. And smile as you do this. Smiling makes a key difference. Deeply feel your heart being uplifted and calmed as you breathe. You can imagine a color or sparkling light filling your heart with peaceful and uplifting positive energy and love. And you can take that light, color and feeling and experience it going all the way from your heart to your head, taking your delightful, joyful and uplifting feelings and messages of peace from your heart into your mind.

3. As you breathe out, imagine your breath going down from

your head/heart to your gut, taking with it calming feelings and messages. Really feel that letting go, relaxing, calming and peace-filled sense of joy fill your belly. Add a light or color that deeply enhances your gut-felt feelings of peace, joy and contentment.

4. Breathe in *'uplifting calm-joy-in your heart'*, breath out and down *'deep abiding-peace-in your gut'*. Continue doing this, as you smile, swallowing peaceful joy from your head to your gut and feeling so profoundly aligned, peacefully integrated and joyfully calmed.

> "Ask yourself whether you are happy, and you cease to be so."
>
> John Stuart Mill

> "The search for happiness is one of the chief sources of unhappiness."
>
> Eric Hoffer

Happiness-ing — Don't focus on Happiness!

Focusing on happiness can create problems! There's a growing body of scientific research backing up the insights from the quotes above and highlighting how the pursuit of happiness can have a surprisingly paradoxical effect — the more you pursue happiness, the less likely you are to experience the very outcomes, well-being, psychological health, and happy feelings you're trying to achieve.

For example, studies have examined people's attitudes towards happiness and found that those who are most focused on happiness are the least likely to achieve it. Other experiments have shown that the more people try to gain happiness from an experience, the less satisfaction they achieve. In one study, led by psychologist Iris Mauss from the University of Denver, participants' focus on happiness was increased by having them read a bogus newspaper article extolling the importance of achieving happiness. Compared to a control, the people who read the happiness-extolling article later reported less happiness in response to a happy film.

In another study, participants were instructed to make themselves feel as happy as possible while listening to the music of Stravinsky's Rite of Spring, while other participants were simply asked to listen to the music. Results showed that compared to those who simply listened to the music, participants who tried to increase their happiness reported worsened mood.

Other research suggests that a focus on personal happiness can increase self-focus, impair social connection and lead to social isolation. So focusing on your own happiness alone can lead to increased levels of loneliness and disconnection.

Yes, focusing on happiness by and of itself is counterproductive. Instead, as we've explored throughout this book, you need to focus on the underpinnings of happiness-ing — the skills of pleasure, flow, purpose and meaning. When you live from these skills, behaviors, attitudes and processes then happiness is a natural result.

As we discussed at the beginning of this chapter, happiness is not a goal or some *'thing'* for you to put your focus on. It is but a *'measure'* of how well you are doing on the more important components and unconscious competencies of happiness-ing. So use the success strategies described throughout this book and focus on those — and as a result, happiness will flow in your life.

Remember, focusing on happiness as an end in itself is an enemy to happiness, just like focusing on money as an end result is a surefire way to create misery in your life. Money and happiness are both simply a means to an ends; it's what you do with them that counts.

> *"Perfect happiness is the absence of striving for happiness."*
>
> Chuang-Tse

> *"Happiness is not best achieved by those who seek it directly."*
>
> Bertrand Russell

Bringing Your Human Spirit Alive!

As indicated in the previous section, happiness comes, not from focusing on happiness itself, but from living and acting in a way that brings your human spirit alive! This is what the field of *m*BIT is all about and what it brings to the game of life. With *m*BIT you learn to tap into your own innate wisdom and to live from the Highest Expression of you. It's about truly bringing your human spirit alive by living from Compassion, Creativity and Courage as ways of being and doing in your world.

And here's a profound insight… your brains are malleable and changeable. The neural networks of the head, heart and gut brains exhibit neural plasticity and are able to change their structure and function. *'The brain that thinks, changes itself.'* Why is this profound? Well let's explore this in some detail.

> *"The principal activities of brains are making changes in themselves."*
>
> Marvin L. Minsky

Neuro-genesis — Evolving your Self, Evolving your World

It was once thought that you were born with all the neurons you'd ever have and that slowly over time brain cells would atrophy and die off. That the number of neurons in your head would inevitably dwindle. This meant that if you suffered from some debilitating brain disease or damage such as a stroke, you were forever broken and your brain would not and could not repair itself. This has now been overturned, literally turned on its head (so to speak). Science has uncovered that our brains (and not just the ones in our head) grow new neurons, new dendrites and new synapses all the time.

There is an amazing and growing body of research on this process of neural plasticity. As pointed out many years ago by psychologist Donald Hebb, and backed up by numerous cutting-edge scientific studies, when neurons fire together they grow new connections and *'wire'* together. Through a process called *'neuro-genesis'* our brains grow new neurons and make new synaptic connections and new neural structures. This is called structural plasticity.

One example of this was demonstrated with London taxi drivers.

Researchers discovered that taxi drivers having learned the geographical complexities of driving around London had developed larger hippocampi, key regions of the brain responsible for visual-spatial memory. Another powerful example of brain plasticity as shown in recent research, is the increase in frontal lobe connections of people who've learned and practiced loving-kindness meditation.

Our existing neural connections also undergo ongoing change and adaptation, modifying hour by hour the synaptic strength and response of the connections. This is known as functional plasticity. As neuroscientists like to point out, *"Our brain is a verb"*, it's not a fixed object but an ongoing changing and evolving process. I like to think of it as a garden, an ecology, and the thoughts, feelings and experiences that you generate in your life, change the physical structure of your neural networks — of your brains. As Dr. Norman Doidge points out in his excellent book on neural plasticity, *"The brain that thinks changes itself"*.

> *"The brain is a far more open system than we ever imagined, and nature has gone very far to help us perceive and take in the world around us. It has given us a brain that survives in a changing world by changing itself."*
>
> Dr. Norman Doidge

And in keeping with this garden or ecology metaphor, it turns out that cells called micro-glia in our brains monitor this garden and tend it, helping to build new dendrites and synapses for those neurons that are being used and eating up and dissolving dendrites and synapses that are no longer being used. As a result of this *'gardening'*, as the neuroscientists like to say and as indicated above,

"Neurons that fire together, wire together; and neurons that are out of synch, unlink." Another way of saying this is use it, or lose it. And that the brain builds itself based on focus, attention and action. The way you use your multiple brains evolves and changes their structure and their ongoing abilities and propensities for action.

As indicated previously, this process of neuro-genesis not only occurs in the head brain, it's also been shown to occur in the gut and heart brains. This is an incredibly exciting finding with significant implications for you and your life. The point is, by personally using the Success Strategies you've learned throughout this book and by living from Highest Expression, you can and will evolve new neural patterns and circuits within your brains! You will literally evolve yourself for greater neurological capabilities for happiness-ing.

> *"How we pay attention promotes neural plasticity, the change of neural connections in response to experience."*
>
> Daniel J. Siegal

The practice of Compassion creates more neural compassion circuits throughout your brains. The practice of Creativity creates more neural creativity circuits. And the practice of gutsy Courage creates more neural courage circuits throughout your integrated and connected brains. You literally evolve yourself physically, mentally, emotionally and amplify your capacity for higher orders of consciousness, greater levels of happiness-ing and wiser ways of being and doing.

So align your brains and life around your Highest Expression of self. Fill your life with integrated Compassion, Creativity and

Courage. Create a world — your world — that is worth living. One that inspires you. One that represents all you want to have and be. And then share your knowledge and skills with others. Bring the changes you want to create to all your relationships and all the organizations you're part of. In this way, as we all begin to work together we can literally evolve our brains, evolve our selves and make a wise and generative difference to our world.

☑ Success Strategy — Evolving your World with *m*BIT Coaching

This success strategy is not a specific technique. Instead it is a suggestion for how you can amplify your success and happiness in life by utilizing the services of a skilled *m*BIT Coach.

While it's true that you can make amazing and fundamental changes to yourself and your world using the techniques, insights and strategies from this book, you can take it to a much higher level with the assistance of a trained coach. Elite athletes know how important it is to use the services of a coach. Coaches can support you to change, they can guide you in the most fruitful approaches, they can help keep you motivated and they can often see the patterns and processes that you miss in yourself.

People from around the world write to me literally every single day about how their lives have been changed by using an *m*BIT Coach. If this sounds like something you'd like to experience for yourself, then jump onto my website www.mbraining.com and go to the '*Find an mBIT Coach*' section. There you'll see a growing list of *m*BIT Coaches from around the planet that offer their services. Pick one near you and contact them. Many will do coaching via phone or skype, so even if there's not one geographically close, you can still avail yourself of this profoundly powerful experience and amplify your personal evolution through the use of *m*BIT Coaching.

> *"People say that what we're all seeking is a meaning for life. I don't think that's what we're really seeking. I think that what we're seeking is an experience of being alive."*
>
> Joseph Campbell

Awareness Questions — Bringing Your Spirit Alive

Ask Yourself:

- What makes my heart sing and come alive? What passions and dreams bring my spirit alive?

- What makes my head brain light up? What creative ideas and thoughts capture my attention and bring my mind fully alive?

- What moves me deeply? What makes my gut fill with drive, motivation and courageous action?

- What is a way of being, a way of action and a way of living that will truly bring my human spirit alive? What will allow me to flourish and to live a life of true meaning and deep purpose?

Pos ψ Well-Being

In this final section I'd like to share with you the latest research from Positive Psychology. While the field of Positive Psychology first started with a focus on authentic happiness, it eventually came to realize the very same insights we've been exploring both in this chapter and throughout the book — that to gain deep levels of happiness, joy and life satisfaction you need to focus not on happiness, but on purpose, meaning and well-being. As indicated in the previous few pages, it's truly about bringing your human spirit alive. Ultimately the process of *'well-being'* is about the *'Being'* and *'Doing'* of happiness-ing — of creating and living a life of deep purpose and meaning.

So the latest work by Prof. Martin Seligman and his colleagues in the field of Positive Psychology is now focused on what they are calling *'Well-Being Theory'*.

Well-Being Theory

According to Well-Being Theory, well-being has five measurable elements (PERMA) that count toward it:

- Positive emotion

- Engagement

- Relationships

- Meaning and purpose

- Accomplishment

While three of these elements are identical to those proposed by earlier work in Positive Psychology (Positive Emotion, Engagement/Flow and Meaning), the addition of the two elements of Relationship and Accomplishment now round out the components that lead to well-being and ultimately to deep and abiding happiness.

It's not surprising that relationships have been added to the prerequisites for well-being and happiness. Humans are social animals and we all have deep needs for connection, love and contact with others. And the quality of this contact is important. This is why there's been a focus in this book on building strong and high quality relationships with others and why it's important for you to add value to those around you. Strong networks of loving and caring relationships make a difference. And the research supports this.

It's also not a surprise that accomplishment has been added to the list of what generates well-being. When we achieve goals and outcomes we feel good. Creating things, accomplishing results and succeeding in life all bring about positive cognitive and emotional responses. Accomplishment adds to flourishing. This is why we focused on goals, dreams, values and outcomes in Chapter 10. Life is fantastic when you make it so. To do that involves accomplishment. But this is just one component of well-being and has to be done in balance with all the other elements.

You can also see how the components of PERMA fit so nicely with the models from *m*BIT. Relationships are supported by a focus on compassion and connection with others. Accomplishment is about creativity and the gutsy motivation to keeping going even in the face of setback and adversity. Positive emotions link to the heart. Meaning and purpose connect strongly to wisdom and to bringing the human spirit alive. Engagement is about the flow of working with all your multiple brains aligned and operating from autonomic balance and coherence.

When you get all of these processes and elements working together in your life, your well-being soars, you begin to truly flourish and happiness comes easily. So fill every single day of your life with the components, skills and processes of happiness-ing. Be aware of the enemies to your happiness, and when you find them, pattern-interrupt them and replace them with the success strategies you've learned from this book. Build a life filled with PERMA!

Yes, the back of your birth certificate may NOT contain the necessary instructions for how to run your body, your brain and your mind. But from reading this book, you've now got the tools and skills you need to continue to transcend the enemies to happiness and to create a magnificent life filled with deep joy, purpose and meaning.

So I thank you for reading this book and sharing the ongoing journey to happiness and meaning with me. I truly do appreciate every single person who makes the time, effort and value to read what I have written. And I wish you much joy in your continued learning adventures. Let's all work together to create more happiness and make a wise and generative difference to our world.

> *"Happiness cannot be traveled to, owned, earned, worn or consumed. Happiness is the spiritual experience of living every minute with love, grace, and gratitude."*
>
> Denis Waitley

Strengths & Values In Action

Use the following table to determine which strengths, qualities and values to focus on and amplify in your life to support the processes and skills of happiness. Also notice if you have any elements of the absence, opposite or exaggeration of these strengths and remove them from your behaviors and your life.

Enemies to happiness	VIA Strength
Objectifying Happiness	Perspective/Wisdom
	Creativity
Demanding Happiness	Gratitude
Focusing only on Yourself	Citizenship/Loyalty
	Kindness
	Social Intelligence
	Love
Not bringing your Spirit Alive	Purpose/Spirituality

📋 Notes from the Field — Your Story

Ok, it's the end of the book and it's been quite a journey. I've really enjoyed writing this book, I've learned a lot, experienced lots of purpose, flow and meaning during its development and creation. And I've made a difference to the world and hopefully to people's lives. I certainly made sure I followed through and finished what I started, and I also ensured that I only wrote it in a happy way. If I wasn't feeling the joy, if I wasn't in-joy-in-myself during any stage of the writing process, then I stopped and went and did something else. So I ensured that I removed the enemies to writing happiness in my life and replaced them with a process of writing delight. Cool. That's my story... But what about you?

What's your story? You are now aware of all the enemies to happiness, you have the tools, strategies and skills at hand to do the processes of exquisite happiness-ing in their place. What story are you going to unfold now in your life? Take a moment and imagine just how your journey of happiness-ing is going to unfold in your life as you move forward from this point on. Grab a pen, and in the available space of the next couple of pages, write out your *'happiness notes from the field'* story. This is now about you. I left this last section for you. You are the expert of doing happiness in your own life! Enjoy!

Avoiding the Enemies to HAPPINESS

Your Story

Your Story cont.

Your Story cont.

☞ Remember This — The 12 Rules for Avoiding the Enemies to Happiness

In this final section, rather than summarize the chapter, we're going to review the whole book and the overall 12-step process for '*Avoiding the Enemies to Happiness*':

- ✓ Stay away from unfulfilling prophecies — create positive self-fulfilling prophecies and empowering beliefs in your life.

- ✓ Don't celebrate failure — only celebrate success.

- ✓ Remove conflict and incongruence — seek and support alignment and congruence at every level of yourself and your life.

- ✓ Never take away choice — give yourself more choice, control and flexibility.

- ✓ Ignorance is dangerous — knowledge always provides power and choice.

- ✓ Slow suicide will kill you — only do things that add long term value to your health and life.

- ✓ Don't be a victim of your emotions — Control your mind, body and emoting.

- ✓ Greed destroys — go for balance and generosity.

- ✓ Don't sabotage yourself — love and support yourself.

Avoiding the Enemies to HAPPINESS

- ✓ Beware of negative influences — seek positive caring relationships.

- ✓ Don't follow the Failure Formula — go for massive success.

- ✓ Don't focus on happiness — fill with your life with purpose, strength and meaning to bring your spirit alive!

ⓘ Extra Info

Refer to www.enemiestohappiness.com for

- more information about the material covered in this chapter
- additional reading and references for this chapter

Acknowledgements and thanks

I would like to thank and acknowledge all the people who made this publication possible.

This book came about from an idea that a good friend of mine, David McCombe generously shared with me. It's an idea David is passionate about. The story about how he came to this idea is quite impressive and inspirational and I'd like to share it with you.

When David was a young lad, growing up on the little isle of Bute, off the rugged west coast of Scotland, there came a time when he was ready to leave the nest and venture out to the wide, wild world. He would eventually travel to London, get a job, and meet his lovely wife Linda and move to Australia to start a family with her. As a young lad of 17, with amazing wisdom and insight for his age, he decided that he would look around at the people he knew and what they were doing to make themselves happy or miserable. He compiled a list that he called '*the enemies to human happiness*' and decided he would systematically and carefully remove and beware of these enemies to happiness in his life. He called this process '*Avoiding the Enemies to Happiness.*' In their place, he would continuously search for and study those things that produced happiness. In this way he would give himself, and the people he loved, the best chance for happiness and success in life.

When I met David, many years later, our shared passion for human excellence, psychology and personal mastery lead us to a natural discussion about happiness and its enemies. Together we designed this book and went about studying the science of Positive Psychology so that we could bring the latest research about happiness to David's deep and important insights. My background is both in Science (I have advanced degrees in Applied Physics and

Computer Engineering), Psychology and a Masters Certification in Neuro Linguistic Programming (NLP). I also have experience and expertise in writing, training and adult education and I'm the co-developer of the amazing new field of human excellence known as *m*BIT (multiple Brain Integration Techniques). So it was a natural fit for David to offer me the book idea. For this and all his great ideas, passion and input, I sincerely and deeply thank him. Our many nights of brainstorming and research were an absolute delight. David also interviewed and wrote the *'Notes from the Field'* section for Psychologist Dorothy Rowe. It's a great interview.

I would also like to thank, acknowledge and express my immense gratitude to all those people who agreed to support this project by being interviewed for their thoughts and ideas on happiness. Each chapter has a *'Notes from the Field'* section that contains interviews with people who are exemplars of happiness and excellence in my opinion. They are people who have much wisdom and advice to offer and include (in no particular order) Robert Dilts, Judith DeLozier, Dr. Dorothy Rowe, Dr. Mick Webb, Dr. Deborah Rozman, Edward de Bono, Suzanne Beecher, Peter Fischer, Sogyal Rinpoche, Jan Roberts, Dr. Timothy Sharp, Tammy Van Wisse, Thomas "Sully" Sullivan, Marvin Oka, Mere and Ellie.

In addition, I'd really like to thank the many, many people who shared their feedback, advice, thoughts and reviews and helped with the action research of the exercises. In particular I'd like to thank Carole and Arvo Soosalu, Fiona Soosalu, Philip Jensen, Prof. Suzanne Henwood, Jan Marsh, Allison Staggard and Pauline Wong.

I'd also like to express thanks and respect to the developers and leaders of the fields of endeavor this book is based on. Thanks to Prof. Martin Seligman for all his great work in Psychology and his most recent creation and development of the fascinating and important field of Positive Psychology. Thanks also to Dr. Albert Ellis for his magnificent work on Cognitive Psychology and Rational Emotive Behavioral Therapy. In addition, my thanks go to Dr. Richard Bandler and Dr. John Grinder, the original developers of NLP. For me, NLP continues to be one of the most powerful and insightful understandings of human process and excellence. And a special thanks to my colleague Marvin Oka, who worked with me to develop the new and exciting field of *m*BIT (multiple Brain Integration Techniques). Thank you.

I'd also be remiss if I didn't thank the following authors and researchers for their very kind permission to quote or reference their excellent work: Prof. Eugene Gendlin, Dr. John Gottman, Gavin de Becker, Stephen Elliot and The Institute of HeartMath,. I'd also like to acknowledge that Coherent Breathing® is a registered trademark of Coherence LLC and that HeartMath® is a registered trademark of the Institute of HeartMath.

Finally, my deepest love and gratitude to both my parents Carole and Arvo and to my beloved Fiona, whose support, encouragement and wisdom is evidenced throughout this project and book. Thank you. I love you all!

And thank you also, my dear reader, I hope this book makes a positive difference to your life and helps you avoid the enemies to human happiness, replacing them with strategies for success, purpose and meaning.

Legal stuff

As indicated at the front of this publication, the author and publisher have used their best efforts in preparing this book. This publication contains ideas, opinions, tips and techniques for improving happiness, wisdom and human performance. The materials are intended to provide helpful and useful material on the subjects addressed in the publication. The publisher and author do *not* provide or purport to provide you with any medical, health, psychological or professional advice or service or any other personal professional service. You should seek the advice of your own medical practitioner, health professional or other relevant competent professional before trying or using information, exercises or techniques described in this publication.

The publisher and author, jointly and severally, make no representations or warranties with respect to the accuracy, reliability, sufficiency or completeness of the contents of this publication and specifically disclaim any implied warranties or merchantability or fitness for any particular purpose. There are no warranties which extend beyond the descriptions contained in this paragraph. The accuracy and completeness of the information provided herein and the opinions stated herein are not guarantees, nor warranties to or towards the production of any particular result, and the advice and strategies contained herein may not be suitable for every individual.

You read this publication with the explicit understanding that neither the publisher, nor author shall be liable for any direct or indirect loss of profit or any other commercial damages, including but not limited to special, incidental, punitive, consequential or other damages. In reading or using any part or portion of this publication, you agree to not hold, nor attempt to hold the publisher or authors liable for any loss, liability, claim, demand, damage and all legal cost or other expenses arising whatsoever in connection with the use, misuse or inability to use the materials. In jurisdictions that exclude such limitations, liability is limited to the consideration paid by you for the right to view or use these materials, and/or the greatest extent permitted by law.

About the author

Grant Soosalu

Grant is an international Trainer, Leadership Consultant and Executive Coach with extensive backgrounds in Organizational Change, Training and Leadership Development. He has advanced degrees and certifications in Psychology, Positive Psychology, Applied Physics, Computer Engineering and System Development. He is a qualified Total Quality Management (TQM) Trainer, and has achieved Master Practitioner Certification in the behavioral sciences of Neuro Linguistic Programming (NLP) and Advanced Behavioral Modeling. More recently Grant was awarded a Graduate Coaching Diploma in the newly emerging field of Authentic Happiness Coaching.

Grant has wide ranging expertise and experience in the educational sector as a Lecturer, Coach, Training Developer and Facilitator. He also has extensive backgrounds in Business Development, Senior Technical Consulting and Project Management. Grant provides coaching and mentoring to CEO's and Senior Executives around the world.

Currently, Grant is a Consultant Lecturer at a leading Australian University where he runs workshops and programs on the applications of Positive Psychology to Conflict Resolution, Risk Management and Organizational Change. Grant also runs a successful consulting company providing services to organizations predominantly in the finance sector.

Grant is the co-developer of the exciting new field of *m*BIT (multiple Brain Integration Techniques) and has published articles and papers in International Journals, in the fields of Coaching, Leadership, Philosophy, Applied Physics and NLP.

References and resources

Extensive references, bibliography, suggested readings and additional resources for the work described in this publication can be found at either:

www.avoidingtheenemies.com

or

www.enemiestohappiness.com

Information on the new field of multiple Brain Integration Techniques (*m*BIT), including free articles, whitepapers, exercises and mp3's can be found at:

www.mbraining.com

And if you'd like to read Grant's blog, go to:

enhancingmylife.blogspot.com

Made in the USA
Charleston, SC
19 April 2015